THE
MADNESS
IN
SPORTS

The Madness in Sports

Second Edition

Arnold R. Beisser, M.D.

Director, Health Training Center
Los Angeles, California

Clinical Professor
Department of Psychiatry
University of California, Los Angeles

THE CHARLES PRESS PUBLISHERS
Bowie, Maryland 20715

Editor-in-Chief: R. Murray Chastain
Production Editor: Kathye Pettebone Long
Text Designer: Gerard A. Valerio
Cover Designer: Don Sellers

The Madness in Sports
Second Edition.

Library of Congress Cataloging in Publication Data

Beisser, Arnold R
  The madness in sports.

  Bibliography: p.
  1. Sports—Psychological aspects.   2. Sports—Social
aspects.   I. Title.
GV706.4.B44   1977   796'.01   77-10552

ISBN: 0-913486-83-3

Prentice-Hall International, Inc., London
Prentice-Hall of Australia, Pty., Ltd., Sydney
Prentice-Hall of India Private Limited, New Delhi
Prentice-Hall of Japan, Inc., Tokyo
Prentice-Hall of Southeast Asia (Pte.) Ltd., Singapore
Whitehall Books, Limited, Wellington, New Zealand

Printed in the United States of America

77 78 79 80 81 82   10 9 8 7 6 5 4 3 2 1

To Rita

Contents

PREFACE TO THE SECOND EDITION

Sports in America have undergone significant changes since the publication of the first edition of *The Madness in Sports* in 1967. These changes lead us to wonder whether sports still serve the same psychological and social purposes for which they were originated. It is time to reconsider old meanings of sport to athletes and fans, and to interpret them in the light of new data. The amount of time, energy, and money devoted by Americans to sports has continued to increase annually. Television audiences for sports events continue to increase, and the number and variety of sports events available through this medium continue to expand. The financial investment in professional sports in the last quarter of the twentieth century shows an astounding growth, with television contracts in six figures, enormous salaries for players, and new superstadiums. The skill with which sports are played has raised the level of play to heights that could not have been conceptualized a few years ago. Players, themselves, have become hybrid forms, with 7-foot basketball players and 260-pound football players no longer considered unique.

These modern-day gladiators continue to be idolized and imitated, their comments serving as potent forces for selling everything from deodorants to political candidates. Their views on morality, sex, and politics are eagerly sought after and widely quoted. The ideal of the scientist or statesman-philosopher is now rivaled by that of the player or coach-philosopher.

Only a few short years ago black athletes were severely limited or excluded entirely from major professional sports; today, they dominate professional basketball and, to a considerable extent, football. In addition, their involvement in most other sports is growing rapidly, and the ranks of coaches and managers had opened for them by the last quarter of the century. Perhaps of most significance for both white and black people is that most of us have stopped counting the relative numbers of each on teams.

The field is opening up for women as well. Women's sports, originally an area virtually ignored, are growing in popularity even more rapidly than sports in general, reflecting the new acceptability of the role of the female athlete. Although there is still much to be done to reach sexual equality, women are now acknowledged for their sports prowess professionally, as well as on the college and high school levels.

Not all of the changes in sports have positive social value. Many sports are becoming increasingly brutal and violent. This violence is no longer limited to the field of play, but now extends to the spectators as well. Violent attacks by spectators on players are no longer rare or unique events, but now cause serious concern to all who attend sports events.

In the last few years many Americans have become dissatisfied with the limitations of the role of spectator and have returned to participant sports, thus reversing a major trend. Joggers may be seen on most city streets today, neighborhood tennis courts are jammed, and exotic sports from the Orient have attracted many dedicated participants. At the time the first edition of *The Madness in Sports* was published, tennis was a relatively minor sport; today, it is both a popular television spectacle and a popular sport for participation by both men and women. This trend returns sports to the control of the individual and away from the mega-industry of sports.

This new edition addresses these developments and interprets them in light of traditional values in sports. The important concepts and information from the first edition have been expanded upon, and new developments and ideas added that provide important clues to the direction our society is taking and the options that will allow us to influence the way we will change.

As in the first edition, case histories of athletes and fans that I have treated as a psychiatrist are a major source of data. Many of the case histories occurred several years ago in a different social climate. Attitudes toward racism, sexuality, and other important issues have changed. Nevertheless, the psychological struggles within the individual in relation to sports remains similar, and, therefore, the cases are retained in this volume to illustrate those timeless issues. Another source of information has been my experience as a consultant to several coaches, teams, and administrators of sports programs, both amateur and professional. These experiences have been personally rewarding and have enriched my understanding of the exceptional, as well as the ordinary, athlete and team. A third major source of data is one available to anyone who watches television and reads the newspaper: the remarkably detailed reporting of every aspect of athletes, teams, and sports. In fact, there are few things in American life about which we are given so much information.

A number of books on the psychology of sports have appeared in the past decade, but, to my knowledge, this remains the only one which deals with the issues from the intrapsychic perspective of the athlete and fan as well as from the psychological and social observations that can be made from viewing sports. As with the first edition, the book will be of interest to behavioral scientists who are concerned with motivation and psychodynamic understanding of sports. It will also be of value to those athletes, coaches, and physical educators who wish to understand the significance of sports in greater depth. Finally, it will have appeal to almost everyone who has paused to wonder what all of this commitment and activity we Americans have to sports means.

I wish to thank the many people who have assisted and contributed to this work: my patients, the coaches, teams, and administrators with whom I consulted, and the sports writers who have, on occasion, called me to discuss items of mutual interest. I am especially indebted to Virginia Milhem for her skill and the care she used in the preparation of the manuscript. The encouragement of my wife, Rita, has been an important factor in making this book possible.

THE
MADNESS
IN
SPORTS

Introduction

Thought is born of failure. Only when actions fail to satisfy human needs is there ground for thought.

—L. L. WHYTE, *The Next Development in Man*

There is a great deal in contemporary sports that is nothing short of "madness," which includes all of the various meanings that may be inferred from the word. There are moments of mad joy in sports. The exhilaration and intense pleasure experienced by players and fans are among the great appeals of sports. An athlete may be in a state of ecstasy when playing "over his head"; he has a sense of mastery and transcendence which approaches a religious state. Fans, who participate only vicariously in the action, may become hysterical with excitement when their team wins the Big Game, as, for example, after the Pittsburgh Steelers' first Super Bowl victory.

Journalists have often noted this frenzied excitement associated with major sports events. They call the baseball World Series "October Madness," and football bowl games are known by such names as "Super Bowl Madness." The enthusiasm and commitment of both players and fans reach such heights that some observers have described these occasions as a form of national insanity erupting with seasonal regularity.

In support of their favorite teams, spectators engage in very strange behavior which in other circumstances might be considered "crazy." They parade with slogan-bearing banners, dressed in strange hats and odd clothing; they decorate themselves with magical symbols related to their teams and favorite players; they engage in a whole range of wild tomfoolery, reminding one of madmen or rebellious children. They may place their jobs in jeopardy, neglect their families, or remain transfixed for hours in front of a television screen.

Sometimes the involvement becomes so complete that it is serious. At such times the more literal meaning of madness may be invoked. Individuals may become so preoccupied with sports that all other aspects of their lives are left impoverished, and their personalities develop so one-sidedly that they cannot get along in the conventional world. They may be unable to develop enduring personal relationships, and instead are preoccupied with a sports fantasy world which overshadows the real one. Sometimes they become so disorganized and out of touch with reality that they actually become psychotic. The vanguard of this group may be found in almost any neighborhood bar, as fifty-year-old men nightly relate high school football exploits that took place more than thirty years before. They may recall such events more vividly than those occurring about them now. Their present lives are empty when compared with those thrilling moments.

The collective enthusiasm and preoccupation of Americans with sports, whether satisfying and joyous or a prelude to depressing emptiness, may have serious implications for our whole society and its future. How much of a nation's energy and involvement can be expended on an activity like sport without threatening the integrity of the rest of its social and economic life? Some have wondered if our preoccupation with sports is not a major symptom portending our lemminglike rush toward collective destruction. The social dilemma of sports is that while they provide many of us with a degree of pleasure, commitment, and meaning which otherwise would be lacking, they may also be leading us in directions that we would not deliberately choose if there were other viable alternatives.

A century ago we believed that madness had only negative connotations, and we ostracized those whom we labeled as mad, sending them to special institutions. Today we have come to realize that this madness may also express parts of all of us, and we appreciate its value for what it may teach us about ourselves. We have come to realize that in order to get along in the world you have to be "a little bit crazy" and that those of us who unquestioningly accept the conventions of our society may be more irrational than those who do not. The purpose of this book is to examine some of our accepted attitudes about sports and what they may signify for us as individuals and as a society.

This is a book about athletes, athletic teams, and sports fans. It is different from the usual journalistic treatment of sports in that it seeks to go beyond what is reported in the sports pages of the newspapers. It examines the thoughts and hearts of those who have been engulfed in American sports. It would not have been written had I not experienced a unique series of events which caused me to stop and wonder what it all meant and forced me to synthesize a view of sports from my varied experiences as a psychiatrist, athlete, fan, and reporter. Today there is a need for a greater awareness of the psychological significance of sports, since they strongly influence us throughout our lives. The impact begins during the early years of growth and development, and sports occupy much of the leisure time available to many adults.

INTRODUCTION

Sports were of major importance to me when I was growing up, just as they are in the lives of many American boys. They were probably the most important single activity in my life. I fell asleep each night with a fantasy of breaking away from the starting blocks on the track, of dashing into the foul circle to shoot a hook shot, or of leaping to catch a long pass in the end zone. To me, school was made up of sports, which were the reward, and studies, which were the price one had to pay to play them.

My love of sports continued into my early adult life at college and later at medical school. While I was an intern in a busy general hospital there was little time for leisure, but what was available was spent in sports—in a make-shift basketball game after midnight or, if there was still some daylight, a quick set of tennis on a neighborhood court. There were always a few friends eager to join me, wherever I was. I looked forward to these moments of play at odd hours, for they carried with them a pleasant nostalgia after a hard day, and it was like coming home and relaxing.

When I was twenty-four, the Korean conflict had begun. Since I was a Naval Reserve officer, I was alerted for recall to active service. I resigned my hospital position for a week's vacation of playing in a tennis tournament. The week was extended to many months by the military game of "hurry up and wait," and the period was climaxed when I reached a lifelong goal of winning a national championship. I wrote home that I had accomplished what I had wanted to in sports and that I didn't think I would play seriously anymore, for there were more important things to do.

Two weeks later I received my orders. The day after I reported for active duty, my life changed more than I could ever have anticipated, for I was stricken with polio and housed in an iron lung, unable to move at all. The tank continued to do my breathing for nearly two years, and I was never again to walk: I was almost totally paralyzed. Now physically limited, my principal activities became thought and reflection.

My initial thoughts were of what had been familiar sources of pleasure, and significant among them were thoughts of sports. I became aware that when action is blocked, the energy is transformed into thought. Although I was half a century later than Freud in making this discovery, I doubt that it was demonstrated to him any more dramatically than it was to me.

Had it not been for the suddenness of the cessation of my athletic activity, I believe there would have simply been a gradual dissipation of the intensity of my interest in sports. Other activities which were becoming more important to me would have taken their place. But I was not to experience this slow transition, for one day I played, and the next day I could not move at all.

As soon as I was able, I began to prepare myself for a return to medical practice, this time in the field of psychiatry. My study of human behavior led to a natural synthesis with my interest in sports, and I became curious about the psychological and sociological function and meaning of athletics. My active participation in sports was transformed into thought, and I began to attempt to understand not only my own interest and experiences in sports, but also those of athletes I knew and heard about within the framework of my growing knowledge of the behavioral sciences. I began to realize for the first time the full influence of sports on the development of the individual personality. I realized that sports were a most important social influence to shape my values, goals, and ideals, and that I was not unique in this respect. The time and commitment that I had devoted to sports had probably made them more influential in what I was to become than religious training, schools, teachers, or the community in which I grew up. They provided a vital supportive social framework where growth directions were determined and shaped. I realized that I would repeatedly return to the sports scene for guidelines, for deciding how to manage my life, and for determining what was good and what was bad. I could see the impact of sports on others, as well.

As I watched sporting events, I began to view them with a fresh perspective, no longer encumbered by my intense involvement. I became aware of the way an athlete competes well or poorly under pressure, how a coach or a crowd may influence his performance, and the symbolic meanings of each. I realized that the psychological condition of the athlete is just as important as his physical readiness in determining his performance. I became aware of the influence of parents and siblings on the athlete during his developmental years in his choice of sports, his style, and his ability. I began to understand how losing can be more important than winning to some athletes, and how others construct elaborate rituals when winning to magically ward off retaliation from dim, nearly forgotten figures.

During my years of active competition, I had very little interest as a spectator in the performance of others, and was bored by sports statistics. Now I became a fan. As a passive observer, I enjoyed a vicarious excitement in watching competition. The psychology of the fan as someone who can gain pleasure from identification with the players, without the actual stress of competition, became clear to me.

The most profoundly revealing insights came when, as a practicing psychiatrist, I was able to study athletes who had become my patients. The intimate relationship of psychotherapy was the major method of investigation, and a segment of my psychiatric practice became specialized for former athletes. They came to me as someone knowledgeable in sports, but I was surprised to find the degree of identification they felt with me as one whose athletic career had abruptly ended through illness. I learned that action-oriented athletes tend to equate emotional difficulty with physical disability. Moreover, their emotional difficulties often begin with such events as graduation from college, retirement from sports because of age, or the assumption of new responsibilities that preclude continuation of their customary athletic roles. In short, they, too, had become physically separated from an important source of satisfaction.

Participation in sports served as an integrating personality force, and when deprived of this force, psychiatric symptoms appeared. In the course of psychotherapy, the psychological meanings of the individual's sports activities became clear. For some, the athletic field was a place where certain desires, unacceptable elsewhere, could be acted out; for others, sports were a means of relating to people in what was otherwise a forbidding world. Sports were a way of pleasing or identifying with parents for some; for others they were a way of rebelling, in a socially acceptable way, against parents or the culture in which they lived.

It has been necessary, of course, to disguise the identities of the athletes described, and some important case histories had to be left out entirely because widely known dramatic events would surely be recognized. The illumination these cases offer has not been lost, however, for later sections of the book utilize anecdotes that are a matter of public knowledge, gleaned from the sports pages, to make specific points derived from more confidential information.

I have been privileged to act as a consultant with coaches, teams, and others interested in the psychology of sports. This has provided me with another unique perspective in viewing the athletic scene from the inside, working with those who are at the height of their career; thus, I have been able to test the validity of some of the retrospective observations I made of athletes during their psychotherapy. For the most part, I have found a great deal of consistency in the observations from these two different perspectives.

The first half of the book reports several case histories and their significance; the second half relates these individual cases to psychological theories about play and work, and places them within the social matrix of contemporary America. My purpose is to heighten awareness of some of the conventionally accepted views of sports and to present some of the dilemmas they contain.

1.

The Paradox of Sports

In World War II the attacking Japanese troops thought they knew what Americans held most dear. They made their banzai attacks not only with weapons but with shouted invectives meant to demoralize. One of those cries was "To hell with Babe Ruth!" So far as I know, they did not defame the religions of America, vilify our economic system, or condemn motherhood. Instead, they selected a sports hero as representative of what Americans held in highest esteem.

It is doubtful that the battlefield shout, "To hell with Babe Ruth," created more than mild amusement in the American troops, for in that time of national peril, concern for basic rights and freedom was predominant. But the level of sports enthusiasm in the United States had led Japanese intelligence officers to believe that athletics were what Americans loved most.

Not long ago, while on a visit to the United States, a European economist became strangely puzzled. Aware of America's proclamations to the world about the vigor of its commitment to the capitalistic economic system, he searched in vain for a financial section in the local newspapers. An American informant could easily have directed him to it, for in many newspapers it is, in deference to American reading practices, fastened to the end of the horse racing results at the back of the sports section. The priority, so casually accepted by Americans, can be puzzling for visitors.

Sometimes it can be bewildering even for a newspaperman. James Reston of *The New York Times* once came to California to cover a heated gubernatorial race. He complained he was hard put to sample popular opinion. "When a political reporter asks around here who's going to win," he reported later, "the answer is invariably 'the Dodgers.' " It may be fortunate that few political elections occur at the same time as major sports events. Otherwise perhaps the relatively small percentage of American voters who go to the polls would be even further reduced.

There is no lack of evidence, in all kinds of odd places, of the overwhelming importance of sports in American life. In many American newspapers the sports pages constitute the largest specialized daily section. One tenth of the *World Almanac* is devoted to sports. Both in newspapers and in the almanac, the sports sections are greater in volume than the sections about politics, business, entertainment, or science. Radio programming now consists largely of sports, music, and news—and even the news includes sports results. A large segment of television viewing time on weekends is filled with sports. Major networks compete for the privilege of showing sports events, so that frequently the three major networks simultaneously cover different events in the same sport. Major spectacles such as the World Series or the football bowl games capture almost the entire viewing audience. A number of bowl games formerly played on New Year's Day have been rescheduled because network viewing time was filled with yet other bowl games.

Other television programs are changed frequently in an attempt to satisfy the insatiable public appetite, yet year after year football, baseball, golf, bowling, and boxing are among the most viable attractions. Few programs have survived longer than the *Game of the Week* or an All-Star this-or-that. Only old movies exceed old sports events in popularity as fillers.

It is not only in the mass communications that our dedication to sports is apparent. Americans take their sports any way they can get them—even live. Cumulative annual attendance figures for football, basketball, and baseball exceed a billion. Regular participants in golf, tennis, and bowling number many millions. Participation in school, club, and team sports has been a part of almost every American's life.

In education many public schools require more time in physical education, usually meaning sports, than in any other subject. From grammar school through high school, athletics represent one sixth or one seventh of the curriculum. Team sports are, for many pupils, the most important aspect of their school life.

OF PLAY AND WORK

How could this remarkable-state of affairs have come about? In the Puritan tradition, the early American churches vigorously opposed sports. As Thomas Macaulay neatly put it, "The Puritan hated bear-baiting, not because it gave pain to the bear, but because it gave pleasure to the spectators." Blue laws were passed forbidding sports participation during times when men were expected to be at worship. Today, the Sunday doubleheader or the televised professional football game of the week has all but replaced the Sunday sermon. Churches now have gymnasiums and sponsor their own teams.

The smiling face of Bob Richards, the former Olympic pole-vaulting champion, has become a symbol of the marriage of the former sworn enemies. Today he peripatetically shuttles between his two callings, the pulpit and the Wheaties Sports Foundation.

The concepts and language of sports are so familiar and pervasive that they are used as metaphors to clarify other aspects of American life. In order to demonstrate his loyalty to the President's policies before his own confirmation as Vice President, Gerald Ford said, "You don't go out and tackle your quarterback once he has called the play." Later, when he became President and was concerned with inflation, Mr. Ford told his cabinet members to hold the line on spending. "I will hold every department responsible. You have the ball, you must carry the ball. If you don't score, it's your fault." Similarly, in the Eisenhower, Kennedy, Johnson, and Nixon administrations, the press often referred to the President as the "quarterback" and "team captain." The cabinets were frequently called "the team." (I have never heard a quarterback referred to as a president for clarification.)

In the world of business and finance, salesmen are told to "keep your eye on the ball" and to have "team spirit." Medical research programs are often launched with slogans such as "winning the fight against mental illness" or "knocking out cancer." Even the field of human behavior has been invaded by the sports metaphor. A popular way of conceptualizing self-defeating behavior is "games people play." Such usage is so commonplace that we rarely give it a second thought.

Recently, when Americans began to voice their concern about an inability to find meaning in traditional values, much was written about the need for a new national purpose. A widely circulated cartoon commented on this. It showed two baseball players standing before a cheering multitude of fans. One was saying to the other, "But I thought baseball was our national purpose." The joke, as I have already suggested, is not so far from expressing the true state of affairs.

In his classical work on wit and humor, Sigmund Freud observed that "in jest truth emerges."* For various reasons of conscience, embarrassment, fear, and integrity, people tend to push certain issues out of their awareness. But these issues are not lost and may in fact reappear when the psychological guard is down. Sports interest is one of these. Indeed, Americans tend to be somewhat embarrassed by the intensity of their feelings about sports. They express concern about the priority of sports in schools and the idolatry of sports heroes, but this concern does not seem to diminish their fervor.

Why should there be this inner doubt, this lurking sense of embarrassment? In a preliminary way we can take our bearings at once. It is usual to

---

*Sigmund Freud, "Wit and Its Relation to the Unconscious," *The Basic Writings of Sigmund Freud*, trans. and ed. by A. A. Brill (New York: Random House, 1938), pp. 711–727.

explain modern sports as a complex outgrowth of play, arguing that the play of children and primitives, through cultural refinement, became what we know as sports. To play may be defined as "to engage in sport or diversion, to amuse oneself, to frolic or gambol; to act in a way that is not to be taken seriously." By definition, then, play is not a serious activity and should not be considered too important. If this is so, we must conclude that Americans occupy themselves, to a large extent, with activities they consider unimportant.

We deepen our understanding of play by contrasting it with its traditional opposite, work: "continued exertion or activity directed to some purpose or end; especially manual labor; hence, opportunity for labor; occupation." Work is "an undertaking; a task." In the very meaning of the words, work, in contrast to play, is clearly something to be taken seriously.

In the earlier history of America, the Protestant ethic idealized work; play was one of its rewards. Every boy heard, "Get your work done so you'll have time to play," and play without work was a forbidden fruit. In the latter twentieth century, a shrinking workweek, vacations, and retirement plans present problems for those still influenced by the spirit of the nineteenth century. The "Sunday neurotic" has made his appearance: the person who is effective at work and depressed with his leisure. He can enjoy his play only when he "steals" time for it; otherwise, guilt interferes. As a clandestine activity he can enjoy it, but when it is allowed or expected, he cannot. The man who has worked hard for retirement finds his free time, which was sought so diligently, to be empty and devoid of meaning. In the ambivalent attitude toward the playboy—publicly scorned, privately envied—we find the traditional view of play.

Today the relationships between work and play are greatly changed.* A considerable part of unskilled and semiskilled labor has been replaced by automation, making steady work unattainable for many Americans. For many of the ten to twenty million chronically unemployed, not working has become an acceptable state. During the great depression of the 1930s, the unemployed worker was guilt-ridden and filled with an overriding sense of personal inadequacy.† Contemporary unemployment compensation lines are surprisingly different. There is "an unmistakable air of conviviality"†† among many regulars and resentment against authorities for inconvenience. Unemployment does not, of course, preclude a man's interest in sports; the

---

*There are also generational differences. Those born in the first part of this century carry with them the spirit of the previous century and idolize work. Those born later tend to doubt its purpose.

†Mirra Komarovsky, *The Unemployed Man and His Family: Effect of Unemployment upon the Status in 59 Families* (New York: Dryden Press, 1940).

††Gregory P. Stone, Ph.D., personal communication. Stone, a sociologist, joined unemployment lines to observe.

commitment that in other times would have been reserved for work may be focused instead on the team of his choice.

The complexity of modern technology and the mandatory retirement age have produced profound attitudinal changes, even in those who find steady work. Added educational requirements prolong the period of career preparation and diminish productive years. At the other end, increasingly early retirement seems to leave only a fleeting moment for production. Quite the reverse is true, however, of sports and play, which grow with every reduction in work. Even while we are at the office, production sometimes seems to pale in significance when compared with extracurricular activities like the coffee break, so sanctified that practically nothing has precedence over it.

While work diminishes, preoccupation with sports grows. In the footrace of time, work led the way, with play following slowly behind; but in this century, wearing the colors of sport, play has taken the lead.

Still the anachronistic definitions of work and play prevail, in part because of "cultural lag." We continue to say that work is serious and play is not, but contemporary behavior makes it appear that the opposite is more nearly true. Word and deed are fractured, leaving a void symbolized by the person who withdraws and wants nothing to do with either work or sports, or the revolutionary who seeks to change the system. But most Americans do not withdraw from sports; instead they approach them with the vigor and dedication formerly reserved for work.

Play and sports, by definition, are nonproductive, carefree, nonserious activities. But for the professional athlete they are handsomely productive. With fringe benefits such as commercial endorsements, the professional athlete can be generously rewarded in our culture, beyond most other professionals and at least on a par with the executives of big business. Only a few athletes attain this preeminence, but the potential is there for all.

One may explain the willingness of fans to pay for their sports events—and they pay handsomely—on the basis of entertainment value received. But does entertainment alone account for spectators who willingly endure inclement weather and personal sacrifice for the sake of a sport? Does it explain, for example, the loyal New York Met fans who steadfastly supported their team in baseball's most miserable showing, or the rioting that accompanies the Stanley Cup competition in ice hockey? Clearly, one must look for motives deeper than casual amusement to understand the fans' loyalty, commitment, and willingness to sacrifice.

Whether for pay or school loyalty, modern sports are dominated by the spirit of work—by long hours of learning signals and plays; by arduous, bruising, bonebreaking practice; by absolute obedience to coach or manager, all in preparation for the big game. Is the word "player" really appropriate for an athlete engaged in such activities?

There is a fascinating illustration of the complete reversal of work and play in athletics. Those sports that began as play, such as ball games, have now lost the playful and lighthearted characteristic and have assumed instead all of the qualities of serious, hard work. Hunting and fishing, in contrast, began as the soul of work, and so they remain for primitives—serious, productive, and necessary for survival. But in our culture, hunting and fishing have assumed the true spirit of play; they are carefree, amateur, diversional recreation.

THE PARADOX OF SPORTS AND PHYSICAL FITNESS

If the psychosocial functions of sports are paradoxical, we can at least find clarity and continuity in their physical benefits? Proponents of sports activities equate them with physical fitness and consider this the important justification for their existence. Nothing should take precedence over our nation's health and fitness, it is said. We must do everything possible to ensure the fitness and health of our nation's youth. This is a point of view with which few will disagree.

The basic tenet of this position is that sports activity leads to physical fitness. Unfortunately the relationship is not confirmed by close scrutiny. If there is a correlation, it may be more nearly inverse. For example, in a 1962 statement on the nation's physical fitness, President Kennedy referred to studies by Kraus and Weber at Columbia-Presbyterian Hospital over a fifteen-year period. Using a standardized physical fitness test, they tested several thousand children and young adults and compared the results obtained by American and European youths. Their conclusion was a disturbing one: while only 1 percent of the Europeans failed, 35 percent of the Americans were unable to pass the test. Yet sports are not ordinarily a major or required part of European educational systems.

The decline in fitness of American youth can also be demonstrated within our own borders. At Yale University a physical fitness test administered to incoming freshmen revealed that 51 percent passed in 1951, 43 percent in 1956, 38 percent in 1960, 35 percent in 1965—a 16 percent drop in fourteen years. The test used, it may be added, was not an overly rigorous one.

These discouraging results have occurred despite the growing importance of sports. Thus, the expected relationship between sports and physical fitness cannot be confirmed. It may even be possible to demonstrate that a negative relationship exists.

The picture is even less encouraging for adults, since the fan sitting in the stadium with a hot dog in one hand and a bottle of beer in the other is hardly contributing to his own fitness or to the nation's. It cannot even be argued that many of our most popular sports are for the physical benefit of the athletes. On the same day in 1961, the oustanding stars of both the National Football League and the American Football League* were classified 4F by their respective draft boards because of chronic injuries. Benny Paret and

Davey Moore both died from injuries received in the ring, and although they are extreme cases, there have been many instances of long-range effects of boxing on the boxer.†

Even the physical benefits of sports, then, are doubtful. If there really is a logic behind the American sports mania, we are not, apparently, going to find it in any correlation with physical fitness.

OF MEN AND BOYS

In growing up, a boy is provided with many models of adult behavior. Some are explicit and deliberately offered, and others are only implied. The models come from a variety of sources: parents, teachers, peer groups, movies, television, history books, and novels. A major part of the growing-up process is sorting the impossible roles from those that are possible. Many such models can be rejected with relative ease. At some point, for example, it is useful for a boy to realize that the American cowboy is an anachronism with little or no place among practical adult activities. In the case of the cowboy role, a boy is aided by society in his task of selection. He soon learns that, outside of books and movies, he is not likely to encounter a cowboy—one just does not often see cowboys in the flesh.†† In addition, the adult world, while patronizingly tolerant of a youngster who is playing cowboy, is actively opposed to adults playing cowboy.

How different the situation is in sports! The adult world not only looks with favor on the role of athlete but deliberately fosters it. American youths are explicitly prepared for the athlete's role in exquisitely accurate miniaturizations of the professional team. Little League baseball and Pop Warner football are almost exact duplications of major professional sports. The uniforms, the publicity, the arduous practice, the complex plays, and, most of all, the pressure of adult expectation make the role of professional athlete not only a future possibility but a present reality.

I once sat down with a former professional football player to watch the telecast of a football game. Anticipating a college or professional game, we sat uneasily for several moments watching, with only a vague realization that there was something amiss and not knowing what it was. We then realized that the players were children and that this was a Pop Warner football game. So completely was the adult sports role simulated, even an expert could not tell immediately that these were only boys.

---

*Paul Hornung and Jack Kemp, backfield stars for the then league-leading professional football teams, the Green Bay Packers and the San Diego Chargers.

†Sercl and Jaros, European physicians, reported evidence of chronic brain damage in nine percent of boxers, even among those who had had only a few fights.

††See "Appearance and the Self;" Gregory P. Stone, in *Human Behavior and Social Processes*, ed. Arnold M. Rose (Boston: Houghton Mifflin Co., 1961), p. 86, for the importance of costume in these models.

The role of athlete is thrust upon boys at ever younger ages. A football-shaped rattle is now available to get infants started on the right track. Before children can read, they wear replicas of sports uniforms. Once they can walk, training begins in earnest.

A boy will have daily encounters with sportsmen at all stages of his development. Older brothers, coaches, fathers, and fans are all eager to show him how the game is played. There is probably no adult role in which each stage of development is so omnipresent and clearly visible as the athlete's. In a world filled with social discontinuity, there seems to be a place for everyone in sports.

On the other hand, work roles seem to have little if any continuity. In our specialized society, a child often has very little real knowledge of his father's work. To begin with, the child never sees him at work. The extent of first-hand knowledge is that the father leaves home at an appointed hour, about the time that the child goes to school, five days a week. Beyond that, everything is hearsay.

I once witnessed a colleague attempting to explain his work as a psychiatrist to his seven-year-old son. The frustration of the father was exceeded only by the bewilderment of the son, until finally, in desperation, they agreed to go out later and play catch. This, unlike the father's work, was something they could quite easily share.

Although the function of a psychiatrist may be especially esoteric, this scene occurs thousands of times with stockbrokers, bank tellers, scientists, and factory workers. Even if there is a product involved, there may be little hope of a father's conveying any real understanding of his work to his son. The little boy who says, "My daddy makes missiles," would hardly be able to answer a second question. In fact, even his father may have only a hazy notion of how his job fits into the total operation.

At home on weekends, a boy may see his father at a form of work, but it is strange work, for it may be helping with the housework or gardening or performing some of the more nostalgic simulations of work represented by the do-it-yourself movement. Here a son may see his father make things, usually inferior to the manufactured product and costing a little more.

Of course, there are a few fathers whose jobs, usually remnants of nineteenth century crafts, can be carried out at home in full view of their families. But such jobs are diminishing in relative numbers, and such fathers represent a minority.

Boys are more apt to see their fathers at play or at work simulating play than at the occupation that provides them with a livelihood. This play often takes the form of sports, with parents and children sharing the role of spectator, or with parents as spectators to their children, or with a father instructing his son in athletics. In such circumstances, a boy's interest in sports is carefully nurtured, but we may well ask to what end this preparation is directed.

A CBS television documentary in 1961, "The Secret Life of Sam Huff," depicted the hard life of a professional football player. It was about the daily life of the then New York Giants' middle linebacker, and it detailed the punishing drudgery endured by the professional athlete. As the program reached its climax, Sam Huff turned dramatically to the television screen and said that pro football "is for men, not boys." If the men are the ones playing football, what are the boys doing?

The present-day ideal for boys is no longer the Horatio Alger success story; the notion, true or not, that every boy can be President is less exciting than it used to be. In place of this traditional ideal has come a new dream, the dream of Peter Pan, of perpetual youth, with every boy a major leaguer.* If a boy learns to play well enough, he may drink from the fountain of youth and continue to play as a professional athlete. For playing, he will be more handsomely rewarded than if he had worked.

Unfortunately, even though almost every boy is rigorously prepared for the role of star athlete, very few can achieve it. But the preparation is continuous through childhood to adult life. Unlike other models, which eventually are discarded as impossible or impractical, the role of sportsman is in some form continually and firmly reinforced by society.

There is something, a kind of consolation prize, for those who fail. They can become fans, and most of them do. They continue intensely to follow the progress of athletes and teams. Emotionally, if not physically, they remain ever ready if the call to play should come. Spectators and athletes join hands with entrepreneurs to keep the hopes of all alive. In sports there is, indeed, something for everyone.

Although there is something for everyone in sports, it is unfortunately not enough. The spectator's role maintains a continuity of interest in sports, but often at the expense of other activities in which there are opportunities to participate more actively. To the fan, much of life seems insignificant in comparison with the excitement at the stadium. He lives in a sitting position, viewing the action through field glasses from afar.

Even a star professional athlete sometimes recognizes the paradox of his greatness. Roy Campanella, before his nearly fatal automobile accident one of the greatest baseball catchers of all time, noted that there must be a lot of "little boy" in a professional athlete to allow him to play. In a more critical tone, Bill Russell, the great player and coach in the National Basketball Association for many years, described the dilemma this way: "We're a bunch of grown men playing a child's game by complicating it. Silly, isn't it?" Even in greatness, the player's role sometimes seems a form of arrested development and may prove embarrassing.

Whatever their deficiencies, the roles of fan and athlete are more viable

---

*Another perpetual youth fantasy, the rock music star, has emerged in the 1970s.

and exciting for Americans than most others. Sports occupy a treasured position so cherished and guarded that there is a reluctance to study their real significance. There have been relatively few attempts to examine the social and psychological significance of sports in America and even fewer that have studied what this sports madness portends for our future. In contrast to the serious literature on sports, there is an overwhelming mass of writing which reports the results of contests almost instantaneously. That race to keep up with the results and almost never to look beyond is not without significance, for as Freud long ago observed, people are reluctant to make any penetrating examination of activities that give them pleasure. Even though the activity may have many limitations and may even create problems, it is experienced as being better than nothing, and a deeper understanding of it is vigorously resisted for fear that the insight will deprive one of the pleasure.

The psychological literature on the play of children provides a further contrast, representing one of the largest areas for psychological study and serving as a principal vehicle for the study of personality development. Is it not curious that sports—adult play—should be exempt from the same scrutiny? Instead they are treated as facts to be reported and accepted at face value.

Despite this apparent reluctance to find out more about the meaning and motivation of American sports, there are compelling reasons for a search. The United States is the second great nation in history to spend great amounts of time and resources in elaborately producing spectator sports. The first was Rome during the period of its decline. Whether or not the same fate will befall us is a matter for conjecture. Sports are an overwhelming influence in the lives of Americans, and if our society is to progress we must know what we are doing and why. It is to that end that this book has been written.

As we have seen, Americans feel embarrassed about recognizing the importance of sports, for it is contrary to traditional concepts of what should be important. As traditional work becomes less familiar and serious, sports assume the characteristics formerly associated with work. Player and worker become paradoxical terms.

This confusion has its strangest influence on growing American boys, many of whom have been carefully prepared for a life of dedication to sports. Although thoroughly familiar with sports activities at ever-earlier ages, most American boys have little firsthand knowledge of modern occupational roles to which they might more reasonably aspire. Many prepare themselves in sports for roles that will never be realized, and as has-beens by their teens, they join the army of spectators. There they become more fully occupied in watching from afar than they ever are while participating in activities that require more immediate involvement.

The effect of these paradoxes on the personality development of the individual is that the transition from boy to man becomes a contradictory journey to nowhere. Play is unquestionably an important aspect of personality development. It is a way of trying out new roles and of symbolically mastering childhood anxieties. In most societies the organized play of children prepares them for adult roles and activities. American competitive sports prepare youth instead for maturity as spectators who watch rather than participate in the significant and meaningful activities in society. Unfortunately, the role of spectator is limited, and it therefore estranges one from the satisfaction of total involvement with life.

Case Histories

2.

The Athlete as a Patient

The part of my psychiatric work that has been with athletes has been interesting and rewarding for me. I feel enriched by these experiences. In the following chapters are descriptions of some of the athletes with whom I have worked. Naturally, the names and details of their lives have been altered to protect their anonymity.

There have been many public images of the athlete. For a number of years he was considered big, dumb, and inarticulate; more recently he has been characterized as a tough but shallow businessman who exploits sports for all he can get. Perhaps these stereotypes do fit a few athletes; however, I am convinced that they are not appropriate for most. This leads me to believe that some of these myths are the result of "sour grapes" on the part of a public that envies the success of the athlete. It is understandable that those who did not "make it" feel better by assuming the athlete is limited in other ways. It is the same phenomenon as the erroneous belief that the genius must be intellectually brilliant but limited in his physical and social capacity.

Most of the athletes I have known have been bright, well educated, and articulate. They have been socially aware and sensitive, broadened by their wide-ranging experiences. The successful athlete has many opportunities that contribute to his sophistication, for he travels widely and meets a great variety of people. However, when an athlete becomes emotionally upset he shares with all of us the same human problems and struggles. Everyone needs to feel respected, to have satisfactions, and to make something meaningful of his life. When one of these elements is lacking, he may find himself in conflict and need to find new ways to live his life more fully.

In that sense, the athlete is much like anyone else who seeks to develop himself through psychotherapy, but in another way he may experience his conflict more acutely. Some of the paradoxes in our society may be more sharply manifested in the athlete because of his success. For example, he may not have experienced the transition from the pleasures of youth to the satisfactions of maturity until much later in life. In addition, his perceptions of the relationship between work and play may be confused, since he may have been able to keep them undifferentiated for a long time. The nature of the star image, which elevates the athlete to adulation by others, may also leave him unprepared for the relative anonymity that follows. All of these may interfere with developing mutually satisfying relationships with others, and with the recognition that life is more then a mere sport or game.

Earlier in this century there was the belief that mental health and mental illness were very different. As we learned more, we came to realize that there is no sharp distinction, but rather a wide spectrum of possibilities in between. Today, we realize that the factors that promote a sense of mental health and well-being may be quite different from those that promote ill health, making the situation even more complicated.

A number of major studies have examined the problem. The Midtown Study examined a segment of the general population in Manhattan to determine the extent and nature of mental health and mental disorder. The Sterling County Studies similarly examined rural populations in the maritime provinces of Canada. Both of these studies revealed astonishingly large numbers of people who had the kinds of problems and conflicts that lead people to seek help from a psychotherapist—up to two thirds of them—yet many, even most, did not consider themselves to be disturbed. The presence of conflict appeared to be a less important determinant of discomfort than the nature and extent of the supports the person experienced in his community. Those people who lived in orderly, well-organized, and integrated communities felt better about themselves than those who lived in disorganized, chaotic ones.

Different people may find different degrees of organization and coherence in a community, and this will depend upon the individual's unique, subjective experiences. The person who has a sense of commitment to some aspect of his community may have a sense of coherence and meaning for all of it. This commitment serves as an anchor point to the individual for a conceptual organization of the community. In otherwise disorganized communities, sports and team identification may provide some individuals with this sense of order and commitment. The individual is able to find meaning, and therefore health and well-being, through his athletic involvement.

When an athlete's or a fan's involvement in sports is interrupted for some reason, he is in danger of losing his sense of order and meaning in life. His once-orderly community life becomes fragmented and chaotic. Thus, many of the athletes described here became upset when they were deprived of their full participation in sports. For the person who has enjoyed this sense of meaning and order, its loss may be especially devastating.

However, we all have similar needs and impulses. The healthy person has been able to find a means of satisfying them in society, a means that does not create too much conflict between himself and others. We all have aggressive impulses when frustrated. The healthy person may express them in sports; the criminal expresses them in naked, unrestrained forms that put him in conflict with society; the neurotic is in personal conflict about his impulses, and struggles with whether or not to express them. When the athlete loses one of his socially rewarded means of obtaining satisfaction, he may express his impulses in a way that is destructive to others, or he may experience them internally as conflict.

3.

The Boy Who Played the Game Too Well

One morning several years ago, an overworked colleague complained bitterly to me about the inappropriate use of psychiatric hospitals. His irritation stemmed from an experience the night before when he had been called at a late hour to admit a young college athlete referred for psychiatric hospitalization. My colleague insisted there was nothing wrong with the young man aside from his having had a disappointing basketball season. He described how the youth had appeared at the hospital and cheerfully requested admission with a letter from his psychiatrist. He had been attending a nearby college, was in his senior year, and was captain of the basketball team and star of the previous year's championship team. This year, however, amid public expectations of athletic greatness, he had failed even to approach previous performances. He did not reveal much disturbance on admittance to the hospital, and it was easy to understand how my harassed, overworked, and tired colleague had little sympathy for someone who looked so cheerful and whose major disappointments were about "play."

The day following this conversation I had occasion to visit the young man in his hospital ward. He was an impressive sight, towering six feet seven inches, his lithe muscular frame topped by short blond hair. A handsome youth, almost too handsome, he was a caricature of the all-American boy, the sort who might be found on the cover of a teenage magazine. His name was Cal. He greeted me with a breezy "Hi, Doc, what can I do for you?" Even to a psychiatrist, blasé from long experience with incongruous behavior, this was startling. Strong, cheerful, seemingly composed, Cal's only expressions of concern were sympathetic remarks about the other patients and gratuitous offers of help to the professional staff. It was not until we moved into an office, behind closed doors, that his mood changed. "Doc, I let everybody down, especially myself. I don't understand what's happened to me," he began. This is the story he told:

In his college town, Cal was considered potentially the greatest basketball player in the school's history. The coaches and sportswriters who saw him as a freshman, a sophomore, and then a junior said all he needed was "maturity," which would undoubtedly come the next year when, as captain and leader of the team, he would realize his ability. There was mention of All-American honors. Most of the players were returning for this climactic senior year, and so it was taken for granted that the team, which had had a good previous season, would have an even better record this year, especially since they were led by their experienced and popular, if sometimes erratic, star.

Although he considered statements about his ability unwarranted, he was nevertheless pleased by them. Personal success, however, was something Cal rarely acknowledged. He attributed what came his way to his teammates and underplayed his own role. The fact that he insisted he was not as capable as everyone seemed to think was accepted as the becoming modesty fans have come to expect of outstanding athletes.

So appealing was his manner that in this fateful senior year he was elected fraternity president. Although he was not the driving organizer usually elected, his "brothers" recognized the prestige he would bring to the house because of his athletic prowess and campus popularity. They arranged his duties so that he would not be burdened with the administrative details of office and could devote himself fully to the basketball season. After all, he was their most celebrated member. He seemed pleased with his lot, although he deliberately avoided thinking too much about the coming athletic season.

As the year began, its significance began to dawn on him. A single thought haunted him: "This is my senior year; it's the end of the line." He felt that after this season there would be nothing ahead—no future. This recurrent thought concerned him so much that he could think of little else.

Although he was never one to discuss his problems with others, he became so preoccupied that he did mention this fear to his buddies. They were quick to point out his potential in professional basketball, business, and coaching, and dismissed his concern as further evidence of the modesty that made him so popular. They didn't understand, and so thereafter he kept his concerns to himself.

He began this most important season amid the fanfare of a campus anticipating a championship. In the past he had not been an extremely high scorer, only because he was such a dedicated team player. He always led the team in assists and had a more-than-presentable eighteen-point average. He always said he would rather "feed off" than shoot. As he saw it, the team was far more important than the individuals on it.

The previous year's chief scorer had graduated, and so in the sports chatter and speculation everyone assumed that the burden of this function would be carried by Cal. During practice, much coaching time was spent preparing him for this role. Cal, however, found it difficult and did not shoot any more in the first few games than he had during the past season, in spite of his coach's remonstrances. As the season wore on, he took fewer and fewer shots. His performance became at times ludicrous, since he would feed off even when he had a setup. Rather than take a cinch shot while standing alone under the basket, he would dribble out until he could feed off. The crowd roared its disapproval at this strange behavior. His game average dropped to ten points and then to five points.

The more pressure he felt, the more he refused to shoot. It was not that he was uncooperative, for he agreed wholeheartedly with the coach's instructions, but with every growing demand he felt compelled to be more of a team player, despite the fact that the team wanted him to score. Through it all was the growing, haunting thought, "This is the end of the line; after this season there is nothing."

He believed he could master his growing tension by working out harder. This was the way he had solved problems before. He took extra workouts and practiced fundamentals almost every waking hour. If he had any energy remaining, he would run up and down the empty basketball court. Even now, as he sat sprawled in his chair in a mental hospital ward, he said, "I'm sure if I just could have worked out harder, I could have handled this thing."

As his playing became worse, he began to believe there was a physical basis for his discomfort, perhaps the flu or even heart trouble. Each morning he appeared at the college infirmary with a new set of minor physical complaints referable to every organ system in his body. He said, "If someone just could have told me it was something physical, I would have been the happiest person in the world." But no one did, and he continued to decompensate.

The solution still seemed to him to be harder workouts. One day, in spite of running and jumping vigorously in practice, he felt no relief. He put more effort into running, but it did not seem fast enough. He felt a rising sense of panic, and ran to his car, got in and drove off as fast as he could. Somehow he felt if he could get going fast enough he would feel better. Out into the country he drove at a furious speed. Then, as his tension turned to confusion, he slowed the car and finally returned to town, to drive aimlessly, slowly, for several hours more.

Finally, stopping at a service station, confused and bewildered, he found the telephone number of a physician who was one of his fans, and called him. The doctor came immediately to see him and sedated him. Lying in the college infirmary in a hazy state, a new solution to his panic emerged. If this were not his senior year, if the end of college and of the team were not in sight because of graduation, then things would be as before.

The next morning he took steps to drop some courses so he would not graduate on schedule. He also made another decision which he said he could not understand at the time. He spoke to his adviser about switching his major from physical education to psychology. Before this, he had scrupulously avoided psychology courses.

This plan was, of course, doomed to fail, and now new problems emerged. Dropping courses terminated his sports eligibility and, instead of bringing him closer to his teammates, separated him from them precipitously. In addition, he had to contend with the basketball coach's outrage and the team's and the fans' perplexity. Now he felt like a freak. Eventually he was referred to the college psychiatric consultant who, in turn, recommended his hospitalization.

What had happened to this collegian, this All-American-caliber basketball player, this fraternity president? What had happened to this sought-after man-about-campus, and why had such a promising future turned into no future at all? Why had college, the preparatory phase of his life, turned out to be the end of the line?

As he talked, it became clear that his future seemed completely blank. He had never given more than momentary thought to what he would do after college. In fact, he behaved as if school would never end. Even more curious, it seemed that his past, too, was blank. It became apparent that he had blocked out his past and future with a curtain of sports. He had fantastic detailed information about sports and athletes, and the events of his own sports career were remembered in the tiniest detail. Each morning he "memorized" the sports page. The performances of great athletes were extremely vivid to him, and their records were the vital statistics of his life. With such a preponderance of objective, factual material accumulated, he had no room for thoughts of his or anyone else's personal life outside of sports. Thoughts about his parents and his relationship to them were vague, so vague as to seem nonexistent. To questions about his feelings, he usually responded that he did not know. So massive was this wall of repression that only the simplest and most benign events were available to him.

Those few personal events he did recall resulted in blind alleys. For example, he remembered that when he was eight years old he slept for a time in the same room with his grandmother. One night she became seriously ill and a doctor was called, but several hours later the old woman died. The undertaker came and took her away. He reported he slept undisturbed through this eventful night, and he was surprised the next morning to find her bed empty. The emptiness was like his own past and future. His surprise at hearing the events of that night was like his surprise in realizing school would not go on forever. He was completely unprepared for events outside of the sports realm.

He was known as "Cool Cal," a nickname that followed him through his athletic career. During games he always appeared relaxed and unconcerned. Moreover, he was always reassuring his teammates to "take it easy" or "don't worry." So widely known was this assurance that his fans used to shout their encouragement by friendly mimicry:

> Take it easy,
> Take it easy,
> Co-o-o-l Cal!

He scrupulously avoided things that were serious and was known as a clown, for it seemed that the more the tension grew in a situation, the more he joked. He rarely contemplated what was happening, but made light even of serious situations. His actions were almost always interpreted by others as colorful.

Although Cal's early childhood was one of enforced seclusion, imposed by his mother, as he grew older he developed a legion of "buddies" who shared his interest in sports. He was one of a group of inseparable companions, and by the time he reached high school he was an expert athlete and was already well known. He achieved all-league honors in high school in three sports: football, basketball, and baseball. Although his sports interests were all-consuming, he nevertheless went rather successfully through the motions of other student activities. He became president of the student body. He attended school dances and other affairs with a variety of girls but never had a "steady." In spite of the fact that he was sought after and at times literally "chased" by girls, he avoided any intense involvement with the excuse that he didn't want anything to interfere with sports and never wanted to let the team down.

His sexual experiences, too, were in the service of team sports. He was not really very interested, and those few occasions when he did become involved he did so only to be part of the team. Sometimes after a game, he and his buddies might pick up some girls, and on a few occasions they even went to houses of prostitution.

Although his interest and proficiency included all sports, his participation was limited to team sports: football, basketball, and baseball. He tried tennis, golf, and track, the individual sports, but found them dull and empty. On one occasion he was enticed by the track coach to run a quarter-mile for practice. In this first and only attempt, Cal ran within two seconds of the school record. The coach's joy turned to frustration, however, when he found Cal had no interest whatever in track. Arguing, pleading, threatening were all to no avail. As Cal put it to the poor, bewildered man, "It's no fun running out there all by yourself."

Even though it was predicted that he could have done equally well in football and baseball, basketball was Cal's choice in college over the less vigorous and sometimes slow deliberateness of baseball and the hostile contact of football. In basketball he felt a strength derived from the closeness to the other members of the team. His most meaningful relationships were with his basketball teammates, who were his buddies and with whom he enjoyed the team play on the court. "Feeding off," which was later to reach such compelling proportions, had always been the most fun. Nothing held such satisfaction as weaving skillfully down the court to hand off or to pass to a teammate for a score.

There were some ominous signs pointing toward his eventual hospital admission. They were deeply submerged, however, by the brilliance of Cal's athletic achievements and the superficial characteristics that made him, among his peers, a popular, colorful, all-American boy. The most outstanding was his inability to make even simple personal decisions, avoiding them until a decision was forced. At home, his mother was only too willing to take over, insisting that her decision reflected Cal's desire. In college, his buddies performed this function.

Now, as his amateur collegiate playing days drew to an end, he was faced with decisions only he could make. In characteristic fashion, though, he blanked these out of his mind, and consequently life lost its meaning and he became aimless. He could no longer use vigorous sports activity to fill the void between the past he had to forget and the future he feared to approach. Neither coaching nor professional sports, both of which seemed reasonable fields for him to enter, held the slightest appeal.

Cal's family story seems bizarre because of its extremes, and yet it is similar in nature if not in degree to that of many American families. The story begins with dissatisfied parents. His mother was a career woman with a certain bitterness toward the new baby for having interfered with her orderly life. He was an unplanned child and remained an only child. She could not warmly hold, feed, or cuddle the baby, but she became preoccupied with fears for his safety. Intolerant of her own bitterness to the point that she had to conceal it even from herself, she overcompensated by controlling him and being overprotective. Unable to give warmth and love to him, she willingly assumed the responsibility for restricting him.

His father responded more positively to his new role. A thread of freedom, warmth, and mutual regulation developed between him and the boy. Perhaps as much out of opposition to his wife as out of affection for the child, he took over many of the traditional mothering functions. (This is the case in many American homes where the mother's working blurs the accepted roles. When both parents work, sharing the traditional paternal functions, both must share in the mothering functions.) Cal's father despised his own work for its tedium and enthusiastically put much of his energies into being an avid sports fan. The warmth and companionship between father and son developed against a background of sports.

Our young athlete learned one thing well from his father: how to fill an empty life with sports, a phenomenon not uncommon in American homes. When his mother talked and nagged, his father ignored her and read the sports page. As Cal put it, "There is a lot of not-listening at my house." This fact was amply illustrated when at one point in Cal's therapy, father, mother, and Cal were seen together. Cal sat between them, nearer his father, looking furtively toward his mother from time to time with a perplexed expression. As his mother spoke, his father turned his head away and whistled a silent tune, occasionally interrupting impulsively.

During Cal's childhood and adolescence his proficiency in sports grew, and this interest consumed nearly all of his energy. In his relationships with teammates he found something akin to the closeness of mothering, which in his experience was really the fathering experience. It was here that he learned what was to be his greatest joy in basketball, "feeding off" to a teammate.

As was inevitable, though, the golden dream of perpetual youth collapsed—for permanence and growth are mutual contradictions. The transition from boy to man could not be delayed. The experience that signaled impending disaster occurred during the summer between his junior and senior years, when one of his lifelong friends married. Cal was in the wedding party, and as he stood beside his friend, a feeling of faintness came over him and he had the thought, "It's all coming to an end right here." This was the clue to what he could not tolerate—the transition into manhood which meant he would have to be responsible for himself, for his pleasure, for his aggression. These could no longer be diffused within the team. He had to stand alone.

Cal played games to perfection; he had skill, sportsmanship, and color. But to him it was not really a game; it was everything. It was not a preparation for his future life, but life itself. Without school sports, life had no meaning. Therein lay the flaw in his character and one of the neurotic problems common in sports.

It was only over the course of his next year in therapy that the deeper meaning of the story behind this cloak of emptiness began to unfold and become understandable. "Cool Cal" was the prototype of the American ideal, a fine athlete who carried sportsmanship and team spirit to an extreme. He was, in short, a boy who played the game too well.

The conflicts that lay within this all-American boy with the blank past and the void future were anticipated by three dreams. He told the first of these dreams in one of the earliest therapeutic interviews, for it was a vivid dream and he had had it many times. He dreamed that a vicious gray wolf was chasing him; terrified, he ran and ran and ran. With the wolf nipping at him, he had to run faster and faster, but nowhere could he escape his pursuer.*

---

*The wolf has an honored place in writings on dreams. One of the classic cases in psychiatric literature is Freud's "Wolfman," so named because of the patient's dream about wolves.

His only hope was to run ever faster. Before a conclusion was ever reached he would awaken, frightened and perspiring. This first dream suggested something of the function of his athletic activity and how Cal, when his breakdown began, hoped that exercise and flight might lead to a solution.

The second dream, reported a few weeks later, was described as being like *High Noon*, the Western movie in which a law officer, amid great tension, awaits the return of the vengeful outlaws on the noon train. In the dream, Cal and four of his buddies were waiting expectantly in the upper story of a barn to "gun it out" with attackers who were expected at four o'clock. He felt confident at first, but as the hour approached he became fearful. The tension mounted until just before four o'clock, when he awakened from the dream. His gang was clearly the basketball team; four o'clock was the fourth year of college, his senior year. With the team he felt potent and confident, but as the fateful hour approached, his fright grew.

In the first dream the frightening object was the wolf; in the second, the object of fear was unknown. The third dream screamed out the identity of the subject he held in terror. In addition to the content it revealed, the dream shrouded his primitive fears so poorly that it demonstrated the extreme fragility of his personality structure and its tenuous protective defenses. It, too, was a dream of flight. He was driving his car, and his father was sitting with him. "I was driving like hell and had it down to the floorboard, but I was scared and no matter how fast I drove, I couldn't get away. My mother, stark naked, was chasing me and she was almost catching me."*

Cal was an only child. His parents were in their late thirties when they married, and it was almost ten years later before they had their son. It came as something of a surprise to them when his mother became pregnant, because both parents had given up their hope for an heir. His mother, with very little formal education, was a self-taught bookkeeper, very efficient and proud of her ability. She was reluctant to give up her job even though she was quite uncomfortable during the pregnancy. In addition, she was plagued by the obsessive concern that the child might be defective. As the time of delivery drew near, her tension increased. Her labor was difficult, but a healthy child was delivered. From the first, however, his mother would not hold him, for she said she was afraid that she might drop him. She was also too nervous to breast-feed him. It is not surprising that as an infant he was fretful and colicky. The mother's tension mounted and her usual control threatened to break down. She was able to regain her composure by returning to work only a few months after the birth of the child.

Although there were relatives and housekeepers, Cal's father willingly

---

*The terror in dreams often represents a twisted wish, here suggesting the incestuous nature of the problem. This also raises a question about the seemingly warm relationship of father and son who might be expected to be rivals.

took over much of his care. He had worked as a civil servant in the Post Office Department for nearly twenty years, and the only promise his job held for him was its potential for retirement. He was disgruntled and often berated himself for not having found a more satisfying occupation. He felt trapped between a job he despised and a wife with whom he could not cope.

He found one avenue of escape which was acceptable to both his wife and the community where they lived. He was a sports fan, rarely missing any local sports events and often traveling to nearby cities to see them. Sports were his main source of satisfaction, and they recalled to him the pleasant days of his own modest athletic career.

In addition to providing his newborn son with some of the routine care babies need, Cal's father was able to combine this with his own pleasure. When Cal was still an infant, he would wrap him in swaddling clothes, take along some baby bottles, and head for the nearest sports event. At home, he held his son in his arms while listening to sports events on the radio. Thus, the father provided many of the traditional mothering functions of feeding and cuddling against the background of an ever-present athletic contest. The sounds of sports were soon associated with warmth, tenderness, and comfort, calming the infant.

One area in which Cal's father had no part was that of controlling his growing son. His mother, an orderly, neat woman who "couldn't stand a mess," willingly assumed the responsibility for training functions. She had long ago abandoned the hope that her husband would be able to take charge. She felt it was up to her, and where she had been uncertain and fearful in feeding and holding young Cal, where authority was required she acted decisively. The child's response was to suck and bite whatever he could reach, including crib sidings and clothing. She felt this behavior disturbing, and dealt with it harshly.

Her fears that something would happen to him were almost realized when Cal began to walk. One day when she crossed the street to mail a letter, he followed and was almost struck by a car. The mother's fright was quickly mobilized into action as she placed stringent controls on him. Cal was literally kept indoors for much of his early life except when he could be accompanied by an adult. He was sickly, and coupled with his mother's intense concern for his safety, he developed into a shy and inhibited child. He spent his time sitting immobilized, lest he displease his apprehensive mother, and his movements became awkward, clumsy, and indecisive.

The redeeming factor in Cal's life was his relative freedom in sports. Sports were his father's realm, and by unspoken agreement, his father had complete autonomy there. His mother's concern about safety was peculiarly isolated to exclude sports. Although her obsessive concern for his safety kept him from ever having a bicycle, from the time he started school he was allowed almost complete freedom when playing sports or games. More important even than the excursions Cal took with his father to sporting events was his freedom to express otherwise constricted physical desires when in his father's company.

At first Cal was awkward and inept as he attempted to learn the intricacies of athletics, but his tentative attempts at playing became gradually freer. He found that it was safe to participate in sports and also they lacked parental prohibitions. He received approval and encouragement as his father spent long hours patiently instructing him in the proper way to throw a ball or hold a bat. His cautious experimentation grew into exuberant skill, and as his ability and confidence grew, his absorption in sports was nearly complete. Thus the stage was set for the surprising disintegration of a promising life.

Riesman* has described the growing number of "other-directed" middle-class people who are guided more by associates of the same age and social class than by family, by traditions, or by desires for achievement. The pressures of these peer groups are reinforced by television, comics, and other mass media, and by parents whose dearest hope for their children is for them to be popular.

The disorder that tends to affect such people is role diffusion, for their roles are defined by the group, without whose support they suffer a loss of identity. Erikson† has described as the nuclear problem of adolescence the dilemma of choosing between identity and role diffusion. Adolescents characteristically cling together in gangs for identity support, but the difficulty grows if in adult life one relies on the group for role definition and identity. The group cannot always supply this support, and, further, it does not always believe its definitions. If a person relies completely on signals from others for his direction, he is vulnerable if he receives conflicting signals or if he is directed toward a goal that might be personally threatening.

For Cal, graduation meant individuation, that is, becoming a unique person responsible for his own pleasures and choices. It meant alienation from his primary nurturing, the team. Seeing his buddy make the fateful choice of marriage was the beginning of the end. "Feeding off" was one way of trying to secure "feedback," to ensure his place within the team.

His desperate clinging to peer relationships was necessary because of the frustrating failures in infancy and childhood to develop trust, autonomy, and initiative. The major consistent thread of security in his growth and development occurred within the context of team sports: the memory of being fed and held by his father at games, the liberty he was allowed in sports by his mother, and ultimately the identity he felt with the team.

---

*David Reisman, *The Lonely Crowd* (abridged edition), D. Riesman, N. Glazer, and R. Denney (Garden City, N.Y.: Doubleday & Company, 1953), p. 37.

†Erik Erikson, *Childhood and Society* (New York: W. W. Norton & Company, 1950), p. 307.

The dynamic forces of his development fitted almost too perfectly into the culture of his peers. He was wafted into a remarkably successful, if temporary, school career. He seemed to accept quite literally the only half-believed expectations of his peers. He was a caricature of the collegian in appearance, athletic ability, sportsmanship, and even sexuality.

His success is both a tribute to and an indictment of the institutions that supported him, for while they did not serve him permanently, they did offer something in place of nothing. The tragedy was that the pressure toward sports was so powerful that they replaced all other possibilities.

If Cal had had a modicum of success at other stages of development, his regression would not have been so devastating. As it was, he had little in the way of alternative personality skills to employ, even temporarily. The fact that he had no alternatives distinguishes Cal from so many other American boys. His case highlights the problem of giving up some of the satisfactions derived from sports for other opportunities for satisfaction. This is a problem experienced by a great number of youths. It thus serves less to set Cal apart from his peers than to emphasize his similarity to the group.

A FOLLOW-UP NOTE

The person whose pleasures come mainly from action often finds words a weak substitute. Such action-oriented people may initially find psychotherapy of dubious value, since it relies heavily on verbal communication. When a psychological disorder hits a person of this type, he finds himself in a serious dilemma, for although action has been his principal source of gratification, it has now failed him. Talking, directed toward the goal of understanding and opening up a wider choice of action, not only is alien for such people but is a threat to their principal protective system. Their past strength came from the instant response of action, and the therapist, who asks for thought before action, may be striking at the patient's deeply held fear.

If someone is oriented toward action, it does not necessarily mean that he is impulsive and unable to delay action successfully. The healthy person uses thought or speech as preparation for action, and these faculties serve him well when his usual behavior has failed him. His action is deliberate and is directed toward the goal of choice.

Cal learned early in life to distrust words as idle, ineffective chatter. The joint interview with his parents bore witness to how this was learned, for each parent ignored the words of the other. In his experience, only action had meaning. When he was unable to cope with a situation, his only quest for solution was physical—through "working out." When this failed, he was certain that his disability was physical.

By the time Cal entered the hospital he had had an unrewarding experience with psychotherapy, equally unsuccessful drug treatment, and electrotherapy. The challenge in treating him was to overcome his distrust by choosing areas of therapy in which he had strength, so that his shaky defenses would not be threatened. In talking about sports, he felt on reasonably safe ground, and so this became the focus of individual interviews. Often these meetings took the form of discussions of recent football or baseball games. Superficially, this might seem far removed from his problems, but in such discussions the important elements of his difficulties were present—the team, isolation or membership, winning or losing, the coach—all of which symbolized the important issues in his life.

In addition, in his ward treatment community Cal was able to reestablish relationships with a group similar to the team. He received support from his new "teammates" in facing his problems squarely. As could be expected, he was a good "team member." In his job assignment in the hospital recreation department, he was able to develop work skills and to face the emptiness he anticipated in work.

After several months he returned to college, graduated successfully, and is now teaching in a junior high school with most of his assignments in physical education. When last seen, his hope was to move into high school physical education and coaching.

When Cal went back to college, plans were made to continue therapy there. However, as could be anticipated, he quickly became involved in activities and lost interest in therapy as he felt better. I have seen him periodically, usually at my invitation, and although he seems grateful for these occasional visits, he has shown no desire for more intensive therapy.

Although his work performance is reported excellent, he still feels his life is not very meaningful. He is keenly aware of his isolation from his buddies, all of whom have married. He dates occasionally but rarely seriously. Looking back upon his illness, he sees it as a bad dream and still wishes it had been physical. Nothing in his present life has been able to compare in appeal with his college playing days, so nostalgically recalled.

4.

A Family Legacy

can't say I had ever had a conversation with Jack, and yet I felt I knew him well—in the way one knows an athletic hero. We both attended the same college, and bits of information proclaiming his football abilities would pass along the student grapevine until his comings and goings were as familiar to me as those of a roommate. Such a relationship between students and football star is a strange one. Students greeted him and he returned the greetings perfunctorily; much was known about him, but he knew nothing of his greeters.

I felt a strong kinship with Jack. Even though the college was large and our sports interests were different, in the gymnasium we shared a fraternal spirit. We spoke little to each other, and yet each knew who the other was. Our relationship was not personal and did not continue beyond the gymnasium. Thus when his wife (whom I had never seen) called me many years after college, I found it hard to place her. She explained that her husband had been seriously depressed and, too depressed to make the call himself, had asked her to call me for an appointment. When she said Jack remembered me from "better days," a flood of thoughts rushed to my mind. What did she mean? Whose "better days" was she talking about? Did Jack know I was physically handicapped and in a wheelchair?

Then I began to remember Jack from college. He had been known as "Jolting Jack," probably the most spectacular blocking back in the school's history. I could see him making one of his patented leaping moves, which took out two or three key men with a single block. He was more exciting to watch than the ball carrier. In the days before platooning he was also a defensive spark plug, moving up and down the line, encouraging the line with words and slaps. He seemed as wide as he was tall, burly and rough on the field, but surprisingly youthful in street clothes.

The anticipation of seeing him filled me with a mixture of feelings—he reminded me of pleasant college days and of the admiration I had had for his athletic ability; I was curious and concerned that someone who seemed an invulnerable specimen could become so depressed.

As he was led into my office by his wife, I immediately sensed my professional role. This was not a college reunion but a serious situation. I did not see the rugged football player I remembered. Rather, a drawn, thin man led by his wife moved slowly into my office. His short stature was apparent, not his strength. Although the day was hot, he was bundled up in a sweater with the collar turned up and looked as if he were preparing for a freeze. He stared blankly at me for a moment, stood motionless, and then forced a weak smile and began to cry softly and tearlessly. The only audible sound was an occasional whimper.

I began to see Jack regularly, and his history slowly unfolded. Since college he had played pro football for one short season. He hadn't done well; in a game of giants his short stature and relatively small size had been too much of a handicap. He had a series of minor injuries and his professional career ended. Returning home, he went to work in his father's automobile parts store. Although a failure in pro football, he was still a hero to his hometown, acclaimed as one of the best athletes they had ever produced. Old friendships were renewed and he basked in the recognition of the townspeople. He joined the Chamber of Commerce and the Elks, and led the boosters of the high school football team. Informally, he helped coach the team, working especially with the blocking backs and the linebackers—his old positions. He felt like "one of the boys" and they accepted him as one, calling him by his first name.

The one dark spot in his life was his job—he hated the work. It was sheer drudgery trying to sell things to people, and still worse organizing automobile parts. He felt life would be horrible if work were the only thing to look forward to. The only saving factor of the job was his enjoyment in talking to the workmen and customers. Otherwise he performed his job in a perfunctory and listless manner. As could be expected, tension developed with his father-employer. His father accused him of being a "playboy," but was certain he would grow out of it in a short time.

Jack was one of the town's most eligible bachelors and made the most of it. His sexual exploits were fabled, sometimes bordering on the heroic, with two consecutive dates in one evening. After a couple of years he began dating one girl steadily. Although he had his pick of the town's lovelies, he did not choose a pretty girl but, as he said, "one who wanted me more than any other girl did." She was always waiting for him, never disagreed with him, never seemed too upset if he was inattentive. He felt sure he could trust her. He did not know who proposed to whom, but, at any rate, they were married in one of the drunkest, wildest, and most celebrated local events of the year. Jack, the football hero, was married.

Jack's life continued very much as it had when he was single. He spent nights out with the boys, went to poker parties, participated in alumni groups and other clubs. He found to his pleasure that his popularity was even more enhanced by his marital state and his faithful companion. The wild sexual escapades of bachelorhood had become a strain for him, and he was now quite happy to confine his sexual activities to his wife while still enjoying the companionship of his friends.

Toward the end of the second year of their marriage, Jack's wife announced that there would be an heir born to the family. Jack was wild with joy. He let out a whoop which was the beginning of a three-day celebration, with mountains of cigars and cases of liquor. He had great, even grandiose plans for his child, whom he saw as a continuation of the family football dynasty.

This was a momentous event for Jack's father, too. He hoped that fatherhood would stimulate the maturity he had anticipated in his son. He recognized his own advancing age and looked forward to retirement. The plan he then initiated was to have far-reaching consequences for his son. Jack was gradually given more and more responsibility in the business, with the idea of his taking it over. This seemed appropriate to Jack, and he tried to work hard at fulfilling his job. However, the sense of emptiness within him grew in proportion to his increasing responsibilities. He was now haunted by a repetitive thought that there was "nothing to look forward to but a life of work."

This was an idea he dared not share with anyone. He was able to go through the motions of work with reasonable success, and so no one knew of his torment. The once-spontaneous smile was now a forced part of his facade. Jack puzzled about many things. He had once reveled in the adulation and praise he received, but now praise about his work seemed hollow and meaningless, giving him no satisfaction. But to the town and to his family, Jack was progressing as they had expected and everyone was pleased.

When first married, Jack and his wife had moved into his family's home. This seemed a practical idea since all the children were married and the big old family house was nearly empty. He had been away from home a long time and felt somewhat excited about returning. He was a little surprised at the intensity with which he found himself insisting it was the right thing to do, but once they were settled the tension seemed to leave. His wife, as always, was agreeable, since this was how Jack wanted it. Sometimes he thought to himself (secretly, of course), "This is the life. I have both my mother and my wife." His mother hovered over him as she had always done before, and continued to be solicitous.

Jack's wife also cherished some private thoughts. She had agreed to this arrangement only because she had wanted to please him, but tension developed between her and Jack's mother, since she could not appreciate the mother's ways. Try as she would to make the best of things, her anger increased. With the coming of the baby she talked seriously with Jack about getting a house of their own. Actually, Jack had also thought of their moving out, for he was becoming sensitive to some of the remarks his friends were making about his living in his parents' home. Still, he could not avoid the desperate feeling he sometimes had of wanting to stay at home with his parents. Although he did agree to look for a new house, it was without enthusiasm. Eventually he and his wife were able to find their own home in one of the new upper-middle-class areas of town. To Jack, however, it never seemed like home.

With this move, Jack seemed to change. His wife sensed something was wrong. When they were alone, he pouted when he didn't get his way. More disconcerting, his wild enthusiasm for the baby had now turned to disinterest. With the couple's increased responsibilities, his wife expected more from him. She hoped he would do little things around the house and was worried and annoyed that he seemed to resent this. They had harsh words about it.

Jack, too, was self-critical. He was angry at himself for his lack of interest in the home and in his coming child. When he felt tense or low he would return home to "visit the folks." This generally helped him feel better.

Although both Jack and his wife saw the changes that were taking place, they entered into an unspoken pact to say nothing about the situation. This did not smother the irritation, however. Although she regretted it many times afterward, she found herself yelling, "What did I marry, a man or a little boy?"

Her remark struck a vulnerable spot in Jack because it expressed his own unspoken concern. He repeatedly told himself to "act like a man," but the more he tried, the worse things became. His few remaining pleasures began to slip away. In his weekly poker parties with the boys, he had always been a fierce competitor and hated to lose. Now he found himself uneasy if he won a big pot. He didn't want to be ahead, but was comfortable only when he just broke even. All joy was taken out of playing, but he still went through the motions. Only his wife knew of his inner anguish.

When his wife went to the hospital to have the baby, Jack was very tense but was reassured by his friends, who told him all expectant fathers worried. He sat out the waiting time with two old high-school football teammates and actually began to feel pretty good while waiting, talking over old times with them. When the news came that he was the father of a fine baby boy, he was numb. After whoops of joy, one of his friends went to the phone and called Jack's father, giving Jack the phone to make the announcement. In a stunned voice he said, "Dad, we have a little boy." As he listened to himself his voice sounded very distant and strange. The voice on the other end of the line cheered loudly, and even in his dazed state he had to hold the receiver away from his ear.

His father's mood changed and the voice at the other end became solemn.

He announced the decision he had made several months ago. "Son, I've been waiting for this moment to tell you. I'm going to retire. I'm stepping down in the business. You're in charge now, my boy. It's all yours." Jack didn't comprehend. It all seemed strange, as though it couldn't be happening to him. He held the telephone receiver for a moment that seemed interminable. Finally, he turned mechanically, abruptly said, "Thanks," and hung up.

His two companions became concerned about Jack's strange behavior and the expression of bewilderment on his face. They watched him carefully; then, not knowing what else to do, they shouted more congratulations and pounded each other on the back, shouting, "Oh, we'll really tie one on tonight! How about that, Jack, old boy!" But Jack hardly heard them.

Over the next few weeks, Jack's feeling of being stunned and distant deepened to sadness. His stomach hurt, he was concerned about his bowel movements, he had trouble sleeping, and he would awaken very early. He didn't hear what people were saying to him because he had become preoccupied with himself. He hated to go to work, and when he was there his depression was occasionally punctuated by periods of irritability. He was edgy and kept noticing the astonished looks on people's faces when he would suddenly burst out with an angry remark. He couldn't concentrate, and felt as though he had to get away, but his usual haunts—certain favored bars and clubs—didn't make him feel any better. The poker parties were empty, his friends were distant, and even football held no interest for him. Visiting his mother didn't improve his mental state. He seemed to lose interest in everything, felt useless, and castigated himself, saying, "I'm not much of a man. I wish I were half the man my father is."

Even worse, he was tortured with recurrent and terrible thoughts about his new child. He would lean over the crib to look at him and view that innocent face, when suddenly a picture would flash into his mind of throwing the child against the fireplace or strangling him. He had the same kind of thoughts about his wife. When he saw her in bed or caring for the baby, he would say to himself, "Don't kill her, don't!" He began to think she was suspicious of him and that she knew his thoughts. He resented her attention to his son, and was irritated if she slept late and angered if his meals were delayed or if things weren't exactly in order when he got home. He hated himself for such ideas. They seemed completely alien to his image of himself.

His depression deepened. He tried to find solace by reading his long-set-aside Bible. He began attending church again, but found little comfort. In fact, he believed himself so unworthy that he could not continue going, and rejected the pastor's offers of help. It was his family physician who suggested a psychiatric consultation. Of the names suggested he seized upon mine, since it triggered some vague, nostalgic "last hope" of someone who would understand his ordeal.

When Jack saw me in the wheelchair on his first visit, he could see that we both had had an abrupt halt to our sports participation. It was easy for him to understand that the cause of my experience was paralysis, but the cause of his was beyond his comprehension. My paralysis was a physical expression, an understandable counterpart to his psychological conflict. I had clarity of reasoning and a paralyzed body while he had a paralyzed mind and a strong body.

He asked me over and over how I had managed to come to terms with a life devoid of old, meaningful activities. While I tried to keep the focus on his dilemma, I was keenly aware of my own, and our working alliance truly became one of mutual exploration. Jack asked me questions I had not dared ask myself, and touched certain unhealed wounds I had superficially treated. Indeed, how had I managed my own sudden transition from an active physical life to an enforced sedentary one?

I worked with Jack early in my career as a psychotherapist when I believed, as I had been taught, in the importance of the therapist's anonymity to his patient. The therapist was supposed to be a blank screen on which conflicts could be projected and objectively examined. But there could be no such anonymity here. He could see that we were both involved in a situation that touched our individual lives deeply. How absurd to use the popular technique of reflecting questions when our encounter had such evident importance in my life as well as his!

I have summarized the major events in Jack's life that had precipitated his agony and depression: marriage, the birth of a son, and success in business. His emotional paralysis occurred in the wake of events expected to bring only joy to a man's life. But in the context of his life they meant something quite different: severe depression, thoughts of self-destruction, and frightening homicidal wishes toward those he loved most. This led to his beginning psychotherapy, that process of self exploration filled with vicissitudes, but also with the gratification that growth brings.

Certain traditions in Jack's family played a vital role in the formation of his personality as well as that of each of the other siblings. He was the youngest child, with older brothers and one old sister. His brothers, being quite a few years older than he, had clearly set the pace for him. They had been fine football players and had played blocking back, as Jack had. They had also attended the same high school and college. Jack did not depart from the path well-worn by his brothers until after college. They had not returned to the family home after college, but had moved to other states and were apparently happy, economically successful, and devoted to their families.

Jack's sister, on the other hand, was two years older than he and lived near the family home with her recently acquired husband. As Jack saw it, the family had always been divided into two smaller family groups, each separate. His two older brothers and the father represented one family unit, and the other consisted of himself and his sister and mother.

While the adults were technically the same in both families, the dominant roles were reversed. Some differences were subtle and some were not. During the twenties, Jack's father had become a very successful businessman and had amassed a considerable fortune. He was a dynamic community leader and a patronizing patriarch at home. When the prosperity of the twenties was followed by the depression of the thirties, the family fortune was lost, leaving him a broken man. He was shattered and helpless, and for over a year he sat at home just shaking his head in disbelief. Jack's mother moved in to fill the vacuum. She had been a flighty socialite before, but now had to assume the responsibility abdicated by her husband. During the darkest period she took in washing to support the family, and occasionally worked outside the home during the day.

It was only in recent years that Jack's father had partially regained his former business position. The older boys had grown up under the tutelage of the dynamic, confident, and prosperous father. Jack, who was only two at the time of the financial losses, knew only the indecisive, doubting father who relied completely on the mother. Thus, the two family groups differed in leadership; the older was his father's family and the younger was his mother's.

There appeared to be an unspoken agreement between the parents about this. Jack recalled vividly that when, for example, the family went to an amusement park, he and his sister had to stay with their mother and watch while the older boys and their father went on "dangerous" rides like the roller coaster, the ferris wheel, and the whip. To Jack, the older boys and his father were adventurous, with a devil-may-care attitude, but his mother was the hovering, ever-present, worrisome, fretful, concerned woman.

Jack's father was a great sports fan and, as a former player, football was his favorite game. He was proud of his boys when they played, and he never missed a game. He had shown the older boys all he could about the fundamentals of the game and had offered steady encouragement to them. When Jack was old enough to begin to play, his father was still suffering disillusionment and so could offer Jack little support. Jack missed this acutely, for he longed for the day when he would be close to his father. His desire to emulate his older brothers was intense, since he hoped in this way to win his father's interest. He tried to tag along with the brothers when he could. Although they were rough and sometimes teased him, on other occasions they encouraged him and taught him some fundamentals of the game. This never sufficed, however, to take the place of the father's attention he had missed.

Jack's mother never attended an athletic event, for she was afraid the boys would be hurt. Although in the family tradition she was supposed to "steel herself" at home while the men were away in danger, she succeeded in making her suffering clear to all concerned. She was fearful and trembling whenever a game was played, always anticipating the worst. When one of the boys did have an injury, minor though it was, she hovered over him and exaggerated its seriousness. Jack clearly recalled the feelings he had when he was too young to watch his brothers play football. He had had to stay home and watch his mother wait and worry. It seemed an injustice that she should suffer so much while they played.

As an infant, Jack was less robust than his brothers. He had suffered from severe recurrent respiratory ailments, sometimes hovering on the brink of death. His mother was very apprehensive that pneumonic disease would someday take her youngest son. As a result, she always bundled him up in heavy coats and sweaters to make certain he would not get a chill. He never left the house without a final check and her approval that what he wore was warm enough. To sneak out without approval usually ended in his mother's creating an anxious, hand-wringing scene.

In a way, the crumbling family fortunes had set the stage for such over-concern, for the loss of plenitude once held is more devastating than consistent poverty. Jack's early feeding experiences were a focus for the family economic struggles. His mother believed she could demonstrate that they still had plenty by stuffing him just beyond his capacity. In those depression years the world was a capricious and unfriendly place. Jack's mother wanted to protect her youngest son against its dangers in every way she could. In her daily warnings to Jack she also tried to make it clear that although the outside world was filled with sources of illness, injury, starvation, and freezing, she would always take care of him. She hoped this would offer him the sense of security she did not feel herself.

As he grew older, Jack took over the responsibility for worrying about his personal safety. He would engage in a personal dialogue before he went out, asking his own questions about whether his clothes were warm enough and whether he had eaten enough. He never liked to cause his mother undue worry, and did his best to heed her warnings about being careful. He knew it would cause her great pain if he were sick, and it bothered him even more to think how she would care for him tenderly, despite her own hurt, if something were to happen to him. Yet this also made the thought of being sick or weak vaguely appealing, for it meant his mother would be especially solicitous.

Paradoxically, in order to fulfill the male expectations in his family, he also had to be rugged. He found he was aggressive and in frequent fights with neighborhood boys. The fights and his occasional injuries became his personal compromise between the two families, representing the pleasures of infancy with his mother and the desire to emulate his older brothers and his father. The sense of being drawn toward both weakness and strength left Jack with a feeling of cleavage in his personality. This tenuous balance was sometimes tipped in one direction or the other. On occasion his fear of injury and illness became a self-fulfilling prophecy of disaster.

Another event gave heightened significance and perhaps more fundamental meaning to Jack's dilemma. His parents were devoutly Catholic, and when they determined that it would be unwise to have any more children, they agreed to sleep in separate rooms to avoid temptation. Jack's father moved in with the older boys and Jack joined his mother in what had been his parents' room. While sleeping with his mother was the realization of fond hopes, it also filled him with apprehension, for he knew he was depriving his father of a valued position. An angry look from his father would freeze him in panic. Although in later years he was to find ways of partially mastering this situation, he always carried a residue of terror and guilt from these events. They set the stage for the tragedy that was to befall Jack as an adult.

One way Jack dealt with having replaced his father was by taking on his father's characteristics—identification—most obviously by emulating his father's fervor for sports. Discussions at home centered around football, with the dinner table often becoming the setting for spirited and sometimes heated conversations about the relative merits of teams and players. The living room often served as a simulated practice field for check blocking and play learning. Jack, his father, and his brothers thus shared this overriding family interest. His mother, though, remained a direct descendant of the long-suffering women of the world who fearfully, but pridefully, watched their men go into battle.

It was predestined that Jack would be a football player and that he would be a blocking back. In this family this was as much a part of being a male member of the clan as wearing trousers. Nothing was more important to the family than his learning football skills. His developmental years became an apprenticeship, and his progress in school was measured, not by grades or courses completed, but by the success of the team on which he played. Ordinary events were relative to the fall football season, spring training, or the dormant time in between. By the time he reached junior high school he had mastered many of the game's fundamentals and was an outstanding player. He progressed through D, C, and B classifications and finally on to varsity football. After high school came college and then professional football.

Jack's attitude toward studies mirrored that of his brothers. It was necessary to keep a certain scholastic average to participate in the real business of school, which was athletics. He was bright enough to keep his grades at a passing level and to keep himself from becoming too emotionally involved in his schoolwork. His school performance was further enhanced by the quiet respect he always showed to adults. Unlike so many of his teammates, he was not rowdy or discourteous in class. He slid through school without involvement, and it took only a spurt of study in his senior year to get him into college. He was always well liked by his schoolmates and was regarded with the respect accorded an all-league star and team captain.

Jack felt at ease in most situations, developed some lasting friendships, and was popular with his peers. However, he felt best on the football field. All else was subordinate to the physical contact he had there. Whether in practice or in a game he sensed a special kind of thrill in executing a perfect block or hitting a ball carrier low and head-on. He had a feeling of almost orgiastic pleasure when he felt the solid crunch of leather against leather. He was dimly aware that he entered each play with a fear that he would be injured or with the peculiar certainty that this would happen. Then, when he survived, he felt the profound relief of a condemned man who had received a reprieve. To the fan in the stands, he was the symbol of aggressive football.

During the first few weeks of psychotherapy, Jack talked endlessly about his shortcomings and failures. Each hour was filled with self-castigation. He reevaluated his entire life, making it an object for self-criticism, distorting pleasures and successes so that they would reflect badly on him. Obscure motivations that formed only minor parts of his whole life loomed large and sinister to him. He called himself weak and cowardly, remembering his fear of being hurt while playing football. When reminded of his aggressive play despite his fear, he concluded that he had blocked and tackled hard just because he wanted to hurt the players on the other team. He condemned himself as unprincipled, sadistic, selfish, perverse, and without virtue.

What affected him most deeply were his thoughts of hurting his wife and child. This seemed to be the most dramatic demonstration of his basic evilness. "I'm no man; I'm like a monster. What kind of an animal would want to harm his own family?" He was preoccupied with his failure and his lack of responsibility. He pleaded to be "put away forever" so he could never harm anyone and would not be a burden to his family. He said that if he really had any "guts" he would have done away with himself long ago.

In a profound depressive reaction like Jack's, life memories are sorted out anew. Those memories conforming to an inner sense of evil and worthlessness are remembered, while those of any positive value are discarded. Although these retrospective accounts are usually unreliable when compared with objectively derived information, they nevertheless reveal important ideas and feelings that ordinarily go unspoken. These are the unintegrated, troublesome fragments of the personality.

For our understanding of this case it will be of value to synthesize some of its elements. Marriage, involving fatherhood and taking over his father's business, reactivated a whole group of unfinished conflicts in Jack's life. Maturation should naturally have carried him toward independence, success, and self-reliance, but when Jack tasted these he was terrified. It seemed to be a recapitulation of the time when he had replaced his father in the parental bedroom. It brought back feelings that his father's weak, defeated condition was his fault rather than the result of financial reversals in the great economic depression. As a child he could turn to his mother for protection from his fears, but as an adult he could not.

His memories focused now on actions he interpreted as being homosexual (despite the fact that he had never had any homosexual relations), instead of being those of a man, a father, and a husband. This selective remembering

served a dual function, the more obvious being to confirm his sense of bad-
ness. The second function was to shield himself from the responsibility of
displacing his father. If he were to see himself as a homosexual, he could
avoid seeing himself as a competitor to his father, the man.

I began my work with Jack over twenty years ago. Since then many
changes have occurred in American psychiatry, and my own orientation has
also become somewhat different. There are now available a group of drugs
that are helpful in depressions and contribute to a more rapid recovery. Although electrotherapy was already being used when I first treated Jack, it
was not utilized because of family objections. The most important change,
perhaps, would come in my approach to psychotherapy. Today I would be
much more active, focusing on the interchanges of the moment between
therapist and patient. Thus, although this description of Jack's therapy is
faithfully reported from my notes, it is somewhat anachronistic in relation to
my present approach to therapy. My interest at the time in reconstructing the
past life of the patient does provide specialized information which is useful
in understanding the psychodynamics of sports.

Jack gradually developed more trust in me as we met, and he dared to talk
about things he had shamefully hidden before. His depressive symptoms
gradually decreased and his mood slowly began to elevate. One of his fears
had been that telling me about his terrible thoughts and evil intentions
would have a contagious effect and they would hurt me or make me "sick."
He was relieved when this did not happen and was pleased when I understood what was troubling him. Later, however, this praise for my objectivity
was to turn to criticism: I was not sufficiently sympathetic and com-
passionate. At first he saw me as warm and understanding and his family as
disinterested; then I changed in his eyes and seemed cold, while he portrayed his family as helpful.

As the depression lifted and he talked more freely, his self-castigation began to be directed outward. His father was the first main target for his anger.
Jack criticized him for being both threatening and weak. He said his father
was cold, callous, and unconcerned. "He never really gave a damn about
me." He revealed the strange belief that he had actually "killed" his father on
the day of his own son's birth, when his father announced he was giving the
family business to him. When he first experienced anger toward his father he
was stunned, and there was a mild recurrence of his depression. Then gradually he was able to appraise his feelings more realistically. The shadows of
his expectations and disappointments were projected on me, and the relationship between his attitudes toward me and his father was slowly clarified. However, when he became more at ease with this image of his father,
his mother became the recipient of his hatred. During the time in therapy
when he hated his father, he saw his mother as faultless and spoke of her in
idealized terms. He eulogized that it was only her love that had sustained
him through the years, and only his concern for her had kept him from com-

mitting suicide in his darkest moments. Closeness to her, however, contained elements of anger for her overprotection. He gradually began to complain that her concern had kept him infantilized and fearful. Her long-suffering fearfulness had caused him to feel guilty for any slight discomfort he may have caused her. He moaned that she wanted him to feel guilty, because that was her way of tying him to her. "That suffering business, that's a way of controlling me." He recalled that her constant concern for his eating habits, his bowel movements, and his need for warmth had scared him. There seemed to be no middle ground. He had to either completely give in to her and do as she thought best or get away from her entirely. He said his brothers had felt similarly bound to his mother and remembered his next older brother saying he had left town to make a "clean break"; if he had not he could never have had a life of his own. For a long time Jack vacillated between extreme opinions about his mother. On one hand she was a dominating ogre, while on the other she was the gentle, sweet, devoted parent. Only very slowly was he able to see her as she really was—a collection of mortal faults and virtues.

Since he was grown now, with a family of his own, his dependence upon his parents was emotional rather than physical. This made them relatively safe objects to be angry with and to examine. Their images could be destroyed by his words with relative freedom, since they were no longer the only persons in his life. Once destroyed, they could be reconstructed more realistically.

His resentment toward his wife, however, was more immediate and therefore more threatening. Anger toward his child seemed so reprehensible and irrational that it was impossible even to talk about it. Any criticism of his wife or child was immediately followed by symptoms of guilt and depression. He was gradually able to understand that he had expected and demanded the same smothering relationship with his wife as he had with his mother. He feared this and yet was drawn to it, but his wife's failure to comply with his efforts to reconstruct the mother-son relationship with her led to his anger. When his own son was born, it became even more difficult to act as a child to his wife. These disappointments led to murderous thoughts of doing away with both of them.

Transference to the therapist of attitudes and feelings for significant figures in the past is vital for the progress of therapy. The therapist slowly clarifies the distorted impressions until the patient at last sees him realistically. Jack's transference of unrealistic attitudes to me was altered somewhat by the reality of my disability and my need for a wheelchair. This disability had helped in the formation of an early rapport, as he believed I could understand his problem better. I also appeared less threatening to him. Later, he was concerned about me because I seemed more vulnerable to attack. At first, Jack saw me as the understanding, all-giving, idealized recapitulation of his mother; at another stage I represented the cold and disinterested father whose favor he sought, but who had always been somewhat distant. Later still, he projected upon me the image of the smothering parent who prohibited him from taking risks and from enjoying himself. During this period he saw me as restricting even his sexual pleasures and as trying to make him feel guilty and indebted to me.

Therapy continued for almost two years, initially in the hospital and thereafter on visits to my office. After several months, Jack was able to return to work, and his old problem with work became the central issue of his later therapy. With all his good intentions of returning to the responsible role of father and husband, he continued to despise work. The best he could muster was, "This must be my cross to bear." He contrasted himself to his father, who had developed a successful business, while Jack felt he himself was a freeloader without drive. During Jack's hospitalization and subsequent therapy, his father had returned to head the family business. When Jack went back to work, he was again working for his father. Now, however, he began to recognize that it had only been in his declining years that his father had developed any satisfaction from his work. The fact that his father had experienced similar problems and had resolved them was encouraging to Jack. Heretofore he had been unwilling to examine his father's work attitudes. A turning point came when his father, due to failing health, definitely decided that he had to step down from the business. If Jack could not take over, he would sell out. Jack decided he would like to take over the business, but on the same basis as anyone else might. He drew up a contract with his father, arranging to buy him out over a period of years, during which his father would step down gradually. The gradual changeover, its mutually agreeable businesslike nature, and the fact that Jack was in control of the transition made it possible for him to complete the task. His therapy was complete when he was in full charge of his business. Work was never truly satisfying for him, but he was able to see himself as he was, disliking the routine managerial aspects of his work, but enjoying his contacts with people. His greatest satisfactions came from his family, lodge activities, and once again, poker parties.

Jack maintained a vital interest in sports, but with some significant modification. Formerly, football had been all-consuming in its importance. He had never missed a game, and in a vain attempt to recapture his lost playing days, he had spent considerable time working out with the high school football team. Now, with increased responsibilities at home and at work, there was a growing distance from and objectivity toward football. He was still a student of the game and an active alumnus of his college, but other interests began to take priority. Football and other sports became, appropriately, recreation and leisure pastimes rather than life's major activity.

I occasionally hear from Jack, usually at Christmastime. The last time I received a note from him, he had been asked to talk to the high school football team about school spirit. His theme was to be "Don't forget, boys, it's a great game, but it's only a preparation for living."

In each stage of an individual's life, different problems and satisfactions are available. If one is unwilling or unable to meet the challenges of a new stage, he often tries to make it into an old one that he managed more adequately. Sometimes the new stage can be remolded in the image of the old, but often the people involved are unwilling to be molded. In these cases, the individual begins to descend his personal developmental scale in a quest for peace, attempting to find some stage in which he is comfortable. This was our football player's experience. Well adapted to playing football, he was unable to face the problems of middle adult life. He stood on the childhood side of a great gulf separating him from the satisfactions and responsibilities of parenthood and work. To bridge this gulf, he had to encounter an awesome but vulnerable father toward whom he held murderous wishes. At the same time, he felt pulled backward toward being his mother's child again. His wife and baby were unsuitable and unwilling subjects to be made into the images of the past, and seeing them as obstacles that were blocking his quest for comfort, he grew furious with them. Since it hardly seemed right to express his rage on them, he turned it on himself. Although his forward motion was temporarily suspended and he seemed to move backward in time, he had a strong need and desire to overcome his conflict. This desire was the motivating force that eventually made progress possible. Bridging the gap between boyhood and manhood was finally accomplished in a controlled and mutually agreeable arrangement with his father. His goal, not unlike that of many young men, was to take over his father's business, but before he made the step he carefully examined it with me, wanting to avoid any impulsive act.

During the course of his measured steps, he looked at the experiences leading to his present predicament, using the microscope of psychotherapy. This searching revealed much that was hidden. One contradiction of long standing in American life is that the main setting in which overt expressions of physical affection between men are publicly tolerated is the same setting in which the castigation of homosexuality would be the most severe—in the athletic stadium or the gymnasium. When seminude men gather in a gym they desperately need to deny their positive feelings for one another and displace the restrictions of conscience onto projected objects of scorn. Jack had experienced great sensual pleasure from hugging and being hugged by his teammates in the enthusiasm of victory. As a defensive linebacker he derived similar pleasure from patting them on their squatted buttocks and their backs. These pleasurable sensual feelings were acceptable within the framework of the game and to the thousands of spectators who watched him, but outside the sports arena, with heightened needs for such pleasures, he critically and derisively reevaluated his feelings. In the service of his depressive symptoms, his actions became demonstrations of his perversity. He believed he must be "queer"—perhaps the most derogatory term among athletes.

Another significant pleasure came for Jack when he was playing, driving hard into an opponent while tackling or blocking. He then had intense feelings of satisfaction and a vague sensation that he had won; he felt strong for "taking his man out." In this situation alone he could engage in aggressive competition and remain free of guilt. It was actually a safe realization of his fearsome competition and murderous wishes toward his father and brothers. The adulation of the crowd encouraged him in his violent aggressiveness and helped absolve him of guilt. It was that guilt which was to arise anew while Jack was working with his father, since in this situation his conscience could not be ignored. Not only did he fear his fantasies of doing away with his father, but he magically feared the expected retaliation. In his psychotic state, when his father turned over the business to him he felt that his fantasy had been realized and that he actually had killed his father. The very psychological qualities that had made him a successful hard-hitting football player spelled disaster when the rules of football became the rules of work and parenthood.

Jack had to be a football player to assume the expected role of the man in the eyes of his parents and siblings. So strong were these expectations that they even determined the position he was to play on the football team. However, he had no such clear guideline for his role as a father and a worker. There was a discrepancy between the words he had heard spoken about responsibility and success and the behavior he had seen in his models. He was confused by his father's withdrawal from the role of aggressive businessman and by his brothers' fleeing from home. His sexual identification with the masculine members of the family was weakened in his developmental years by the division of the family into two groups based on age: he, his sister, and his mother formed one unit, while the masculine unit was made up of his father and older brothers.

Jack eventually found a suitable identity of his own, which was not so stereotyped as the models he had been given. His innate strength and purposefulness, coupled with the psychotherapeutic experience, allowed him to become more nearly a whole person. He could meet the demands of his conscience and yet experience the satisfactions available. This was accomplished largely by his learning to leave the past behind him.

5.
The Killer

Although the origins of tennis are obscure, the game is known to have been played in many ancient lands with somewhat differing rules. It was played in the ancient court of Persia, in the dry moats of castles in the Middle Ages, and in nineteenth-century England on Major Wingfield's famous court that was shaped like an hourglass. In all of these different settings there was one note of social continuity: tennis was a game of the aristocracy. Called "the royal game," it was popular among European kings and their courts, and it is recorded that Louis X of France died from a chill contracted after playing tennis.

Just before the turn of the century, Major Wingfield's form of the game was transported to America by way of Bermuda. In the new world it continued to be associated with the upper classes. Tennis clubs sprang up wherever the wealthy congregated, and the principal American tournaments were played at exclusive clubs in rich vacation resorts such as Newport, Southampton, the New Jersey shore, and Palm Beach. Today's professional tournaments continue to be played at fashionable resorts and clubs around the world: in San Juan, Hilton Head, and Las Vegas, as well as the stately old clubs.

Although tennis courts are now available to nearly all Americans, the game still carries the connotation of the social class of its origin and retains a certain snob appeal. The availability of public courts apparently has not affected the image of the game, since those who choose to play still seem to be given a peculiar sense of social elevation.* So, although it is a tough, competitive sport available to masses of people, it has, paradoxically, maintained a close relationship to leisure and wealth.

Wherever aristocracy or pseudoaristocracy are found, so too are found those pretenders, the "social climbers." The first inroads into the exclusivity of tennis were made by a group of modern-day courtiers, the "tennis bums." They were men and women of modest means and modest social position who coveted the status and the material benefits of wealth. The nature of their seeking also implied a preference for reaching the prized position by receiving personal favors or the condescension of the privileged, rather than by conventional hard work.

The historical relationship of the game to the aristocracy, the muted applause that substitutes for cheering, and the meticulous attire that is the standard uniform have provided tennis with the additional connotation of being a sissy's game. Yet, like any of the major sports, if played well it is physically demanding and requires great stamina and technical excellence. In fact, there is probably no more grueling athletic activity than a five-set tennis match.

The social mythology of a sport is a major factor in its being selected by participants. The pool hall, the football field, the bullfight arena, the baseball stadium, and the skiing slopes have unique appeals based on their social environments and the images of their contestants. A sport may symbolize the personal psychology and the social striving of the individual who selects it. This often holds true for the tennis player.

When Ken came to my office seeking psychiatric help, he had been experiencing anxiety and tension for several months. This condition had developed when he had, according to plan, entered his brother's business. He was tall and tanned, with handsome features. His tailored sport coat, covering a tieless shirt, gave the impression of meticulous disarray. Although he had come to me with a burning purpose, his manner was a veneer of studied casualness; he found it difficult to get to the point. The psychiatrist becomes accustomed to this in patients, and so I listened to his warm-up talk of tennis, of recent and upcoming tournaments, of how he had heard that I was a psychiatrist, and of a number of mutual friends.

Ken was not a complete stranger. I had seen him play several times in tournaments and could recall him on the court. The meticulous dress, seemingly casual attitude, and powerfully aggressive game with its booming service and hard-hit volleys were impressive. But I was struck also by the worried look on his face while he played. As I turned my attention to him now, I

---

*Many players and tennis fans have been working toward popularizing the game. Perhaps the most concerted, well-organized effort to date has been made by World Team Tennis, a professional tennis league which encourages loud cheering and has discarded the genteel, time-honored method of scoring in favor of a streamlined system meant to make the game more attractive. The initial match for the Los Angeles entry, the Strings, more nearly resembled the premiere of a Hollywood movie than the beginning of a tennis competition; it was complete with spotlights, a razzle-dazzle master of ceremonies, and a round of jokes from one of the Strings' most enthusiastic supporters, Johnny Carson. Not surprisingly, the league has met considerable resistance from those who wish to maintain the aristocratic image of the game. Attendance was poor during 1974, the first season.

could see the deep furrows in his brow, now relaxed, which helped me to realize that he was the same "Killer Ken." So worried at play, so casual in a psychiatrist's office!

As if on cue from me, the furrows appeared, the worried look came over him, and he began his narrative. Now in his late twenties, he had ranked high among the nation's tennis players for several years, winning a number of national titles. About a year ago he married and a few months later entered his brother's advertising business. Although on the surface he seemed unchanged, he began to feel constricted and tense, longing for his tennis-playing days.

Most disturbing of all was a change in his relationship with his brother John, seven years older, with whom he had always been very close. Their relationship, especially after their father died, had been more like father and son. They had planned since childhood to go into business together. Now that the dream was a reality, it turned out to be a nightmare for Ken instead of a happy culmination. He became increasingly tense with his brother, sometimes feeling that he was being picked on. Such thoughts he quickly dismissed, though, because there was no factual evidence. He was touchy and had even "blown up" several times. This was foreign to him, since in his recollection he had never lost his temper before. His brother, somewhat bewildered by this behavior, tried to talk to Ken but was rebuffed and avoided. Ken harbored a secret fear, he revealed later, that in some way he might be provoked by his brother and inadvertently harm him. This seemed quite incongruous to him, since he was really very fond of John.

The boys had grown up in a small town north of Los Angeles. Here they had been confronted with two very different worlds—a rich one and an austere one. Ken's father, Charlie, worked as caretaker on a wealthy man's estate. Their family home was modest to the point of austerity, although it was set in the center of a broader world of luxury and wealth. The "Boss," in a moment of democratic magnanimity, had decreed that "Charlie's kids" could do anything his kids could do. So Ken and his brother were allowed to move freely between the two worlds, seemingly accepted in both. To the casual observer, the Boss's order was followed to the letter, but for Ken and John, there was never any doubt about the real situation. At home, before they went into the Boss's world, they were always cautioned to behave, not to offend, and to act like gentlemen. They had a vague realization that when they played with the Boss's children they had to be careful, for in some way their family's survival depended upon their good deportment. They were models of good behavior.

The Boss was genuinely fond of these boys, for they were handsome, well-mannered, alert, and good athletes—all that he admired and wanted in his own children. As a result, he often held "Charlie's kids" up as models to them. As could be expected, they did not take kindly to these unfavorable comparisons, and the seething anger that developed in them became the price "Charlie's kids" had to pay for the freedom they were allowed. But in any conflict between the Boss's children and Charlie's, the former had the ultimate weapon—they belonged there.

When he was five years old, Ken had come to his mother with tears in his eyes and, bewildered and ashamed, had asked what a servant was. His playmate, the Boss's son, had scornfully put him in his place with this word. The Boss would never have tolerated such an overt display of snobbery, but in their conspiracy of silence, Charlie's family would never have reported any interfamily conflicts for fear of offending. In later years, as the children of the two families grew up, their differing social roles were maintained by innuendo rather than by such direct pronouncements. Clearly implied differences always lurked beneath the Boss's egalitarian decree.

The smiling facade that Charlie's family showed the Boss did not reveal the intense competition between the families. Charlie's family was very close and united in mutual support and seemingly in agreement on all issues. But this in itself produced many tensions within the home. The closeness of the family and the code that prevented any expression of discord to the outside world forced them to handle problems within the home. There were thus few opportunities for the dissipation of tensions outside of the family.

Charlie was a good-natured fellow who easily accepted his subservient role; for him the most important thing was peace. He wanted peace in his own family and between his family and the Boss's. He approached his existence with an air of calm. Charlie's wife, although warm, encouraging, and protective of her brood, was more ambitious and envious of the benefits of wealth and position she saw. The family often spoke of how fortunate they were in their circumstances, but there was never any question that the men in the family, Charlie and his two boys, could please her by seeing to it that she had more of the good things of life. Nothing was more important to the members of this small family than gaining Mother's favor. Charlie, for example, bought her gifts that were beyond his financial ability. Although these tokens were promptly returned to the store, there was little question of her secret pleasure from these gestures which told her that, if he were able, Charlie would provide her with a life of luxury. This was their little game of make-believe. It was through the boys that she entertained the greatest hope of someday realizing her ambitions. Charlie's wishes for the success of his boys were mixed with his own feelings of envy for the favors his wife gave them.

There was no place in this family for spankings or other severe punishments. Any overt competition outside the home was restricted because of the need to maintain the family's "proper place." Yet at home the rivalry for Mother's favor was intense. One way the men of the gamily dissipated their tensions was through mock wrestling contests. As fathers will do, Charlie engaged in friendly contests with his boys. He was actually stocky and powerful and had to mute his own efforts to make the competition more nearly equal. Ken's brother John always seemed aware of his father's latent strength and never really entered enthusiastically into these wrestling matches. But Ken's efforts were undiminished by the reality of the situation. In fact, although he was small, his enthusiasm was so great that sometimes he actually was able to get the advantage of his father. He could get a stranglehold which caused Charlie to gasp for breath and, half-playfully, admonish Ken, "You're a real killer, Ken. You're dangerous." Ken experienced his father's comments with a vaguely formed mixture of emotions: guilt over possibly hurting the father he loved and pride in his own strength.

In school, Ken and John tried to conform to the apparently inconsistent standards set by their parents in the home. They wanted to be popular, in keeping with their father's values, but they also strove for the more material successes for which their mother yearned. Ken learned from his brother some of the techniques to accomplish these seemingly incompatible goals. Though he was an excellent and industrious student, Ken made a considerable display of disinterest in schoolwork and grades for the benefit of his classmates. Meanwhile, he was very enthusiastic about sports. In their school, the "in" group of boys felt that being "a grind" was subhuman, and athletes who were poor students were of the highest social order. Thus the sometimes paradoxical standards of the family were matched by an equally contradictory set of standards at school. Ken and John, however, found satisfactory solutions. They were good athletes and members of the "in" group, and they overtly scorned scholarship but studied secretly. They were careful never to be seen carrying books home and always disclaimed any responsibility for their high grades. If confronted, they would reply with measured casualness that they could not help it if they were lucky.

On the estate, too, as they grew older, they developed some opportunities for achievement without incurring the wrath of the Boss's family. The Boss loved sports and insisted that his brood, which included Ken and his brother, participate vigorously. It was the only opportunity on the estate outside of the family circle for the open expression of the competition that burned so strongly. Tennis was the big sport.

Each week a tennis professional came to teach the Boss's kids. Ken and John were allowed to watch and later to practice with their privileged playmates. The caretaker's children maintained a respectful distance from the lessons, but they were always present and they observed carefully. They caught on quickly and practiced hard. Both Ken and his brother improved more rapidly than the Boss's children. Ken was especially precocious. His brother, just as in the wrestling with his father, seemed less determined and more willing to accept second place.

Ken became so expert that he began entering tournaments, with the Boss's insistent sponsorship. Of course, when first encouraged he modestly insisted he wasn't good enough. Privately, he could barely contain his enthusiasm at the prospect. One of the contingencies was that he play doubles with the Boss's son, but this was a small price to pay.

He began playing local tournaments with immediate success. Bursting with pride, he would bring home a medal or a small trophy signifying victory and give it to his mother. He could always anticipate her expressions of joy, as she experienced his success as if it were her own.

Ken's brother was also quite willing to sacrifice his own tennis ambitions to be Ken's sparring partner and adviser. The competition between the two boys was obvious only occasionally. Then, in moments of anger, they played against each other furiously. It was at these times that the tensions arising from the closeness of the family bonds became fully apparent.

In the beginning of his fifteenth year, two very important events occurred in Ken's life. He realized his dreams of success when he became tennis champion of his age division through a sparkling series of outstanding victories and was heralded as a future tennis great. But victory for Ken came with defeat for someone close to him: his father developed tuberculosis. His father's illness seemed to realize his own worst fears that someone dear to him would suffer as a consequence of his success. Ordinarily even the events of early childhood were clear and distinct in Ken's memory, but these two events had become so confused in his mind that he was not certain which had taken place first. The extent of his father's illness was minimized by everyone at first, but over the next few years the telltale signs and their ultimate conclusion became clear.

Ken saw his formerly robust father shrink in size and wither away. He was now away for extended periods in the sanitarium. Ken was stunned and nearly overcome when he saw his father and the tragic changes that resulted from the illness.

The Boss was sympathetic, and even though Ken's father was no longer able to work, he allowed the family to stay on in the caretaker's cottage. But now they had to subsist on the rapidly diminishing family savings. His mother went to work; fortunately, Ken's brother was now nearly finished with college.

When old Charlie was finally laid to rest, it was a great relief for everyone. Seeing him suffer and wither away had been agonizing, and his slow, lingering death left a deep scar on the tight family group. Ken seemed more affected than the others.

Economic times were good, however, and as soon as John finished college he was able to assume the burden of the family's financial problems. He did this so successfully that his mother was able to stop work, and Ken was once again free to pursue his academic and tennis careers.

But a strange thing occurred in the way Ken now approached tennis. He had always been a tenacious, steady player who won primarily because he outlasted his opponents. Now, however, he could not stand long, drawn-out matches. Either he won quickly and decisively, or he did not win at all. He began to play the serve-and-volley game. In his matches, points were decided by a stroke or two. If he got into an extended match it was an agonizing experience for him, and he could think of nothing except ending it.

This change in the way he played caused Ken's star to fade for a couple of seasons. He became known as a teenage has-been whose principal assets were a bludgeonlike serve and a hard volley. He went all out on each point, hitting for the winner. The point was practically always decided without a rally.

He lost his confidence, too, and questioned his own ability. This was something that had never happened before. Inevitably his hard, reckless play produced some sensational victories. If he was "on," he seemed to be able to beat almost anyone. His confidence gradually began to return after he defeated world-class players easily on several occasions. However, he was just as apt to lose to a mediocre player if he happened to get into a long match. As he put it, "Long matches just didn't seem human." Although he was very strong, when he found himself in a tight struggle on the court he became concerned about his health and sometimes even about the health of his opponent. He often found himself short of breath.

Ken utilized well the social skills he had acquired in childhood on the estate and became one of the most popular players in the game, with both fans and players. His mannerly casualness did not betray the intensity of his competitive spirit. His tournament record continued to be spotty, however. There were dramatic, decisive victories over outstanding players but also seemingly inexplicable losses to inferior players. His nemesis remained the problem of not being able to win long, agonizing matches.

Ken got along well with both men and women and developed quite a following with the latter. At the tournaments where he played, there was always a ready band of admirers to greet him when he came off the court. They provided him with a plethora of sexual opportunities. Although his fellow players took advantage of such opportunities, Ken was different. He was chivalrous and protective of women, and he preferred long-term, stable relationships. As a result, he tended to avoid many of the available opportunities. He felt uneasy if he satisfied himself sexually and not his partner, and he bitterly resented other players who "took advantage" of girls. He was always cautious lest he hurt someone.

In his midtwenties he met an attractive girl at a tournament, and a serious romance bloomed. She was the daughter of a wealthy industrialist and was an ardent tennis fan. Their courtship extended for many months, and eventually they were married. She was a warm and intelligent girl and deeply loved her husband. Ken had not been unaware of the material advantages of this marriage. Although he was genuinely fond of his wife, he found himself obsessed, first with the desire for material advantages which could come to him from their marriage, and then with self-castigation for taking advantage of the situation.

After a tennis honeymoon, the young couple settled in an apartment in her family's home. From the beginning, Ken felt ill at ease there, as though he did not belong. He could not "let down," even though his wife encouraged him to do so. In her parents' home he felt like an outsider, in the same way he had felt ill at ease entering the big house on the Boss's estate in California. As a result, the young couple developed some strange habits, spending a good deal of time in hotels and motels where Ken did feel comfortable.

Although he had dreamed of a life of leisure, when it became available to him he could not accept it. The solution seemed easy, and he decided now to go to work in brother John's advertising business, as had been their plan for years. They had always said they would one day work together, and when they finally made the decision, both looked forward to it eagerly. Ken's wife was pleased, too, because she thought that at last he would be happy.

Ken's life showed a pattern of extreme social mobility, with his ascent occurring largely through tennis playing. Sponsored by the Boss as a boy, he achieved recognition, and then married into wealth, all mainly because of his ability to play tennis. His upward mobility was the result, not of work, but of play.* Moving from servant to leisure class left him with the anxiety of not feeling at home anywhere.

And now here he was in my office. His appearance did not betray the extent of the turmoil he felt within, for he had learned early in life to show on the outside only what he wanted to be seen. But he experienced great tension and anxiety beyond anything he had ever felt before. He reported that since entering his brother's business he slept very little, and when he did, he had a recurrent dream which troubled him.

He said he wasn't sure, but believed he had experienced the dream from time to time since childhood. Now, whenever sleep did come, he dreamed this:

> He was climbing a steep mountain with another man. It was dusty, rocky terrain. They climbed together. Then he could see an avalanche coming. By running up ahead at an angle he avoided the avalanche, which passed just behind him; but it carried his fellow climber down to his death. He stood on the mountain motionless and became aware of eyes in the front and in the back of his head. With the front eyes, he looked up the rest of the mountain where he wished to go, while with his rear eyes he looked back with regret to where his companion had been. He would then awaken.

---

*Jan Huizinga, a major theoretician about play, notes that play is unreal and not serious. It is the introduction of reality into a player's life that so often leads to difficulty, for he becomes responsible for his actions and their consequences. Old conflicts, which could be denied as unreal in play, are reactivated and must be dealt with anew.

Ken's story was that of a boy who had grown up in a specialized social milieu of wealth and luxury. The main people he knew outside his immediate family, the estate owners, impressed him as having a different set of concerns from his, and he looked to their life-style as an ideal to be sought. They were unconcerned about the mundane activities of survival which occupied his own family, and they were interested primarily in living a good and meaningful life. He was impressed with the disparity between himself and his playmates, and he surreptitiously coveted what they were born with.

Ken and his family were like an isolated minority on the estate. They remained there by virtue of the Boss's grace. Although they were allowed privileges, it was always apparent that these could be revoked at any time. Ken was always aware of the differences between his position and that of his playmates and between his family and the Boss's. In some respects it was like living in a medieval feudal society.

But there were important differences between Ken's society and the feudal one. The clarity of roles between servant and master was blurred by other factors which allowed him to hope he could have what belonged to the Boss. The Boss decreed that there was equality among all of the estate children and encouraged competition among them. As Ken moved into the world beyond the estate, he became further aware that it was possible for him to change his social position. His appetite for success had been whetted long before.

His own family relationships had already prepared him for his view of the world in which he lived. His family was a microcosm of the way he saw himself in the world. In the immediate family the males, Ken, John, and his father, were competitors for the favors of his mother. The disparity between his social role on the estate and that of the Boss's family was no greater than that between himself and his father and brother in the home. They were Goliaths and Ken was David. In the home, just as on the estate, there was an egalitarian decree. There were mock wrestling matches in which his father and brother pretended they were no more than equal to Ken. Ken's brother never took the pretense seriously and recognized full well the relative differences in size and strength between himself and his father. But Ken took the game seriously and believed he could win. His enthusiasm, if not his strength, led to occasional apparent victory when wrestling with his father, who had then dubbed him the "killer."

Another factor amplified the tensions of competition: the code that one must be careful not to complain or offend. This confined the expression of tensions to within the family, since when one was outside the home one always had to be on good behavior.

As Ken grew older, another opportunity to express his desire for competition outside the home developed. The game of tennis became almost the perfect expression. On the court, as long as he kept his sportsmanlike demeanor, Ken could compete furiously. There he could truly be equal or superior, with the one restriction of appearing modest and polite. As his proficiency in the game increased, other advantages accrued. He was able to live among the wealthy and eventually join them permanently through marriage. His mother, whose favor he sought, was delighted by his tennis progress, and especially by the social advances that accompanied it. Ken had become a successful social climber.

In his successes, however, Ken experienced a vague sense of regret, as though he had achieved something he should not have. This had also been the case in the family wrestling matches, and now it happened when he played tennis. A vague concern for the regretful consequences of victory grew and finally came to fruition with the realization of his worst fears: his father became ill and eventually wasted away to death. Ken felt unconsciously responsible, for, after all, had his father not designated him "the killer"?

Although much of what had taken place was beyond Ken's awareness, it nevertheless had a profound effect on his tennis. His competitiveness was impaired. Whenever a match triggered a dim reminder of his father's slowly deteriorating health, he grew panicky and, not caring whether he won or lost, wanted only to end the match. In matches like this he found himself worried about his opponent's ability to survive and about his own health as well. He confused these tennis battles with long-past competition with his father and its tragic ending. He could allow himself to win only if the victory were quick and merciful.

In aiming to satisfy the dictates of his conscience to be merciful, he ironically regained his nickname. To win quickly, he hit terrifically hard. So devastating was his game because of his attempts to win quickly that he began to be called "Killer Ken of the Courts." As it had done long before, the nickname caused him a mixture of pride and regret.

In spite of his conflict about winning, he had much success. He met all problems, on and off the court, with the same immediate, decisive action designed to finish the situation at once. Sometimes, of course, in his eagerness for an ending, his actions were ill-considered and impulsive. Most of the time, however, his decisiveness served him well.

A series of events then intervened to block the immediate resolution of some conflicts. First there was his marriage, the realization of a courtier's dream. He married a wealthy girl and could really have joined the coveted world of the Boss, but the dictates of his conscience forbade this, and he experienced his success as a feeling of "not being at home."

In a desperate effort at solution, he ran headlong into another recapitulation of the same problem. As is so often the case, the object from which one flees is the very one found in the new location. Ken's entrance into business with his brother immediately precipitated a psychoneurotic reaction. He feared that something would happen to his brother, who was now in the familial position of his father and akin to the social position of the Boss. He feared he would be the cause of his brother's downfall, as he unconsciously believed he had been in the case of his father. He avoided his brother as much as he could, but the tension mounted.

The dream that now plagued him was a metaphor of his psychosocial dilemma. He had not given up the competition with his father for his mother's favor, although these events were long past, and he found in his present situation with his brother and his wife a symbolic representation of this unfinished situation. His social and psychological problems mimicked each other. He stood on the mountain looking toward his advance in the family and in social class, but a second set of eyes forced him to look backward at the evil consequences of his ambition.

At a deeper level, there was the issue of his sexual identification. His mother, in her quiet way, had been the dominant figure in the home, and in accepting her standards, he partially identified with her. The split in his identifications required strange behavior in school. He hid his scholastic ambitions and studying—his female identification—while he displayed his male identification in seeking popularity and competing in sports. Tennis represented a suitable solution to this dilemma, for although it was a vigorous sport allowing him the masculine role, it carried feminine connotations as a "sissy game." Sportsmanship, the counterpart of popularity, was the perfect subterfuge to hide his intense ambition.

In infancy, the excessive protective concern of his mother, the bountiful giver, had laid the groundwork for Ken's future hope that the world could be his. The inevitable disturbance in this union between mother and son led to the doubts and the guilt which later, when reactivated, pervaded Ken's life.

The formulation of a case from historical information may serve as a basis for therapy, but it is not therapeutic in itself. The experienced therapist knows that the problems he works with may be solved in many ways, and it is not necessary to explore every hidden recess of a patient's life. Formulating the factors that lead to neurosis is an important scientific exercise providing a preliminary understanding of what should be handled and what should be left alone. However, the patient needs help with what bothers him at the moment, and a complete exploration of his life may be not only unnecessary but not even in his best interests.

Ken had always solved problems by action. As is the case with many athletes, he was not one to contemplate or to see much virtue in understanding. His smooth social veneer gave way to a vitriolic attack against me for my inability to "do something" immediately to change him. In his scorn for the impotence of my words he relived the wrestling matches with his father. He could only admire someone who was able to overpower him. In therapy, he was not rewarded for his vehemence, nor could he find any objective evidence that he had hurt me. As a result, he began to feel there was enough power in talking, and perhaps even in me, to be useful. Having for the moment found some peace in this relationship, there was a resurgence of feelings directly related to his father. In our interviews Ken spent much time in talking to his father as though he were actually in the room.

He began to see this unfinished situation as distorting his present relationships with his brother and wife. At various times he treated me with the deference reserved for the Boss and competed with me ambitiously to have anything that I had, while feeling regret for his desires. At other times he tried to curry my favor as he had his mother's.

Although his relationship with his brother improved greatly, he made a decision not to continue in business with him. Eventually he entered a related business in which his tennis contacts were advantageous. He thus successfully made a place for himself on his own and even felt more "at home" in his own home with his wife.

From the standpoint of his tennis, a fascinating change occurred. Ken had maintained his old reputation as a court "killer." One day he could upset almost anyone, but just as easily at another time he could lose to a mediocre player. During therapy, he lost his horror of winning long drawn-out matches. A tennis match no longer made him react as though his opponent was his father and to win would be to kill him. A tennis match, long or short, was now only a tennis match. Freed from the compulsion to lose long matches, his tournament record actually improved. Although he had become only a part-time player, in the few top tournaments he played in each year he was often the winner. The only thing that kept him from being ranked highly was the small number of tournaments in which he played. Although certain tennis officials encouraged him to play in more tournaments, some of Ken's intense interest was gone. He now had other interests: a growing family and his occupation. These seemed more urgent.

Ken showed clearly how personal conflict can influence the way an athlete plays the game. There are front-runners, strong finishers, faders, clutch players, and chokers; there are power players, beguiling players, offensive players, defensive players, and an infinite number of other types. The choice of which mode an athlete uses is based not only on his physical attributes but also on the psychological meaning that he invests in the competition.

6.

On Being a Woman and an Athlete

Not until recently have women's sports begun to attain popularity and acceptance from the general public. Although there have been women athletes in the past who have captured the interest and imagination of the sports fan, they generally have been regarded as special curiosities. An athletic woman was called a "tomboy," something between male and female. Within this rigid social climate, the roles of women and athletes were incompatible. The prevailing belief was that any woman who would invade the most masculine of activities had to be suspected of being somewhat strange. Thus, until the latter years of the twentieth century, almost all women athletes were the objects of innuendo questioning their femininity. If a woman became too proficient in her sport, this or that athletic association might even require special physical and chromosomal examinations to determine if she were, indeed, a woman and not a man. Not only did this and related attitudes seriously limit the opportunities open to women, but it also produced a share of social casualties among those who dared to participate. Fortunately, this belief that the role of woman and athlete are incompatible is becoming obsolete, yet for women athletes in the past, it was an ever-present threat. To some degree, these stereotypes can be the source of intense conflict even now. The women's movement is doing much to erase the anachronistic psychological remnants.

During my own athletic days, I had known many of the top women tennis players in the world and had occasionally shared discussions with them about the struggle they felt against sexist bigotry. As athletes, they complained that they were regarded by both men and women as sexual curiosities who must be either lesbian or promiscuous. In my psychiatric practice, I have seen only a few women athletes as patients. Perhaps they have chosen women psychiatrists on the probably correct assumption that another woman would be better able to comprehend the stresses they experienced.

A number of years ago a strange series of events occurred around a promising young woman tennis player. She suddenly disappeared from the sports page, and just as suddenly reappeared over a decade later. Both incidents were without public explanation.

Susan had been champion in her division and had led her age group through each classification. Toward the end of her junior classification years, she began to enter the women's open events. She quickly began to emerge as a major threat to the established champions. Sportswriters, tennis officials, and fellow players all had the expectation that she was about to bloom fully into a great player. In fact, early one spring, in a major event of that time, she unexpectedly upset several of the top-seeded players and went on to win the tournament. This was the first time she had won a major national event in women's open competition.

Then she suddenly disappeared from public view. There was no further mention of her in the sports pages, and the anticipated ascent to championship was ended. The inquiries among fans, "Whatever happened to Susan?" remained unanswered, and she eventually faded completely from public memory.

I had seen her play on only one occasion before her disappearance, but I still remember her clearly. She didn't look like a top tennis player. She did not have the sun-bronzed skin acquired from long hours on the court. Even more remarkable, she played in a restrained way which I can only describe as dainty. She did not bound about the court with the abandon that most top players develop. There were other qualities, however, which clearly revealed the high level of skill and competence with which she played. She was incredibly steady from the backcourt with very sound ground strokes; she could outrally almost any opponent from that position. Although she was not fast, she compensated with a remarkable anticipation that allowed her to reach the most difficult corner balls. She rarely rushed the net, but when she did come in to it, she volleyed with competence. When an opponent had the courage to take the net on her, she was met with precise, net-skimming passing shots both down the line and cross-court. In short, Susan was not a power player, but she played the percentages magnificently.

Her appearance on the court seemed more related to a bygone era in tennis. A Victorian quality about her manners and the way she played reminded one of the great women players of the early part of the twentieth century: competent, restrained, steady in the backcourt, and always genteel in manner. She was an anachronism in the second half of the century. Her uniqueness made her popular with the fans. She was always modest, very private and restrained. But she had no really close friends among her fellow players, and there was no one to ask about her when she disappeared.

It was many months after she had dropped from sight that I heard about her again. Knowing of my interest in sports and athletes, a psychiatrist colleague called me from the East to talk about one of his patients. It was then that I learned what had happened to Susan and the events that had led to her disappearance. Over the next several years I came to know the situation even better. Here is what happened:

After her prestigious victory that spring, she had been invited, along with several of the leading women players in the country, to an informal training camp at a famous private club. This club annually invited some of the best women players in the nation for a couple of weeks of practice and exhibition during a lull in the tournament schedule. This was the first time Susan had been admitted to the select circle or considered to be a peer by the very best players.

She seemed to play well during the first few days, and although it was a difficult feat among this gregarious group, she remained aloof from the others. She was not one to gossip or to share much of a personal nature with her fellow players, but she nevertheless always maintained friendly, although superficial, relationships with them. In no way was her behavior considered unusual.

It was the custom for all of the players to have breakfast together sometime before nine o'clock, and then to play tennis for an hour or two in the morning. On this day, all of the players gathered except Susan. Little note was taken of her absence at first, but since a missing member would deprive someone else in the group of either a partner or an opponent, one of the women called her room. There was no answer. At ten-thirty, when she still had not appeared, the players began to be concerned. They went to her room and knocked on the door. Receiving no answer, they asked the maid, who was cleaning nearby, to let them in. When they entered, there was no one there. All of her clothes and luggage were gone, with one exception: piled neatly in the corner of the room were all of her rackets and tennis dresses. She left no message, and there was no other trace of her in the room. She had disappeared, leaving her fellow players perplexed and wondering.

They called her father to report the disappearance. However, he already knew about it, for after leaving the training camp she had returned home. Her family was astonished by her unannounced arrival, and questioned her about her reasons for leaving the club and about what was wrong. She offered no explanation, but insisted that she would not return.

This was particularly disturbing to her father, for he had been her first teacher and coach and had a large investment in her career. His distress turned to anger, and he castigated her for not following through with her commitments. He insisted that she had a responsibility to the other players, to the tennis club, and to the whole series of tournaments they had arranged together earlier. She did not argue. She seemed oblivious of his attacks and frightened of something even more powerful and terrifying than his rage. This was indeed strange, since she had always followed her father's suggestions in a docile and agreeable way. She usually sought his advice on even the most trivial matters.

Susan's mother and younger sister were like interested spectators as they watched her father cajole, incite, demand—anything to get her to return to tennis. They stood in helpless bewilderment, totally unprepared for these events and for what was to happen next.

Susan remained apparently unresponsive to her father's wrath for about a week, then she disappeared and was nowhere to be found.

Champion tennis players live mobile lives following the sun. They have different relationships in different cities. Each player accumulates a group of followers in each place who are special supporters and friends. In one city it may be fellow players, in another a group of young admirers, in still another a group of older officials and fans. This was also true of Susan.

She had played in a great eastern seaboard city on three different occasions and had become a special favorite of the local tennis officials there. During that period, she had been befriended by one of the local tennis patrons—a wealthy bachelor about forty years old. He was one of that familiar group that follows the players and the tournaments from city to city, often offering helpful advice to officials and players.

He had been very kind to Susan and had taken her and her father, who often traveled with her, to dinner on several occasions. When she played in the tournament last year, she had stayed in this man's home with his mother. He was independently wealthy, and his two major interests—tennis and painting—were little more than hobbies. He was an accomplished artist, but was so awkward at playing tennis that he preferred to be a spectator, rather than actively play the game. He was a quiet, polite man who had never married, and who seemed more like a bachelor uncle to the players, both men and women. This was the man to whom Susan turned in her distress.

When she first disappeared from home she had no clear destination in mind, but aimlessly wandered about the city for a day. In a daze and with no plan, she soon found herself almost instinctively en route to the home of Waverly Gilbert III. Her arrival caught him totally by surprise, but, as always, he was correct and polite.

In fact, he was even glad to see her, for she was one of his favorites. He saw in this restrained, troubled girl a touch of himself, and yet he also saw a potential realization of many of his unexpressed desires. He had become increasingly concerned about his own life, recognizing how sterile it actually was. He was over forty, yet he still lived at home with his mother in much the same way as when he was a child.

When he first saw Susan, he was puzzled by her nervousness and strange behavior. He warmly invited her to come in, and she was soon staying for dinner. She offered no explanation of her unexpected arrival and he did not ask for one, fearing to offend her. After dinner, when she made no move to leave, there was an embarrassed silence. Finally, Waverly invited her to stay overnight, in the very same room in which she had stayed during the tournament.

Waverly's mother was well along in years. She was not so accepting of the strange visit, although she had been fond of the quiet girl and was more than a little concerned about her. She was not pleased by any intrusion into her orderly life and household, but she made no mention of the fact to her son.

The next day, Susan precipitously began to talk to Waverly with an intensity that frightened them both. She declared her love for him and told him how much he had meant to her. She said he was the only person who could save her, and the only person she could trust. She declared that she wanted to marry him, and said that she was sure everything would be all right once they were wed. The poor man had never been confronted with anything like this situation and was completely unprepared for it. He was confused, since they hardly knew one another, but he was also flattered that this attractive, popular girl could care for him. He had never had a close relationship with a woman; he had always kept his distance, and actually doubted his own ability to sustain the kind of relationship that would be necessary in a marriage. Still, there was no doubting Susan's sincerity, and the time had come when he was feeling a bit desparate about his prospects for the future. As she talked, she stirred within him feelings he had never known before. He knew that she trusted him and he felt confident that he could save her; in addition, he was aware of physical feelings that he did not know he had.

When this improbable couple confronted the dowager mistress of the house with their plan to marry, she coldly forbade it. Although she, too, was caught off-guard, she was better prepared for handling such emergencies than Waverly was. Never had she been pressed so aggressively by her usually agreeable son, but she remained adamant. The unrestrained accusations each made against the other were fueled by a reservoir of past, unresolved issues.

The couple, finally acknowledging the futility of trying to obtain the mother's blessing, flew to Las Vegas that same afternoon. They were married in a typical Las Vegas ceremony, with no one they knew in attendance. After a brief honeymoon, they returned to his ancestral home on the East Coast. Each of these two people were desperate for change in their lives, but their needs were very different. They had come together in an explosive way, and they were like sleepwalkers, impulsively following their destinies.

But the 40-year-old bachelor who had been shielded from life, and the 19-year-old woman, afraid and fleeing from an indefinable terror, were unprepared for the complexities and problems of living together. Her sexual experience had been greater than his, but by the standards of her peers her experience had been meager. In her anguish, she was alternately shy and aggressive in her approaches to him. He was able to make awkward attempts at intimacy when she was shy, but was fearfully overwhelmed when she became aggressive. His fear of her heightened her own anxiety to an almost uncontrollable level. She would pace the floor for hours at a time, mumbling things he could not comprehend. He became increasingly upset at his inability to be helpful to her—the role he thought he could assume—and when she seemed to be no longer trusting of him, his hoped-for satisfactions in the relationship seemed to disappear. She had looked to him for stability as someone who was sophisticated and wise in the ways of the world, but she had mistaken shyness for composure and equated wealth with worldliness. Confronted with the collapse of her fantasies, she was filled with terror as she realized how alone she was. Each had envisioned a rescuer in the other and a belief that they could help one another, but neither could comprehend the other's need.

Waverly was at his wit's end. He had gambled on a new relationship after so many years, and now it was in jeopardy. He could not bear to think of it as a failure, because of the shame it would bring to him and his family; yet there seemed to be nothing he could do. He was immobilized and filled with a sense of helplessness. He knew he had to discuss the problem with his mother.

But Susan had her own plan. When she did not come down to breakfast, Waverly was at first relieved, and he and his mother enjoyed the familiar order and tranquility that had recently been interrupted. By midmorning, however, they grew concerned at her absence and dispatched a maid to her room. The maid returned immediately with the report that the door was locked from the inside. In a matter of minutes, a passkey was found and the door was opened.

Waverly and his mother were stunned when they entered the room. Susan lay motionless across the bed, and their attempts to rouse her were futile. Then the maid discovered the empty sleeping-pill bottle by her bedside. An ambulance was called, and in a very short time Susan was on her way to the hospital.

She was in a coma by the time she arrived. The prognosis for recovery seemed bleak, since so much time had elapsed and so much of the drug had been assimilated into her system. The usual emergency procedures were followed: gastric lavage, an artificial airway, stimulants, and other measures. Her response was very slow, and concern for her survival deepened.

But this was not to be the end for Susan. At the moment the situation seemed the most hopeless she began to rally, and her splendid physical condition allowed her to begin a surprising recovery. One of the first people she saw as she began to emerge from her drowsiness was a psychiatrist, who had been called in as a consultant.

Waverly, in the meantime, had found familiar support by turning once again to his mother, as he had always done in the past. He expressed his contrition for having disobeyed her, and she was only too glad to assume her traditional role. Together they considered the best course of action by which they could preserve the family dignity and, at the same time, deal with the unfortunate girl toward whom they felt such a keen obligation. They planned to maintain their traditional gentility to the end of the relationship.

Susan's family had not been called until the suicide attempt. When the suggestion had been made before, she flatly refused. When pressed, she would become panicky and could not be calmed down until she was promised that the call would not be made. When her family was finally notified, her father came immediately to be with her.

When her father arrived, Susan would not speak to him. She pleaded with the nurses not to let him see her. When he finally entered her room, she turned her head away and her face was like a mask, showing no response at all. He spoke anxiously to her and reached out to touch her, but she reacted as though she had no awareness of his presence. Sometimes her face seemed to harden with a controlled rage, but still she said nothing.

In the meantime, she had begun to talk with her psychiatrist. Although she was very suspicious of him, as she was of everyone now, she did reveal a considerable part of herself to him. When she spoke, she rambled in a disjointed way. She said that she was turning into a man and that she could see hair growing rapidly on her face and arms and on the rest of her body. She stated that her breasts were shrinking and that she was turning into her father and could see the changes when she saw her reflection in the mirror. Sometimes she had moments of relief and spoke of these illusions as though they were in the past, but at other times it appeared as though they were still with her. She insisted that her mother, sister, and perhaps some of her fellow tennis players were in the hospital, as she could hear their voices tauntingly calling her "queer," "lesbian," and "gay girl."

She had first heard these voices and had these disturbing thoughts many weeks before while she was at the tennis camp, yet she had revealed them to no one and had shown no evidence of strange behavior. She had believed that somehow the tormenting voices would be silenced if she married. This would demonstrate that she was "normal." So she followed her desperate impulse and married Waverly. When that relationship collapsed, all hope was gone.

With every visit from her father, Susan seemed to withdraw farther. The poor man tried desperately to reassure her, but whatever he did seemed to distress her more. Finally, in a conference with her psychiatrist, it was decided that it might be better if he returned home temporarily.

The marriage, of course, was promptly annulled, and Waverly was able to resume his uncomplicated, orderly life with his mother. He was shaken and even more cautious now than before. He was also truly penitent for having been so unperceptive about the degree of Susan's emotional disturbance, and so faithfully saw to it that she had everything she needed. Her father, on the other hand, harbored unspoken accusations and resentments against his daughter's former husband. Thus, when the Gilberts offered to assume financial responsibility for Susan's treatment, he willingly agreed even though he was well able to handle it himself.

Susan continued under the care of her psychiatrist, Dr. Barton. She was calmed by the doctor's thoughtful manner and by the use of psychotropic drugs. The remnants of her delusions and hallucinations seemed to disappear, and within a few weeks she had recovered to a level that appeared to be little more than an exaggeration of the way she had been before: shy, modest, and restrained.

As she improved, discussions were held about her returning home. Surprisingly, she was quite willing to do so in spite of her earlier withdrawal from her father. Somehow she felt that she had reconstituted in a way that would be acceptable to him. It was at this point that I first learned of the events in Susan's life that had transpired since she disappeared from the sports pages. Arrangements had been made for her return to southern California to live with her family and to continue in treatment with me.

When I first began working with Susan, the characteristics I had noticed when I first saw her play tennis were exaggerated. She was restrained, and kept her eyes cast downward demurely. There was little spontaneity or expressiveness about her; she spoke in a small voice, and what she said tended to conceal more than it revealed. She came for her interviews without enthusiasm, as though she were following orders from some higher power and had no choice in the matter. At the end of each hour, she would wait passively for me to raise the issue of the next appointment. She did not initiate it, but she agreed without interest or reluctance. If I asked what she wanted to do and how she felt about it, she became confused and perplexed. It was as though the question did not make sense to her.

When we talked, our conversations were about the most mundane and superficial events: what time she got up, what she had for breakfast, if she went out, or with whom she talked. When she spoke she reported only bare facts, never referring to what motivated or interested her. At other times she sat in silence for long periods of time, sometimes as long as twenty minutes. I did not press her, for she had had enough of the expectations of others. She needed time and freedom, but she did not know how to handle them, since she did not know how far to trust herself or me.

I asked her about tennis many times, but she had nothing to say about it, or did not want to. She was almost as cautious in what she said about her family, but I gradually began to learn more and more about them.

Her father was a moderately successful attorney. He was very ambitious and had great expectations of his first child. He had had plans for a son whom he would raise to be a championship tennis player, and was disappointed when his firstborn was a girl. Although he was gentle and soft-spoken, he was not warm, and a steely hardness would come over him if he were challenged. Susan's mother was the kind of person one simply did not notice. She seemed pleasant and efficient, and there was little one could criticize about her. There was also little that stood out in a positive way. People thought of her more as an extension of her husband than as either Susan's mother or an individual in her own right.

Susan's father was a tennis player of great enthusiasm and little talent. He had played regularly for years at local courts, but had never played in tournaments. He chose not to compete in something he would not win. The main family social life centered at a local tennis club, where they spent all of their leisure time. Only Susan and her father played. Her mother and younger sister confined their activities at the club to quiet sociability.

There was a special affinity between Susan and her father, and she was always eager to please him. They spent much time together, most of it involving tennis. He accompanied her to all of her matches and she relied on his judgment in whatever she did. Although he dutifully performed the whole gamut of parental functions, it was only in matters pertaining to tennis that he showed any enthusiasm. His interest in the game was the driving force in Susan's career.

He coached his daughter from the time she first stepped onto a court, and he entered her in tournaments when she was only nine years old. She was always the best player of her age group and was considered something of a prodigy. She progressed through the various age levels, always as the champion of each of her divisions. As her game improved, she occasionally had other coaches, but their teachings were always filtered through her father's judgment.

Although not an outstanding beauty, her pleasant nature and her competence on the court attracted attention both from boys in school and from other tennis players. Often this attention developed into dating relationships. Her father seemed to have little concern about this aspect of her life, and Susan seemed to share her father's overriding interest in tennis. As long as she honored her tennis commitments, he was satisfied.

Susan's physical development was normal in every way other than the fact that she did not begin to menstruate until late—almost fifteen years of age—and then irregularly. She considered this to be an advantage, for one of the things that concern women players is that they will have to face an important match while feeling a menstrual low. She had one special boyfriend in school; as though prescribed, he was the captain of the boys' tennis team. They dated; they even sexually explored each other from time to time, but for Susan it seemed without passion.

She was eighteen when she won the important victory referred to earlier, and her father saw this event as an important milestone. He considered himself to be a realist, and he knew that the closeness of their relationship eventually must end. He, more than she, was now aware of her womanhood and its implications, but the subject was never discussed. He sensed his responsibility for her up to a certain point, and then she would be on her own. In his mind, that point was reached when she won the fateful major tournament.

As she traveled to the tennis camp, the realization that she was without clear instructions from her father worried her more and more. She was filled with doubt, since for the first time in her life she did not know exactly where she was going or why. While on the plane, she sat next to a young man of about her own age. Although she had never met him before, she was powerfully attracted to him. She felt herself out of control sitting there with him and, to her dismay, found herself almost automatically engaged in surreptitious petting with him—something entirely alien to this constricted young woman. When they parted at the airport, she kissed him with a passion greater than she had ever before felt. She was appalled by her behavior and frightened by the feelings that had been stirred. The two young people did not exchange names, nor did they ever meet again.

When Susan arrived at her destination, she was at first reassured by the familiar faces and settings and was eager to begin practice. Soon, however, she began to be haunted by strange thoughts. She began to think that her fellow players were not women, but men. She believed she could detect all sorts of male features on them—excessive hair, coarse skin, and crude mannerisms. The closer she looked, the more evidence she found for her fears. She viewed their competitiveness and preoccupation with condition and physical strength as masculine, and not appropriate concerns for women. She was terrified. She began to feel that she was turning into a man, and felt a loathing for herself and her fellow players.

On the night before her impulsive flight, she became so anxious that she was in a panic. She thought she heard some of the other players talking about her and making sexual gestures and invitations to her. Horrified, she knew she had to get out of there. Her first thought was to go home, but realized that was not the answer, since her father had made it clear that she was to be more on her own from now on. As she searched in her mind for where she might go, she finally began to think of the friendly tennis patron in the East, and she was reassured by the memory of his restrained, seemingly assured manner. She was filled with her own sense of passion and need, and felt he could confirm her womanhood. But her selection was most unfortunate.

And now, here she was in my office. Her desperate attempts to find some way out of this crisis in her identity had led her through failure and disaster: a brief, ill-fated marriage, a psychotic episode, an attempted suicide, and subsequent hospitalization. She sat facing me, apathetic and defeated, seeing no clear place to go.

Remembering the severity of acute psychosis and her failing grasp of reality, I listened carefully now to try to evaluate the degree of her current personality integration. The fantastic delusions and hallucinations seemed to have subsided. As little as she talked, it was evident that she was no longer tortured by the voices that called her names, nor did she see evidence that she was turning into a man. What remained for her now was an unappealing reality that offered no place to go. She recalled the acute crisis, and spoke about how fearful she was of becoming a man, offering the explanation that she had been afriad that no man would ever care for her again. She had relied upon her father so heavily, and now she saw that that phase of her life was at an end. In remembering the accusatory voices, she was not now entirely sure she had heard them, but perhaps had only thought so. She explained their presence to herself as the result of her isolation from anyone who cared and could help.

Once, as she spoke, I remembered how difficult it had been for me when illness had ended my tennis career. I commented that I was left with an emptiness and how difficult it had been for me to find that I could no longer participate. For the first time in our relationship, she seemed genuinely touched, and she nodded her head over and over again to show that this was how it was for her, too. She told me that playing tennis without her father's support had no meaning. She had hoped that being at the tennis camp with the other women players would allow her to uncover some new guidelines for managing her life, but she soon found that she did not fit there, and she didn't like the picture of what she feared she would become. She said she was not competitive, even though she had behaved that way to please her father, and that while she didn't know anything else, she knew that a life of competition was not for her. What she had accepted from her father as an important value now seemed wrong for a woman to deliberately choose. She had sought to please her father and to be the kind of daughter he wanted, but now everything was meaningless.

She asked me over and over again how I had managed. All I could say was that with time I had become open to new things and discovered among them many that interested and satisfied me. What she would find, I said, I did not know, but I was confident that if she were willing to endure the uncomfortable sense of loss, she, too, would find something. She was troubled by my not giving her clear directions in the same way her father had done. Indeed, my message was quite different, for I was saying that only she could find the things that would satisfy her. I would be there with her to help. But how was she to discover them? Since she so long ago had set aside her own feelings and emotions, they were now almost unknown to her.

As we continued our sessions together, she gradually became more lively and expressive. It was easy for me to respond to her at these times, for it was a joy to witness the emergence and flower of her experience. Besides, I did like her. She sometimes became quite angry with me for not telling her what to do in a situation. I was not bothered by her anger; rather, I was heartened by it, because I could see that she was beginning to become better acquainted with the way her experience was grounded in feeling, and thus to know more of what she wanted. Her assertiveness heightened the intensity of our relationship.

For many months she stayed at home discontentedly, doing little chores and spending long hours in her room. I had grown concerned about the fact that she did not reach out for new experiences, and feared she might become mired in bitter dissatisfaction at home. One day, over a year after she had first been hospitalized, she surprised me. She said that she was starting work as a secretary in her father's law office. It would not have been my choice, for I was concerned that she might get trapped again in the relationship with her father.

Fortunately, Susan had her own plan about how her work in her father's office should develop. She maintained a rather distant, businesslike relationship with him, and quickly became competent in her work. She refused to go to lunch with her father or even travel to and from work with him. She explained it to me this way: She wanted to know that she could get along in the presence of her father, but she wanted their relationship to be on a new basis, one in which she retained her independence. She knew her own purpose and continued to improve and to work. Two years after her hospitalization she changed course again and enrolled in college, having decided to become a psychologist.

At first I was concerned that Susan's choice of psychology for a profession had been made mainly to please or imitate me—a transference manifestation. She had relied so heavily on her father for signals in the past: was she trying now to do the same thing with me? My hope was that she would be able to choose things that were uniquely hers.

We talked about this many times. Yes, she did want to be like me. No, not only to please me or imitate me, but to help other people to find themselves and what they wanted. That was meaningful work, she said, and something that would fulfill her. Could doing what I did be a new form of constricting her own freedom? No, she was certain that it was a pathway to her own self-discovery.

But before the occupational issue could be settled, there were other unfinished things.

She never talked about playing tennis or her career in sports; she wanted to leave that behind her and to forget it completely. It was still a locked door. One day I asked her if she didn't miss her tennis activities. No. She dismissed the question without consideration. I pursued: "It was a skill that you had developed. Is there no way that you might want to use it now?" She stared at me coldly and said, "You don't," referring to my own tennis career. I was startled by her response, and thought a moment. "True, but you and I are not the same. Besides, I couldn't, even if I wanted to. You could." I was reminding her of the fact that I was physically disabled and she was not. She stared intently at me for several minutes, then said softly, "I have felt that it was somehow not right for me to play, since you can't. You can't, can you?" She wept. My eyes, too, grew moist, not because I could not play, but because I was deeply touched by her feelings for me.

A few weeks later she announced ominously that something very strange had happened to her. I leaned forward. A boy whom she had dated several times had asked her to play tennis with him that weekend. She had avoided any response, confused and not knowing what to do, and she was now on the verge of panic; she had to make up her mind.

The problem was not that she didn't want to play, it was that she did. But she didn't know what to do or how to behave in this situation. She had never, she explained, played just a friendly game. She had never played casually; that had been forbidden. The boy knew nothing of her championship history, and was little more than a beginner himself. She was afraid that she would "blow it," that her competence would ruin the relationship. Should she play down to him? Should she not play at all? She felt as though her skill was a cross to bear, as it had been when she was disturbed.

She became more calm and began to consider alternatives. Perhaps she simply would not play; she would make an excuse. Why, I asked, didn't she just tell him that even though she had been a champion, she still wanted to play tennis with him.

"Too simple. You don't understand. I couldn't. I would be embarrassed. He would be humiliated. I couldn't respect him. He couldn't like me. It's all confused. I just don't know."

"What if you are lots better than he is? It is a piece of truth, isn't it?" I asked. "Besides, if your being too good for him interferes with your relationship, then there can't be too much there."

"But he won't think I'm much of a woman. Maybe he'll think I'm a dyke."

She was right. I did not understand. I had forgotten. There it was. I stayed with her.

"There is nothing that says you can't be an athlete and a woman at the same time."

She paused, sighed, looked relieved, and then began to talk.

"It's all so strange. I really don't have to be what anyone else wants me to be. I don't have to be like my mother; I don't have to be like my father wanted me to be." It was one of those moments of realization that words cannot convey. Of course, she had known these things before, but now it had sunk in at a level that had been walled off.

The next time I saw her, she told me about her tennis date with the boy. She was like a person who was experiencing freedom in a relationship for the first time, unencumbered by a lifelong pattern of "shoulds." It turned out that her date was not only surprised, but pleased, to hear about her tennis background, and he eagerly asked her to show him ways to improve his game. They played together for about an hour, and then were asked by another young couple who were playing on the next court if they would like to play some mixed doubles. Her superior skill made her the dominant player in the foursome when they began to play, of course, but surprisingly enough, she enjoyed it. Again she spoke of the freedom she felt.

She talked at great length about what it meant to compete, and it was clear that she did not enjoy that aspect of tennis. But she had enjoyed instructing the young man, and had a special feeling of giving when doing so. For the first time she appreciated her skill and knowledge in tennis for what she could give to others. The world was opening up for Susan.

Over the next two years she reported playing fairly frequently, not with the old intensity, but for the sheer enjoyment of playing. She played with boys whom she dated, and she played with some of the girls on the women's tennis team. It wasn't serious; it was fun. The tennis coach asked her over and over again to play on the women's team, but she was not interested.

By now our meetings were much less frequent. Susan didn't come to see me on a regular basis, but when some new stress entered her life she might come for four or five sessions, or perhaps on a monthly basis for a while, until she mastered the situation that was bothering her. Increasingly, she used our meetings for her own purposes to test a new idea or share an exciting experience. She had moved from her preoccupation with her deficiencies to the exhilaration of enhancing her own growth.

She was also now beginning to find other means of supporting her own development. In the late sixties, Susan began to identify herself with some of the social issues of day. She participated actively in the antiwar movement. She was hardly a political radical, but she was, with her quiet, firm efficiency, an effective worker in the movement. For her personal development, this led to an even more significant identification with the women's movement. Women had begun meeting together on campuses to examine the meaning of being a woman in our society and to free themselves of the social strictures that had limited them. This sharing of common experiences with her peers had an important liberating effect on Susan, for knowing that she was not alone in her struggle to find a meaningful place for herself as a woman provided great support.

When I met with her during this period, she reported with amazement how she had discovered that this or that friend had had very similar experiences in becoming a woman. She talked about the strange ideas she had had of what was acceptable feminine behavior. Her personality was developing and emerging in a new, exuberant way that was rewarding to see.

It took her almost twice the normal length of time to graduate from college, but when she finished, she decided to go on to graduate school. At this time, however, she decided to study business administration. She hoped to combine her interest in women's rights and psychological helping through a career in organizational development and industrial psychology. She hoped thereby to promote opportunities for women in business.

Women's tennis was becoming popular in a new way. Women's tournaments began to draw large crowds and to achieve wide publicity. Names like Billie Jean King and Margaret Smith became as widely known as the best men players like John Newcomb and Rod Laver. For the first time, a considerable amount of money was to be made by women in tennis. Susan spoke with enthusiasm about these developments and followed them closely, even though she was not a participant.

One summer, between semesters in graduate school, she took a job as a teacher at a children's tennis camp. She enjoyed it so thoroughly that she continued to do some teaching when she returned to college. She was able to support herself quite adequately this way. She worked for other teaching professionals and had a few private pupils of her own. Teaching tennis now seemed to be the perfect amalgam of the various skills she had developed.

As her popularity as a teacher grew, Susan began to work regularly with a well-known teaching professional. Together they provided year-round tennis camps and various instructional aids. During the summer months they traveled around the country offering tennis clinics. A couple of years later her own book of tennis instructions, written especially for young people, was published and became widely used.

I was pleased when she sent me a copy of her book, with a very warm dedication. As I read the book's contents, I realized that Susan had emphasized the fact that sport provides an opportunity for expression. She referred to the special opportunity for young women in the game of tennis. Much of the text discussed the well-balanced life and the freedom to choose whatever the player wishes to make of tennis.

The women's movement and the second half of the twentieth century have expanded the choices available to women. There are still many ways in which women are not free, but much progress has been made. Being a woman and an athlete need no longer present a serious identity and role conflict for women. Whatever path a woman chooses today, she is likely to find a supportive reference group of her peers.

Susan's history is an epiphenomenon of this transitional social period. The vestiges of Victorian rigidity continue to influence what we consider to be acceptably human. Susan was born into a family with little flexibility in the roles of man and woman, and one in which there was very restricted opportunity for exchange in the relationships between the sexes. She had been unwittingly exploited by both her father and her mother to meet their own frustrated aspirations. The fact that she had never fully accepted the role stereotypes of either woman or athlete made it possible for her to discover a new personal synthesis between them.

She was materially aided by the shared explorations with other women in group discussions. Discovering that she was not alone in her struggle was a great relief. Her psychotherapy prepared her to be open to these experiences, but the peer support supplied an essential ingredient. Had she not had the good fortune of being in the right place at the right time, and to have the benefit of such women's group supports, she might have remained stuck.

The last time I saw her, Susan seemed to be thoroughly enjoying her life. But there were new questions about her future which concerned her. They had to do with the old specters of conventional marriage and family. She was in love and she wanted children, but she feared the restriction that either of these might bring. She struggled with the question of whether she was willing to give up some of her freedom in exchange for the support and satisfaction to be derived from a commitment to a man and a family. She had even explored the possibility of children and communal relationship without marriage, but she did not feel that this would be enough for her. Freedom, for Susan, had brought new choices and new dilemmas, but now she struggled with them in a conscious and deliberate way, seeking that which would best fulfill her personal needs.

7.

The Champarbitrary

Almost every mental hospital has among its long-term inhabitants a formerly prominent boxer. His badges of courage—scarred and thickened ridges over the eyes and a vacuous stare mirroring dulled wits—are easily recognized; his is the shell of a once proud, powerful figure who danced about the ring to the cheers of fans. He served them well. But the human skull, admirably designed to house the vital and vulnerable brain which makes its possessor human, can offer only so much protection. Inevitably the pain of the blows is dulled, the pummeling of the skull becomes increasingly vague, and the cheers of the crowd become more distant. Eventually the brain is irreversibly damaged by the blows, the seemingly limitless earnings are plundered by the payoffs, and the fighter stands alone, a hollow hulk. In the end there is the institution, erected by those who cheered, where their discarded creation can be hidden. The damage is done, the brain cannot be restored, and the only issue is custody. Perhaps the Roman crowd that turned thumbs down on a maimed gladiator was more merciful.

Not only is the boxer's danger great, but his rewards are small and fleeting, and the barriers against his getting even these are almost insurmountable. Kirson Weinberg, studying 127 fighters, found that only 7.1 percent achieved national recognition. The financial gains, sought at such great risk, are reduced by training expenses, taxes, managers, and silent underworld partners. What the fighter actually receives he usually squanders recklessly.

And what happens after the boxing days are over? The career is brief, for only the youngest and healthiest can stand the physical punishment. The tragic specter of Sugar Ray Robinson, perhaps the greatest and smartest fighter ever, who, well past his prime, fought in relatively unimportant events in a vain attempt to maintain the living standard of the golden years, exemplified the fate of every boxer. Once his ring career is over, the boxer is ill-equipped to carry on in business and society. He can shine shoes like former champion Beau Jack or sell ties like Kingfish Levinsky. The story of Gene Tunney is one great exception. He retired at his peak, his mind and body intact, and went on to new successes in the business world. Rocky Graziano has also done well. But most boxers undergo a sharp decline in status after retirement.

An examination of ninety former champions and leading contenders, each of whom had earned substantial amounts during his ring career, showed the following occupations upon retirement:*

26	work in taverns	3	bookies
18	trainers or trainer-managers	3	racetrack workers
		2	wrestlers
18	unskilled jobs	2	liquor salesmen
6	work in movies	2	gas station attendants
3	cab drivers	2	janitors
3	newsstand vendors	2	in business

The boxer's lot is not a happy one, and his future is almost always dim.

What makes a man enter a profession that holds such a questionable future? Why does a man subject himself to beatings, fleeting fame, almost certain failure? The dull hulks of former boxers who are custodial patients in hospitals are unable to supply the answers. Their desires, their motivations, their memories, like their money, have long since disappeared. Only a still-alert boxer could supply such information.

I have known several of these ghostlike figures who were once great boxers, but the Champ was the first former fighter I met who retained enough awareness to provide information about his past and his motivations. Unlike his more deteriorated colleagues, the Champ's past profession was not apparent from his appearance. He was of medium height, not overly stocky, and he had a regal bearing. His most characteristic mannerism was the slightly disdainful look he wore, looking through or past those to whom he spoke. It was a pugnacious, challenging stare which suddenly, without apparent reason, would change to anger in response to some hidden association with the past. Just as quickly he could change to laughter and, with a twinkle in his eye, make feinting, bobbing steps backward, as if in a boxing match. Conversation with him was like being in the ring. He first moved

---

*Gregory P. Stone, "American Sports: Play and Dis-Play," *Mass Leisure*, eds. Eric Larrabee and Rolf Meyersohn (Glencoe, Illinois: The Free Press, 1958), p.255, quoting S. Kirson Weinberg and Henry Arond, "The Occupational Culture of the Boxer," *American Journal of Sociology*, Vol. 57 (March 1952), p. 469.

relentlessly in on his opponent, and then, just when least expected, he would back off with some fancy verbal footwork, keeping his antagonist slightly off balance.

He spoke in a slightly hoarse, high-pitched voice, and the words he used did not seem like his own. He referred to the hospital as "this worthy establishment" and to me as "my friend, the good doctor." He never missed an opportunity to use one of his practiced cliches, even if it had little to do with the conversation of the moment. Whenever I talked with him, he would say at least once, in stylized fashion, "May the better man emerge victorious." This was almost a trademark, and sometimes, if there were no other opportunity, he used it in place of "Hello" or "Goodbye." Most of the time his enunciation was clipped, his accent a peculiar mixture of North and South, but when he grew excited, he lapsed into the drawl he had learned as a boy—and then he seemed more genuine. For the most part, though, there was an unreal quality to his speech, and he seemed very distant.

At the time I first saw him, it had been nearly five years since his last fight, with the last few years of his ring career spent in relative obscurity. As an amateur in the Golden Gloves he had been champion, but as a professional he had never been more than a leading contender.

He was seething with anger. When examined by a hospital doctor, he responded to an innocuous request for place of birth with great irritation. "Of course I'm from the South—Birmingham—but I'm proud of it. Some Negroes are ashamed of coming from the South, but I have no bitterness." His answer was like the angry response of a man who had just been attacked.

Even though he had been a promising fighter as a boy, he could not compete in his home state, but first fought professionally in New Orleans, where his manager passed him off as a Mexican, giving him the name of Raoul Dominguez. His strict instructions to speak to no one lest he reveal the secret of his origin proved to be no small order, since it resulted in unforeseen reactions. He won his first fight in impressive style, but when the press requested an interview he fled to his dressing room and locked the door, confused, frightened, and disappointed. The occasion, which might have been expected to be greatly satisfying, turned into one of the most painful experiences of his life. His confusion turned to anger, and his anger to fury. He hated everyone, his manager the most. He couldn't be himself; he didn't know who he was supposed to be; he couldn't even talk. Under the bare bulb in his dressing room he made some vows. He would leave the South and never return; he would become somebody and never be muzzled again.

His manager pounding on the door made him feel trapped. He didn't know how to be a Mexican. He wasn't white, and couldn't return to being an obedient colored boy, and so he solved the problem by leaving through the dressing-room window.

He now began an agonizing journey hitchhiking and walking to Detroit, the only northern city he had ever heard about, because he knew that he had an "auntie" there. During the trip he was near starvation and his physical discomfort helped nurse his bitterness, but it was not at all clear to him against whom his anger was directed. Was it the whites for their discrimination or the blacks for their complicity? He was angry at anyone who reminded him of his humiliation and confusion.

In southern Illinois he was offered food, his first in several days, in a railroad hobo jungle. He felt uneasy but grateful to the men who had invited him to share their food. In a clumsy attempt at friendship, one of his hosts said to him, "Another darkie boy trying to escape up North." In a burst of rage he leaped to his feet and pummeled his host. The man dropped to the ground with a dull groan and the others jumped up to drive him off. As he ran, he glanced back through the trees and saw them leaning over the prostrate form he left behind. He felt no remorse, but only a rhythmic rise and fall in rage. Yet he was puzzled. What had triggered this attack? Was it because he had been called a "darkie boy" or because the man had suggested he was trying to escape? As he trudged along, he kept reassuring himself, "I don't run from nobody."

Arriving in Detroit, half-starved, he found his way to a Salvation Army mission where he spent several days regaining his strength. A kindly member of the staff tried to offer him spiritual and practical guidance and talked about finding him a job. The rage and fear still boiling inside him made it impossible for them to communicate, and the offer of help only seemed to irritate him. His would-be helper finally told him that he was just like a porcupine and that he had better pull in his stickers if he were going to get anywhere. The confrontation had the desired effect, and he began to talk about himself. He explained that he was a boxer and what he really wanted to do was to get himself a fight. His counselor, after trying to persuade him to find a "regular job," at length helped him find the nearest boxing gym.

He arrived at the gym and tried to discover how to get into a professional fight. After a brief workout, even in his weakened condition, his natural ability stood out, and he found a manager with whom he signed a contract that same day. He knew nothing of the terms and was not interested; all he wanted was to "get a fight." He told his manager that he was going to "be somebody" and was convinced that as long as he had enough to eat and could work out and fight, he'd be satisfied. He wanted to earn a "name" for himself, to be recognized.

He considered his speech to be the most shameful aspect of his origin, so he began a serious effort to learn to speak like people in the North. He attended a few sessions of night school, but around other people he was embarrassed and quickly gave that up. It was through his own efforts, imitating others and using a dictionary, that he was able to change his speech. His imitation was very deliberate. When he heard someone who sounded "elegant," he would try to talk the same way, copying the tone of voice and the phrases used. Once, for example, he heard a well-dressed man at a fight speak of "utter nonchalance"; after a trip to the dictionary, he found "utter nonchalance" in nearly everything he did. Many of the words and phrases, lifted out of context, were used inappropriately. Often he had a special word or phrase, recently acquired, which he would use over and over again at the gym. The results were sometimes ludicrous, but those who frequented the gym soon learned that to laugh meant a challenge, and his growing reputation as a boxer made this unwise. Those who ridiculed him learned to do so outside his hearing.

His boxing career progressed according to plan. He chose a new name, emulating one of his idols. With this name he felt an identity he never felt with his other one. His prestige was enhanced, and he progressed through club fighting and preliminaries and finally went on to main events. Within a few years he was a feared contender who had indeed developed a "name."

He liked to think of himself as a scientific boxer, but his reputation was that of a relentless attacker whose assaults were punctuated by seemingly light-hearted taunting and backpedaling. He had his share of defeats, but they were mainly from being overmatched early in his career. His ring future appeared very promising.

His image was now crystallized: the disdainful look, the relentless attack, the stilted speech. It was almost entirely a synthetic front presented to the white man's world. He still had moments when he responded in a more natural manner, consistent with his childhood—moments of uproarious abandon and joy, and others of tenderness when he was with people who shared common experiences, common origins, and common suffering. But these friends satisfied his drive to be "somebody" less and less. It was not with them that his battle raged; it was with the others, those who had made him suffer. The battle became so important to him that the times when he was his old self became fewer and fewer. The look of disdain was with him almost constantly, as was the rest of his armor. Always ready for battle, he kept his guard up.

As his boxing improved and his reputation grew, his desire to become "somebody" increased. A little success only made him more demanding. His contract and his manager, once acceptable on any terms, now were constant irritants, mere impediments to his progress. He had no idea how the fight money was distributed; all he knew was that he was getting very little for his fighting and did not live in the style expected of him.

His dissatisfaction reached its climax one day when arguing with his manager about money matters. Telling him the "facts of life," that phrase so universally used to describe falsities one fears to change, his manager explained that it was essential to pay the right people to protect his boxing career, but that they had to remain anonymous. This explanation meant nothing to the Champ; all he knew was that someone in his position should have more money. Finally, in the frustration of not being able to comprehend this injustice, he flailed out against his manager, dropping him with two rapid punches. When the police arrived, he was booked for assault with a deadly weapon, the usual charge against a boxer who uses his fists. Once again, the skill he hoped would secure his place in the world had instead brought him punishment.

He was released after a single night in jail when his manager (who was able to swallow his pride in the interest of his pocketbook) refused to press charges, fabricating a story that exonerated them both. This was not the Champ's first brush with the police, for there had been several arrests before, on charges ranging from assault to petty theft. The penalties had always been mitigated by his manager, and the Champ was left with a fine, a night or two in jail, and then release.

After this outburst, the manager did make some adjustments in the money the Champ got for his fights, but the basic inequities were still there. Although he was now a headliner and considered one of the best men in his division, he had not had a championship fight. The problem of a championship fight was simple: before he could fight the reigning champion, he had to agree to lose the first time in order to get a return bout in which he would have a chance to prove himself legitimately. To lose a fight intentionally, to give up, would mean that he would have to endure the same kind of humiliation that had caused him to flee from the South: that of not being himself. He absolutely refused. For the Champ, this had nothing to do with morality; it was entirely a matter of pride. With the championship or even the chance at the championship blocked by his stubbornness, he could go only one way, and that was down. His fame began to fade, and it was harder and harder to get fights. His manager, who had been willing to endure a good deal, saw the future fade—and dropped him. There followed a series of managerial changes, but to no avail. His hopes of ever becoming champion were gone, and he became apathetic about boxing.

In the meantime, he had married a quiet, undemanding girl who loved him deeply. They lived quietly, and despite the modesty of his winnings, his wife, a better-than-average financial manager, had saved most of the money. Seeing the decline in his status and the impossibility of a future as a boxer, she finally persuaded him to quit fighting. It was becoming more and more difficult for him to get a good fight, and although she did not use it as part of the argument, she was aware of the increasingly severe beatings he was taking and was concerned about their effect on him.

He went to work for a construction company and was a good worker. His domestic life was tranquil, and he cared adequately for his family, which now included three children. However, he felt his shrinking fame as though it were a physical pain. To compensate for his loss of prestige, he began bragging. He declared first that he should have been champion, and after some months he insisted that he actually had been. Sometimes he would simply say that he was the uncrowned champion because he never got the fight, but at other times there was a formed delusion that he really had been champion of his division. The tricks of his own mind now gave him what he had not been able to achieve in the ring.

The patently false character of his claims resulted in skepticism on the part of his fellow workers. Finally, the knowing looks and jeering smiles when his back was turned became open derision. He no longer seemed so frightening to the men, and they were willing to take a chance and needle him. There were several episodes when he threatened his detractors. At last he could contain himself no longer and lashed out, severely injuring one of his fellow workers. Another arrest followed. This time the charges were pressed and a jail sentence resulted; no fast-talking manager was there to get him off. Although the charges were reduced because of the circumstances and he was released within three months, he was not the same. There had never been a question of his work ability, but now, because of his impetuous outbursts, no employer would take the risk of hiring him.

After he got out of jail, surly and bitter, he spent all of his time around the house. Nothing seemed to comfort him; he grew more distant from his family and became so easily irritated that after a while his wife, too, gave up any attempts to help and withdrew. He spent this silent time going over in his mind all of the injustices that had been done to him in his life. Hate was all he had and he nursed it carefully, but his self-enforced seclusion gave him no object to spend it on. Deprived of boxing, which had once given him an acceptable way of striking back at injustices, his anger ached like an inner wound until his hold on reality was nearly gone.

He began to hear voices yelling, "Kill, kill, kill him!"—the voices of the fight fans—and he was back in the ring, savagely attacking an opponent. One evening while he was watching the fights on television, his wife came to sit beside him, silently participating in one of the few things they could still share. The fight was exciting, and the Champ began to feel himself drawn into it. The voices—which in his fantasy had become the fans cheering him—were louder than usual. He was in the ring, on his feet throwing punches, bobbing and weaving, the fight the only reality. When his wife stood up to calm him, touching him on the shoulder, he whirled and struck her in the abdomen. She crumpled to the floor.

He was stunned by what he had done. The anguish at having struck and seriously hurt the one person who loved him and had stuck by him shocked him back to reality. He awkwardly comforted her until he was sure that she would be all right. Then, without a word, he left in search of a "crazy house," an action which he had been contemplating for many weeks.

At his own request he was admitted to the hospital. The admitting doctor's note said:

> This 34-year-old unemployed former boxer seeks voluntary admission after striking his wife. He is agitated, anxious, withdrawn. Auditory hallucinations are present

saying, "Kill, kill, kill." He is irritable, guarded, and suspicious. The affect is flat and there are loose associations. Diagnostic impression is Schizophrenic Reaction, Paranoid Type.

Because of his history as a boxer, further examinations were made to rule out brain damage. Although there were some questionable findings in the electroencephalogram, neurological and psychiatric examinations and a battery of psychological tests failed to find any evidence of injury.

When I talked with the Champ a few days later, he was less agitated. He started by telling me the details of his ring career, this introduction being necessary to establish that he was "somebody." Hospitalization removes any person from his usual environment and separates him from the accustomed symbols of identity. A strange place, different clothing, very limited private space, and distance from familiar people and things—all make it difficult to remind oneself of who one is. For the Champ the problem was even more acute, but once his "name" was established with me, he felt more relaxed, and over the next several weeks he became increasingly confidential. It was from these later interviews that I learned the details of his life that I have already given. His natural intelligence and sharp memory made him a good informant. Considering his brief education and his life-long pattern of acting rather than talking, he had remarkable insight into his life.

As a descendant of slaves, he knew nothing of his background beyond the rural plantation environment from which the family came. His grandfather had been a slave, later freed, but freedom had changed neither the geographical location of the family nor the social nexus in which they lived.

His mother died when he was an infant, and the women in his childhood had been a series of aunts, sisters, and other relatives, generally kind and gentle, as he recalls, but in his memory lacking individuality, fused in a rather amorphous maternal image of kind, sweet devotion with an elusive quality of "here today, gone tomorrow." For him, mother, mother substitutes, and, later, all women had this same quality: they gave the promise of pleasure, kindness, and warmth, but there was little that was enduring. Women were objects to be sought and held as long as possible, but the threat of their imminent departure was always there.

His father had no such tenuous quality; he was described as a solitary, unique figure. His mother had been his father's second wife, and there was another wife after her. He had something like twenty brothers, sisters, step-siblings, and half-siblings and became quite confused when he tried to enumerate them. The Champ himself was somewhere in the middle. He had kept in touch with only one member of the family, an older brother. His father, known as "Big Frank," was a feared member of the community and commanded considerable respect. He was quick-tempered and at times brutally beat his children or his wife. At other times he was lighthearted and easygoing. Because of his quick-changing moods most people kept their distance from him, not knowing what to expect next. He also had a considerable reputation for sexual prowess.

The Champ regarded him with a mixture of admiration and contempt. He was impressed by the deference with which his father was treated and by the stories of his fighting and sexual adventures. Among his paramours, it was said, were several white women. But in the white man's world Big Frank wasn't big. He bowed and smiled and said "yassuh" and "nosuh."

There were also vivid memories of the beatings he received from his father. Big Frank, when in foul mood, would taunt and tease his children. The Champ recalled bitterly seeing an older sister taunted relentlessly until she would cry. Even more vivid was an occasion when, in her frustration, she made an attempt to strike back and was brutally beaten. On this occasion the Champ tried to defend her and received a beating himself. Similar punishment continued until his early teens. He recalled these assaults angrily, not because of the physical punishment but because of the humiliation that he felt. After such occasions, he would vow revenge against his father.

In his neighborhood, he was known as a tough kid and was often in fights. As his confidence grew, his opposition to his father became more open. The climax came when he was about fifteen and his father nearly sixty. During what his father undoubtedly expected to be a routine beating of his son, the Champ fought back savagely and a stalemate was reached. Thereafter they had little to do with one another, and within a few weeks the Champ left home and went to the city to live with relatives. He never saw his father again.

In all that he said he seemed very alert. He stated that he had had six years of schooling and considered himself to have been the smartest boy in school, which he probably was. Psychological examination showed his intelligence to be well above average.

In the city, he was a laborer with a reputation for being a hard worker. His quick temper and ready fists found plenty of activity in street fighting. His boss, unusually tolerant because the Champ was such a good worker, saw him fight on several occasions. One day he told him he ought to be a boxer and arranged for him to work out in a local gym for blacks. He also introduced him to the man who was later to become his first manager.

It is difficult for a black person to tell a white frankly how he feels about segregation, particularly if he has grown up in the South where the code of conduct between races is very strict. Attitudes of deference necessary for protection are deeply ingrained. During the time I worked with the Champ, he became relatively free to talk about many deeply personal things, but he was never free enough to explain how he felt about being black and what it had meant to him during his formative years. What I know about his feelings in this respect was gained mainly by inference. Once he asked me if I had ever been in the South. When I told him that I had spent a year in New Orleans, he immediately clammed up and talked very little for the next several sessions. He later told me that it had made him very uneasy, but he did not reveal the full force of his concern.

Although the bitterness he felt had deep roots in his relationship with his father, the major target was society—the white man's world. His feelings toward segregation and discrimination crystallized while he was in the Army. Whether his hatred for his father was displaced onto the social immorality of segregation or whether it was the other way around is impossible to say. Perhaps for him the real battle was against the attitude of white supremacy, and only in retrospect did his father symbolize this injustice. He felt the humiliation of segregation as he did the childhood humiliation at the hands of his father.

In the rural environment of his childhood everyone suppressed the frustration of the social hierarchy. In the city and later in the Army he tasted the potential of equality and became unwilling to settle for less. Yet when he first met men who offered him equality in friendship, he mistrusted them and tested the relationship until he destroyed it.

In his sexual life, which had been very active since puberty, he had emulated his father. His relationships tended to be lengthy, and even as a youth he often went with one girl for years at a time. He felt that he was considerate of girls, and he generally was. Many of his street fights, in fact, were in the service of protecting or avenging them. This was not a fleeting stage, since his relationship with his wife was similar to these youthful romances. He was an ardent lover and protector. Knowing that this was his image of himself made it easier for me to understand why his anguish was so great when he struck his wife just before coming to the hospital. It was an experience alien to his concept of himself, and one that made him feel certain that he must be mad.

By the time he left the hospital, the Champ's personality was reconstituted and he had a good idea of what he wanted to do. He continued to be suspicious and disdainful, but the crisis was over. He had no desire for further psychotherapy beyond solving the practical issues of employment and his avocational interests, which he could see as the source of his salvation. Psychotropic drugs played an important role in his improvement. He was able to use me successfully to clarify some of his problems, but there was always a barrier of mistrust. He returned home, went back to a construction job, and was getting along well the last time I heard from him a year later. His devoted wife was his greatest asset. He had found a modest way of returning to boxing as a volunteer instructor at a boys' club. As a teacher, he vicariously lived through his pupils' struggles to achieve mastery over themselves and their aggressions. He also gained respect from the boys, and this was a satisfaction to him.

I knew the Champ in 1959, before the civil rights movement of the 1960s. In reviewing his case, I am now impressed by the many social changes that have taken place since that time and the new perspectives that have evolved. My description of the Champ reflects the situation as it was at the time I worked with him, although I believe that if I were to see him now, things might be different. Both he and I were products of our society as it was then; if we were to meet today, we would undoubtedly each reflect the changes that have taken place in our society and in our individual cultures. He would have the support of a society that now recognizes the special contributions and values of black culture; he might not feel that he had to become something different in order to "be somebody." I, too, would be able to share in the new recognition and enlightenment, and our relationship might be more substantial. We would certainly be able to more clearly understand our mutual predicament in working together, and perhaps this might allow us to experience a more open communication.

It has been said that a successful boxer must be a hungry man. During the great economic depression of the 1930s, this literally meant a hunger for food. But there are other forms of hunger: the hunger for social position or for a sense of security—of being someone—and these hungers can motivate a man to seek his fortune in boxing just as strongly as the hunger for food.

In this country, achievement in sports has provided one of the most effective ways by which a disadvantaged person can improve his social position. Even if the fields of business, professions, housing, and avocations are blocked, the road to social ascent may be open in athletics. Members of groups that are ordinarily excluded from activities of high prestige and economic reward often see the first light of opportunity on the playing field.

Black Americans have occupied a uniquely problematical social position in the United States. Social mobility has been sharply limited in all sections of the country. Major concern for the problem first focused on the overt forms of discrimination in the schools and housing in the South. More recently we have become aware of the more subtle forms of racism and discrimination that exist in employment and in the whole range of social relations in all areas of the country. Progress has been made, but there is still much to do to achieve true social equality.

David Riesman once studied the social origins of Americans who played college football. He traced the social progress made by various ethnic groups which make up our nation through the changing patterns in names of All-American players. In 1889, all but one, Heffelfinger, were white and bore Anglo-Saxon names. The next non-Anglo-Saxon name was Murphy, in 1895; then Irish names became common. Next came the Jewish and Polish names. Today there is a strange mixture of names representing the entire spectrum of ethnic origins, dominated by black Americans whose names usually tell little of their heritage.

The name of Cassius Clay became world famous, first as that of an Olympic champion, and then as world heavyweight champion. But the owner of that name did not sense that it belonged to him, for it did not fully express who he was. He next adopted the name of Cassius X, but that did not seem right, either. He finally hit upon Muhammad Ali, and that seemed perfect. One of the great appeals of the Nation of Islam in America is that it provides an acceptable heritage to many who cannot find a suitable integration in their lives. The importance and complexities of naming are dramatically expressed in the title of James Baldwin's book *Nobody Knows My Name*. The fact that the disadvantaged person whose identity is fragmented and whose social progress is blocked often explodes in violence seems understandable. The criminal and the boxer, or other athlete, both give direct expression to their aggressive feelings, but the athlete is sponsored and applauded by society. As one black athlete said of boxing, "Where else can a black man beat up a white man and be cheered by both blacks and whites?"

When Jack Johnson captured the world heavyweight championship, he was the first black man to achieve such prominence in this country. He became a symbol of hope and represented the promise of the future to black Americans looking toward social equality and advancement. As champion, his flamboyant behavior exceeded the limits white society had placed on black men; as a result, his defense of the championship began to appear like a renewal of the Civil War. A number of "great white hopes" were developed and touted to try to prove Johnson's racial inferiority. Many years later similar significant social conflict was symbolized in the boxing arena. During the rise of Nazi Germany, there was a renewal of this racial battle on the world scene. In the heavyweight championship fight, a black man, Joe Louis, was pitted against one of Hitler's Aryan supermen, Max Schmeling. The victory by Louis in the first few minutes of the fight was a blow to the superman myth.

The first black man allowed to play major league baseball was Jackie Robinson. During his "probationary period" he was forced to quietly endure the most bitter derision. He uttered not a word of protest, even under the severest provocation. Small wonder that once he was firmly established as a major leaguer, he took opportunity to let out some of his pent-up anger at the injustice. In tennis, Althea Gibson was the first black person to play in major tournaments. At first she was frightened and very conscious of her manners on the court, but later, when she had become the best woman player in the world, she became very self-assertive. Today there has been considerable change, for men like Muhammad Ali and Arthur Ashe articulate their perceptions of prejudice and other interferences in human relationships to a thoughtful and often receptive audience. Some of the cherished stereotypes of the past seem to be dissolving, as athletes, whatever their color or ethnicity, can speak their minds freely.

The exploits of Jack Johnson were considered wild when boxing first reluctantly opened its gates to black men. The Establishment was threatened by what seemed to be Johnson's challenge of the existing order, so he was subjected to the most vitriolic abuse. At that time, and for many years after, the black person who achieved success in the white community experienced a profound identity crisis. He was caught between two worlds, yet belonged to neither of them. His success in the white community separated him from his origins, yet no matter how great his achievement, he was still black. Today, black culture has achieved respectability and is viewed by many more people, black and white, as a positive part of our society. A person no longer must forfeit a part of his identity to succeed in the established world, and no longer must live in an agonizing limbo of ambiguity. Many more models are available to black children today and include not only sports, the professions, and politics, but almost every other aspect of American life as well.

The social climate was not yet so open for the Champ in 1959, and his identity was fragmented. He wanted to be considered a scientific boxer by the white world, which he mimicked with his stilted speech, sardonic smile, and stiff, formal movements. Only with his family did his expressiveness and warm feelings emerge, revealing a genuine and relaxed person. He could not find an adequate way to integrate those two separate parts of himself.

The Champ fought to become somebody, and having a "name" symbolized his need. He wanted a name other people would recognize and respect, but one that was also acceptable to him. Like many people with identity problems, he hoped that if he could just find the right name for himself the problem would be solved. At the insistence of his manager, he discarded the name given to him at birth and exchanged it for one that seemed halfway between his black origins and white society: a Mexican name. Later he renounced this name too, and chose the name of a famous old-time boxer. Better than anything, he preferred to be known as "Champ." None of these names ever solved his dilemma, however, for a name is only an acknowledgment of a person, and the Champ did not know who he actually was.

His psychiatric disorder developed when his warm relationships with his family became contaminated by the bitter disappointments that had occurred outside. His hate appeared in the form of hallucinatory voices shouting, "Kill, kill, kill," and he attacked his wife. The separate parts of his identity began to overlap in inappropriate ways. When there is insufficient opportunity for a person to express an important part of himself, it takes an increasing amount of energy to conceal that part. Eventually the pressure becomes so great that it is no longer tolerable.

When the Champ's boxing career came to an end, he tried to maintain his self-esteem with the delusion that he actually had been the champion, but he was ridiculed for his boasting and felt the familiar sting of humiliation he had known so often before. It was the same feeling of humiliation he had known

with his father, in his first fight, in a segregated Army, and in being deprived of a championship fight. To the poor, the educationally deprived and
socially unskilled ethnic minority member, sports may represent an important avenue to social ascent. However physically dangerous the sport, it
holds for them the hope, if not the reality, of finding a successful identity
and a satisfying life.

8.

Superman and Mild-Mannered Clark Kent

One morning as I approached the university psychiatric clinic where I worked for a time, I found the clinic social worker waiting anxiously for me. "I wanted to catch you before your first appointment to see if you could see a case for me today." There was a sense of urgency in her voice as she continued with the details.

The day before, she had received a referral slip from the university urology clinic with a scrawled message: "No GU pathology; recommend psychiatric evaluation." The procedure for such referrals required a preliminary interview with the social worker.

She found the subject of the referral to be a young male student. When ushered into her office, he stood at the doorway, seemingly paralyzed with fright as she greeted him. Invited to sit down, he flushed and remained crimson throughout the interview. He continually looked furtively about, as if seeking an escape, and never once glanced at his strikingly attractive interviewer. She asked a series of routine and innocuous questions, to which he responded by squirming in his chair, glancing toward the door, and stammering and stumbling, unable to formulate a complete answer. As the interview proceeded, his frustration became contagious, making his interviewer uncomfortable also. In desperation, she finally suggested that he come back the next day to see one of the psychiatrists, since he and she didn't seem to be getting anywhere. He was hesitant and noncommittal, but she insisted that he come back. The interview was over.

She related to me that she had become increasingly concerned about him after he left and wondered if he were grossly psychotic or perhaps contemplating something drastic.

My curiosity aroused by both the patient and the effect that he and the social worker had had on each other, I was able to rearrange my appointments so that I could see him later that same day. The moment he entered the office, the situation was considerably clarified for me. He was a handsome young man, clad in tight Levis and an even tighter T-shirt. Bulging beneath this attire were enormously developed muscles which strained at the thin clothing, giving the impression of nakedness. He probably had the most striking physique I had ever seen, but it was almost grotesque. It was no wonder that his demure young interviewer had been unnerved.

On meeting me he was rather tense and stiff, but much less so than I had been led to expect by my informant. In contrast to his interview with the social worker, he did not stammer at all, but spoke rather in a low-pitched, measured voice that revealed a midwestern twang. He made no mention of his unsuccessful interview of the day before and began talking about himself. Evidently the difference in sex of his two interviewers explained the disparity in his behavior.

In his conversation with me, he said that he had wanted to see a psychiatrist for some time but really didn't believe he could be helped. He had always been nervous and had an "inferiority complex." He talked of his discomfort in crowds, in school, and at work, and described symptoms of sweaty palms, headaches, a "queasy stomach," and tension. After a while I asked him why he had first gone to the urology clinic. He glanced quickly at me like a child caught with jam on his face, paused a moment, and then said quickly, "I can't get a hard-on."

The most potent-appearing specimen I had ever seen was actually impotent. As if on cue he began describing his body-building and weight-lifting activities. Since his middle teens he had been a weight lifter, spending many hours each day working out, gradually becoming very strong and proficient. When he was about nineteen he placed second in his regional weight-lifting championships. Body building soon became an obsession. He felt he could really make something of himself and set goals for himself which he reached on schedule or even ahead of time. However, this program did not do for him what he had expected, and he changed emphasis somewhat. He began to believe that weight-lifting competition was insincere, impractical, and maybe even harmful, and so he changed his goals from the amount of weight that he could lift to the development, appearance, and health of the whole body.

In this program, as before, he regulated himself rigidly. He worked out a meticulous development program with weights and exercises for each group of muscles, and he ate only organically grown raw vegetables and wheat germ. He slept ten hours a night and carefully watched and regulated his bowel movements.

This way of life gave him a feeling of control and strength, since he knew "just what was coming in and what was going out." He felt that if his body were sound, his mind, too, would be sound and he would be able to handle any situation at work, at school, or on dates—all places where he often felt awkward and out of place. He obtained considerable reassurance by playing what he called his "comparing game": "Steve may have more money, girls, education, and friends than I have, but I have a better build." One of the most reassuring things was to see others look at him in admiration and surprise. He always wore thin, tight-fitting clothing because of the startling appearance that it created. It felt good to be noticed.

He had considered entering the Mr. America contest, which he believed he had a good chance of winning, but he regarded such official accolades cynically, insisting that the real importance and meaning of his activity lay in what it did for him personally and how it affected his "human relations."

Despite his readiness to tell me about himself, he kept saying he didn't know whether he wanted to talk to a psychiatrist. I explained to him that he did not have to commit himself and that since I could see him only a few times anyway, he would be assigned to someone else if he decided to go farther. This appeared to relieve him somewhat, and he was willing to return for the limited number of times I was able to see him. Evidently he feared relinquishing his control to the clinic or to me.

Mike was born in Assembly, Kansas, a small rural town with just under a thousand people. He pictured it as a very proper, orderly place with pious and righteous inhabitants who made him feel like an outsider. His mother was the "only divorced woman in town," and as he saw it, her status was viewed as scandalous. He was subject to the unique cruelty of which children are capable as spokesmen for their parents. He was teased with innuendos about himself and his parents, and taunted, chased, and threatened during recess and on his trips to and from school. He was the smallest boy, not only in his grade, but in the entire rural school he attended, and he was acutely conscious of his size and weakness. In order to compensate for feelings of complete inadequacy in the community, he entertained a special fantasy whenever he suffered insult and abuse from his peers. One day he would return to his hometown, burst in on his tormentors who would be planning to "get him," and stand like a colossus in front of them, confidently, disdainfully. They would stare at him in amazement and awe, see his tremendous build, and realize his extraordinary strength. In the fantasy one of them would start to smile, but with a ripple of his muscles that smile would quickly disappear. His peers would cower at his motionless stare. In reality Mike feared violence and always fled from a fight. But in this fantasy there was never a fight nor any need to overpower his opponents; his presence alone overwhelmed them.

In my office I saw a muscular, powerful-looking young man who was, in physique, the man of these fantasies. In his thoughts about himself, however, he was still the small weakling. He related a recent situation in which he and his college roommate had entered into a heated discussion about the equitable distribution of cleaning activities in their quarters. The argument reached a pitch at which it seemed that a physical fight would ensue. Despite his much greater size and strength, Mike fled from the room, with the same feelings he had had in childhood. Telling me the story, he said that as the pitch of the argument rose, he felt as though he were shrinking in size, and at the moment he fled it was as though he were still the scrawny little boy in Kansas. Despite the physical change that had taken place in the intervening years and the fact that his formidable appearance made it unlikely that anyone would ever attack him, he saw himself as the weak, frightened child of the past. His own words were, "It's a crazy thing. I look at myself in the mirror and I can see that I am really tremendous, but I turn away and all of a sudden I'm nothing again—I'm just a scared little kid." As long as his size and strength were reflected in a mirror or in the looks of admiration and wonder in people's faces, he felt strong and confident. But without these signs of reassurance he was left with the uncorrected image of himself as a helpless and vulnerable child.

He not only avoided any possible physical contact with men and fled from fights, but also was frightened of physical contact or friendly relations with women. As he put it, "I built myself up into something now, and I just can't afford to lose anything. If I get in a fight I might get hurt and lose a lot of ground. Girls can ruin a guy. I've seen it happen; they'll suck you dry, they'll sap your strength until you are just nothing."

At the initial interview we had agreed we would meet only five times. Although this was because it was all the time I had available, he was eager to accept it as a way of limiting his involvement to a manageable level. Knowing that he would shortly be finished with me, he felt a greater sense of freedom. He had expressed doubt about whether or not he wanted to continue at all, but when it became clear that I would accept his decision, whatever it was, he felt greatly relieved, for he was clearly in control.

After that first session he came eagerly to each of the remaining sessions with a clear, planned purpose. He decided between sessions what he would talk about and even what he would accomplish. He left no doubt about being in charge, and I supported his need without challenge. It was a great relief for him, and he said more than once that never before had he been so free to do what he wished in the presence of another person.

In one session he came prepared to work on his feelings about his mother, in another about his father, then about women, and finally about his future. He thought each session out in detail before our meeting and accomplished much during this preparation. As a result, at the end of each session he had a sense of closure about each carefully prepared subject that he brought up.

He began each session by outlining what he would do during it, and then he would proceed without pause. At first when I would interject an observation about what he was saying or doing he would listen obediently, but I could detect a certain impatience with me. When I asked him about this, he reluctantly acknowledged that it was true. With some encouragement he declared that he didn't have much time, had a lot to talk about, and I was interrupting him. As we talked further about the matter he became more certain and clearer about his desire to control the sessions. He was relieved that I did not oppose him.

It was not that he ignored me; quite the contrary. He watched me as he talked, scrutinizing my every move. When I asked him about this he said that he wanted to be sure I was listening and also if I were being critical. Sometimes he would even ask me if I were critical. His growing openness allowed him to proceed with greater and greater confidence.

Frequently, after a lengthy monologue, he would abruptly ask me a question. Whatever my response, he seemed to be able to turn it to his own needs and purposes, usually with comments such as: "That's just what I thought," or "That's really important." I was often surprised by how meaningful a simple comment might be to him. The important thing was that he was making personal use of everything that was happening between us.

When we had talked initially, we had agreed upon the brief number of meetings with the understanding that he would be able to continue with another psychotherapist afterward if he wished. By the end of the five sessions, however, he insisted that he was getting along much better and felt no need to continue. He said that he felt better than he had ever felt in his life.

At that particular time in my own career, I was skeptical of such rapid improvement; in fact, I viewed it within the framework of the "flight into health" in which someone behaves as though he is feeling better in order to avoid facing more deeply rooted problems. Today, however, I feel much more accepting of the unique ways in which people can make use of experiences with others. Today, as I review this case, I think of it more in terms of what Mike did for himself, rather than what he should have gotten. He had learned several very important things. One was that he could be freer with another person, and that if he expressed what he wanted from a relationship, he was more apt to be able to get it. As he told me in the last session, he had confirmed this with several people. He felt very appreciative of the brief time we had met.

I have already mentioned that his parents divorced when he was three years old. He described his mother as very good looking and having many dates when he was young. During his mother's excursions, his care was generally entrusted to friends, relatives, or even sometimes to his sister, who was five years older than he. He recalled one occasion when his mother was going out on a date and had no place to leave him; she was forced to take him along. He was instructed not to call her "Mother," and she told her escort that he was the youngster of a friend. He was told to lie down in the back of the car and not to bother them any further.

Despite this rather strange relationship between mother and son, she was all he had and the only one who stood by him, and so, in addition to feeling hurt, he steadfastly defended her during the interviews. His sister shared his misfortune but not his sorrow. They bickered and fought constantly; she, being the elder, was usually triumphant.

All of his subsequent relationships with women were tinged with an overwhelming sense of embarrassment so that his experience with the social worker at the clinic was not a unique one. He blushed and stammered almost any time he was with a woman of his own age, and even found it difficult to order in a restaurant if the waitress was attractive. He was handsome and usually appealed to women; but he considered them untrustworthy, and so he behaved passively in his relationships.

He had a rather pious attitude toward the women he went out with. He would not kiss a woman who had been smoking and he crusaded against drinking, two activities that had been of great importance to his mother. Women who smoked disgusted him and made him fell contaminated.

Mike barely knew his father and spoke of him as irresponsible. His father's main asset, according to Mike, was his appearance. Mike described him as a "lady killer," a term that he also applied to himself and to which he gave a literal connotation. He believed, and perhaps correctly, that he had a kind of lethal charm for the women which made him sought after. He saw his path through life as strewn with the broken hearts of disappointed women. "I can't help myself," he said. "Girls go for me, but I have a way of hurting them in spite of myself. Even if I don't want to, I seem to say things or do things that tear them up. I'm a heel with girls."

There was one group of people with whom he felt comfortable: the weak. He felt warmly toward old people and the handicapped. He often volunteered to help the physically frail and weak, and from this activity he gained considerable satisfaction. Meeting a psychiatrist who was confined to a wheelchair had been a lucky accident for Mike.

He was uncertain as to whether he was omnipotent or impotent, and his preoccupation with these fancied images interfered with more realistic attitudes about himself and others. He saw in me a similar duality. Although I was physically disabled, he attributed magical healing powers to me, bestowing upon our relationship all possible variations on the omnipotent/ impotent theme. He was able to revise his images and their relationship to one another into a more functionally realistic perspective through our experience together.

To me, this new perspective seemed as delicately balanced as its predecessor, and I was concerned that it might not last. During our last session, his only response to my inquiry about his sexual impotence had been a smile— more accurately, a knowing smirk. I asked him about the meaning of this nonverbal expression, but he would not say. Then he said he had some other things to talk about. I assumed from this reaction that there had been an improvement, but that he feared to say it aloud lest his new potency might, in some mysterious way, be endangered.

About two years later, as I was coming out of a restaurant, a Mercedes-Benz sports car made a U-turn on the highway and pulled up in front of me. Out jumped Mike. He rushed over to me and began to speak rapidly. He said that he had seen me while driving with his friend, and wanted to say hello. He had thought about calling me, but hadn't really needed to; if he should, when was the best time to call? He said he was glad to see me. I could hardly get a word in, but managed to mutter that I was glad to see him, as well. My eyes drifted past him to the waiting car and to the stunning girl sitting beside the driver's seat. He saw my gaze and gave his familiar smirk. "Things are okay, Doc. See you later." And he was off and gone. I never heard from him again.

DISCUSSION

Body building is rather different from most of the other sports we have considered. While there is competition, it is more like that of a beauty contest, for appearance is everything. The competition is intense, and preparation for one of the many contests is all-absorbing. The body builder may spend the equivalent of an entire workday, five to six days a week, for extended periods in cultivating his appearance.

Although many body builders possess great strength, body building is not designed for lifting weights. The athlete who competes in weight lifting has a very different physique, one designed for lifting, not for appearance. To the body builder, the mirror is a more important piece of equipment than the weights he lifts. In this sense it is perhaps the most individual of all sports.

A number of outstanding body builders have been my patients in psychotherapy, some of whom have attained wide recognition and won important contests. Just as superiority in any sport inevitably sets an athlete apart from those who participate on a casual basis, so does the competitive body builder become set apart from the more casually involved physical fitness enthusiast. His appearance is striking, exciting a kind of disbelief and awe in those who see him for the first time. Their startled expressions are not lost on him; in fact, he carefully watches the faces of those he meets to see the effect his appearance has.

My psychotherapeutic experiences with all of these young men have had certain common characteristics. For one thing, each of them has tended to be self-conscious and to remain somewhat distant, fearful that he might give up some measure of control over his life. As a result, the psychotherapy has been brief in each case. Yet I have always felt that we have had remarkably close relationships, even though some had previously unsuccessful experiences with psychiatrists. Some of them have maintained occasional contact with me for many years, although for only a few sessions at a time. Strangely, my physical disability enabled me to establish a special rapport with them, as though my limitations in strength—the antithesis of their over-development—reduced the threat against which they struggled.

One of these men, in addition to his intimidating appearance, often engaged in fights to prove his strength and prowess. He would deliberately provoke others so that he could administer a physical beating. Yet, as I came to know him better, he revealed how powerless and vulnerable he felt. His overpowering appearance and belligerent attitude were ways of compensating for this feeling of vulnerability. Perhaps vulnerability—his concealed, mine openly displayed—was the common denominator that linked us. Opposites attract and are related.

Mike's goal was to appear strong. His was an effort to compensate—or, more accurately, to overcompensate—for his deeply hidden sense of being small, weak, and vulnerable to attack. The discrepancy between his Herculean appearance and his actual physical power, on the one hand, and his helpless image of himself, on the other, was striking. The fact that he was sexually impotent while appearing the very epitomy of strength was further indication of his conflict.

The psychological concept of a defense mechanism is one of the cornerstones of dynamic psychology and psychiatry. These are psychological tricks one plays upon oneself and others, and they exist outside of one's own awareness. Through them a person is able to defend himself, to avoid unwanted and unacceptable wishes, impulses or self-images. Defenses hide weaknesses, deny anger, displace sexual feelings, and permit one to attribute one's own evil motives to others; they perform many functions that allow a person to maintain a treasured concept of himself. Mike wanted to conceal his feelings of weakness. He felt secure as long as he could see the enormous physical development of his body, either in the mirror or in the eye of another person. Once he looked away from the mirror or failed to see the admiration he sought in the eye of the observer, he was deflated and left with his own internal sense of himself as a frightened child. Lacking an inner feeling of strength, he compensated by showing to the world an appearance of power.

Many men and women are able to effectively compensate for inherent physical weakness or disability. For example, Tom Dempsey, who set the record for the longest field goal in professional football history while playing with the New Orleans Saints, was born without toes on his right foot. He kicked with the aid of a special reinforced boot. When Frank Budd earned the title of World's Fastest Human, he carried the residual leg muscle atrophy of childhood poliomyelitis. As a boy he could not walk, but through practice and courage he developed into the world's fastest runner. Wilma Rudolph, his counterpart among women athletes, fought a similar battle with a childhood illness which retarded her walking for many years. Harold Connolly, the great Olympic hammer-throw champion, is another dramatic example of how a person can compensate for disability. With only one normal arm, he became the best in the field in a sport that ordinarily requires great strength in both arms.

One may also engage in the same kind of attempt to compensate for a weakness even though the weakness disappeared long ago. Mike no longer had reason to feel underdeveloped and insecure, yet he did. Usually one updates his sense of himself consistent with growing strength and competence; Mike, however, required constant input in order to balance the inner messages from his past.

Even when a weakness has been overcome, there is a certain lag in keeping the self-concept up to date. Most of us do not see ourselves as we are at the moment, but rather as we were some time before. The turmoil of adolescence and the fragmentation of psychosis both expose this lag between physical reality and inner experience. In the aging process, some people try to cling to the memory of themselves as they were when they were much younger, and are unable to accept the changes that have taken place. Similarly, a child, upon reaching adulthood, may be stronger and smarter than his parents, yet when they are together he may continue to behave like a child.

Mike was frightened of most women. They stimulated a vague sense of threat, whoever they were—waitresses, a social worker, or women whom he dated. He was convinced that "a woman can ruin your life." He was like Samson, strong and muscular, but his strength was tenuous and could be lost. To him each woman was a possible Delilah, scheming to rob him of his power.

He also compensated for his dread of weakness by carefully maintaining all of his activities within narrow, manageable limits. He carefully measured all intake and outflow of his body: only minutely examined foods were allowed to enter, and the accounts were balanced daily against the amounts he expelled. Close physical contact with anyone or anything stimulated his fear of the potential danger of surrendering some of his control. He feared that if he left himself open, the delicate balance between what he received and what he put out might be disturbed.

His tenuous relationship with his mother had made him skeptical of anyone else's ability to give to him. Although she seemed tantalizingly attractive and a potential source of satisfaction, he usually felt unsatisfied, never having received quite enough from her. Despite his frustration, he had a realistic appreciation for her as the only one who had stuck by him; thus, he had difficulty integrating the intensity of his disappointment and hurt with his affection and appreciation. He saw himself as more like his father, a poisonous "lady killer" who brought only unhappiness to those he touched. He could neither give nor receive in close relationships with women. Under these circumstances, his impotence was more than understandable.

His father had actually been little more than a fantasy to him. What he knew of the man was through the biased eyes of his mother, who had been disappointed. When Mike was young, he had little in the way of solid male experiences with which to identify as he grew older. In place, he selected a comic strip character, Superman, as a figure for identification. He selected the most omnipotent, omniscient figure possible, one who was invulnerable to life's insults. He had fantasies of himself as a Supermanlike figure, the very sight of which terrified his potential tormentors.

Whenever physical threat was reduced, Mike felt relatively safe and comfortable. He had a special affinity with the old and the infirm; he could make contact and offer help without fear of being drained of his strength. He found a certain safety with me which allowed him greater openness than with most others. My physical disability reduced that amorphous threat he found in the presence of others. Perhaps just as important was the fact that he came to regard me as someone who was also strong in other ways, thereby enhancing his own potential sense of strength.

It is easy to see why Mike chose an activity such as weight lifting—one in which there was less peer-group competition, cooperation, and closeness than in team sports. Weight-lifting competition, the comparison of strength between himself and others, had some initial appeal but soon became hollow and unsatisfying. The real issue for him was not to prove through action that he was stronger, but rather to present the appearance of strength, to appear so imposing that he could overwhelm and awe those about him.

Superman is only a comic strip character, yet he touches each of us. He has a two-sided personality, one omnipotent and one impotent in the form of "mild-mannered Clark Kent," the bumbling reporter. In our competitive society, these two sides of personality are everywhere. As we Americans view the world, there must be winners and losers, successes and failures, the strong and the weak. Yet the dividing line is not so much between one person and another as it is within each of us individually. The accident of birth and what follows is a victory, but we all must ultimately lose our competition with death.

9.

A Case of Strength Through Sports

Jerry was a golfer, and in fact a very good one. A young married man, thirty-three years old, he found himself in our clinic under the coercion of the probation department. His feelings about coming to the clinic were mixed; he was angry with the police for forcing him to come, and yet he had the desperate feeling that something had to be done. The relationship between his sport and his coming to a clinic for psychiatric aid was not obvious at first, but the important function that golf served in his life was to become apparent during psychotherapy. This man was the patient of one of my psychiatric residents-in-training, and although I never saw him personally, I heard about the case regularly in my weekly supervisory sessions. The clarity and perceptiveness in the analysis of this case are therefore tributes to my colleague's astuteness.

Jerry's present predicament had a long background, starting on a rain-slicked, crowded freeway, driving home from work. He was in a hurry to get home and was driving fast even though he had a premonition that an accident might occur. And just that did happen. He saw a gasoline tanker swerve and overturn, and so he moved skillfully into another lane to pass the truck safely. Just as he came abreast, however, it burst into flame, showering its fire across several lanes of traffic, including his lane and his car. His arms, face, and a good part of the rest of his body were severely burned before his clothing could be extinguished.

Hospitalization, which lasted almost three months, was a horrible experience for him. Movement was almost totally restricted, and he was faced with the terrible threat of permanent scarring and disability. In this condition his tension rose to terrible proportions. Yet in this situation, as in all uncomfortable periods of his life, from marital discord to losing a sale in his work, he found comfort and consolation in thinking about golf. He engaged in meticulous fantasies of playing the various courses he knew, hole by hole. He would visualize himself standing on the tee, surveying the terrain, considering the distances and traps, weighing the advantages of various clubs, finally making the selection, and then swinging. He felt the whole process and showed remarkable facility for visual recall of the courses he played. These were not idle fantasies, for at each hole he challenged himself to make the ideal play. Practicing and reviewing his plays served the same purpose as actually playing the course. This was how he dealt with unpleasantness.

When at last he was released from the hospital, he was near total recuperation from his burns, but despite the reassurance by his doctors that he would completely recover without incapacity, he had doubts. He was certain that his wrists would be too weak to play and that he would be too frail to compete. Now that golf was actually available to him again, he was afraid to play. He could not turn into actuality the fantasies of practice which had sustained him through his difficult period of hospitalization. Eventually, the prospects of failure and of possible unpleasant consequences of playing were so frightening that his fantasies became blocked as well.

In the meantime, the family income had ceased owing to his illness, and his wife was forced to work for the first time in their married life. She worked as a cocktail waitress in a local bar and restaurant and made good money. Now that thoughts of golf were no longer satisfying and he strongly doubted his ability in anything, his disturbed thoughts became focused on his wife. He began to believe she was going out with the male employees at the bar and providing sexual favors for them and/or for the customers.

In attempting to deal with these thoughts he made renewed, conscious efforts to play his golf courses in fantasy and to achieve some mastery over them. But he could never proceed very far, because now there was the imminent reality that he would be put to the test. If he actually played again he might find out what he feared—that he had lost his ability. Fantasies of golf became replaced by fantasies of his wife's sexual promiscuity. He was consumed by these feelings and began following her to work to spy upon her. Doubts about his own sexual adequacy were now projected on her. He was sure she considered him weak, scarred, and damaged and so preferred other, stronger men. He began to accuse her openly, and they argued and bickered constantly. She reciprocated with retorts that hit his vulnerable spot, making implications about his worth. Eventually she could stand it no longer and suggested separation. This was only further evidence to Jerry that she did prefer other men. He was damaged. He was worthless. Again they quarreled, and this time, in more positive tones, she spoke of divorce.

In his desperation he decided to commit suicide. Searching for a way, he found a bottle of sleeping pills and took all of them. His wife had been increasingly concerned about his behavior and unexpectedly returned home to discover him semiconscious. An ambulance was immediately called and he was taken to a hospital, where emergency measures saved his life. But now his weakened ego was further disturbed by the toxic drug effects, and he became overtly psychotic, shouting, raving, alternately angry and fearful, and panic-stricken. "They" were trying to get him, to immobilize him and put him at their mercy. "They" were his enemies; "they" were the Jews, the doctors, the police. He was so wild and disturbed that physical restraints were used to try to quiet him. This did not work. He leaped from his bed, forcing aside the attendants, and, clad only in his hospital nightshirt, ran out of the hospital into the street. Frantically he began looking for his own car which, of course, was nowhere near. A crowd began to collect, adding to his panic. To him the people seemed like a lynch mob. As he passed a car he saw a gun lying on the back seat. He seized it and brandished it at the growing crowd; their laughter only served to infuriate him. It was many minutes before he realized that it was only a toy gun, and he threw it aside in disgust. The police had been called and now arrived on motorcycles. In his psychotic state he did not feel worthless, as before, but grandiose. He was certain he could outrun the motorcycles, but in case he could not, he formulated a weird plan: he would let a policeman grab him, and then he would seize the man's gun and shoot him. A policeman soon caught up with him and started to grab him. He reached for the officer's gun but was quickly subdued. Wild with fury that he could not carry out his plan, he was taken to the psychiatric facility to be committed to a mental hospital. The effects of the sleeping pills diminished, and he rather quickly reconstituted after about three days. Seeming well enough to be released, he was allowed to return home.

At home, relative calm prevailed for several weeks since he was still stunned by his experience. However, jealousy over his wife began to grow again, and the cycle of rage at her, her supposed lovers, and his own self-destruction resumed. He accused her of being a "whore," and they quarreled violently. His jealousy reached a climax one evening when, with a couple of drinks, the last vestiges of his self-control were released. He dramatically announced to his wife, "You like Alfred Hitchcock finishes, don't you? Well, I'll make a fascinating one for you!" He poured kerosene over himself, dousing his clothing, and then threatened to set fire to himself. His wife was able to get away to call the police, who soon arrived. Jerry's first sight of them filled him with uncontrollable rage. As he said later, "Cops always make me see red." He tried to attack them with a baseball bat but again was quickly subdued and arrested. This time he was taken to jail, where he again recovered quickly and was released on probation. A condition of his probation, wisely, was that he seek psychiatric assistance. And so he came to the clinic, and my colleague began therapy with him.

Jerry was born in the Charlestown section adjacent to Boston, far away from California and even farther from a golf course. His particular neighborhood, a slum area, was known as the roughest in the city. Each of his parents was born in Ireland and had come to the United States as a young adult, having left home because of disagreements with their parents. Immigration westward to what seemed like an adventurous frontier was merely the climax of years of opposition to and stubborn resistance against parental autocracy. When the two first met, they felt a rapport of common experiences. But as is the case with those who bring unresolved problems into a marriage, who seek a partner who can supply understanding that will undo all the past wrongs, the old problems rose anew. The geographical distance between them and their families in Ireland was no barrier to their primary conflicts. They had carried these conflicts with them like traditions, from the old world to the new. The question of who was in command became the subject of their own marital discord. In fact, Jerry's father became the very father he had tried to leave—the hard-working laborer who prided himself on his strength and honesty, whose hard labor was interrupted by church on Sunday and too much to drink several times a week. He was a shadowy figure to his children and after the day's work took little part in family activities. Similarly, his wife took on the characteristics of her mother. She was a formidable woman, a nagging shrew, and literally threw the father out of the house when he was drinking. The battle raged, with sufficient truces to conceive four sons, of whom Jerry was the youngest. By the time Jerry was eight years old, his father had been thrown out of the house for the last time. His eviction, however, did not mean any improvement in the household or any greater tranquility, for now the mother threatened the boys. Although their offenses varied, the threat was always the same: "I'll throw you out just like your father," or "I'll send you to an orphanage." To Jerry this was a fearful threat. He remembered sitting for hours at the window waiting for his mother to return from work, fearing she might not come back or might send him away.

With the father gone the oldest brother was in command in his mother's absence. He was known as the family sadist. One of his "games" was to whirl Jerry, then the most sensitive and vulnerable, around his head and then let him fly into the wall. He also insisted on Spartan behavior from his younger brothers, sometimes forcing them to sit for hours with heads bowed while the family pet, a parrot, dug its claws into their scalps. Despite this brutality, Jerry knew nothing but admiration for his brother. He talked of his great physique and strength and was impressed by the fact that he had posed for pictures as Atlas holding up the world. An exceptional athlete, the brother had specialized in baseball. At home his directions were followed instantly. It is of no casual significance that this brother became a policeman. Only while Jerry was in his psychotic state could the rage and fright associated with his brother be overcome and expressed by displacement to any policemen around him. It was no meaningless statement when he said, "Cops make me see red."

Physical competition among the brothers was encouraged. They fought constantly, and when one was reluctant to fight he was provoked. Jerry was frequently teased, abused, and "tortured" until he could stand it no longer and would break down and cry. When he cried he was further demeaned by being called girls' names and "sissy." He despised his weakness and identified himself, as best he could, with the aggressive role of his brothers, the role expected within the family.

He attended parochial school, as was expected in his family, was compliant, and caused no trouble. In fact, he was a good student. When he was about fifteen his behavior changed, and he rebelled against the nuns who were his teachers. This rebellion reached such proportions that he was finally dismissed from school. His previous good record, however, allowed reinstatement, but shortly thereafter he lied about his age and joined the Navy. One driving force behind his enlistment was the idea that he was outdoing his brothers, especially the oldest one, since none were yet in the service. After a few months, however, his age was discovered and he was discharged. In the meantime, his oldest brother had joined the paratroopers. Jerry was seized by a compelling desire to do the same, but eventually went into the Marine Corps, where he felt pride in being a member of that "tough" organization. He felt at home with the rough training, rigid standards, and firm discipline, although the Marine Corps did stir up some of his sexual anxieties. He had a distinct fear of being approached by a homosexual and carefully avoided any possibility of such contacts while in the Corps. Heterosexual activities out of wedlock were seriously frowned upon by the family, and so he restricted himself for a while to fantasies of glorious sexual victories. His many doubts about himself, however, led him into a moderately active series of unspectactular sex experiences, the principal feature of which was an intense desire to satisfy the girl.

The Marine Corps gave some direction to his life, but this disappeared after his discharge. His hatred of the authoritarianism of the Corps precluded his reenlisting. In his aimlessness he often thought of finding his father, and eventually he did set out to do this. The compelling motivation to find him was a desire to prove his mother's accusations false and his father right. A long, tortuous search ensued which ended in momentary elation for Jerry when they met in Chicago. Jerry persuaded his father to come home with him, hoping to achieve a reconciliation and have the father reinstated. None of the other family members showed any interest, however, and Jerry's hopes were shattered. The father soon left and the following year became ill and required emergency surgery. Since no other member of the family had any interest in him, Jerry willingly signed for the surgery. As a result of the operation his father died, leaving him with an enormous sense of guilt and a feeling of being responsible for the death. Giving consent for the needed surgery now seemed to him to have been a deliberately hostile act rather than an act of mercy.

Jerry had always had one very strange characteristic: he could not stand to be touched, especially if surprised. He would flail out uncontrollably at such times. He said it made him "crazy." Even the thought that someone might unexpectedly touch him kept him on edge. As a result, he preferred to keep his distance from people, avoiding crowds. He was comfortable with contact only when he was the initiator and fully in charge.

A few months after his father's death, Jerry attended a party and was immediately smitten by a girl he met there. He had never felt such passion for a girl before and was spurred to heroic efforts to win her. Engaged at the time, she was attending the party with her fiance, but Jerry talked so hard and fast and so persuasively that she allowed him to take her home. His competition for her was fanatical. His romantic fervor and his professed love and devotion apparently had great appeal for her, and so the whirlwind romance was consummated a few months later in marriage. Throughout the courtship he had proceeded with an almost religious dedication to winning her.

With victory claimed, new problems arose. He began to doubt his capacity to keep her and feared she might find someone else more satisfying. He became jealous of her past loves and interrogated her endlessly about them. He was never satisfied with her responses—if she denied something, he doubted her, but if she admitted anything, he was in a rage. When his fear of losing her and his doubts about himself increased, he tried to win her favor in a way quite different from his courting tactics. In contrast to his previous aggressive ardor, he now tried to win her by being submissive, passive, and curiously compliant. He voluntarily helped her and even took over many of the functions of a housewife, doing housecleaning, dishwashing, cooking, and laundry. In these areas he considered himself more capable than she and was quite content to demonstrate it. Surprisingly, however, throughout all of this their sexual relations remained fairly satisfactory, for he was always eager to please her. Even in their darkest periods she would say, "You may not be too much good in other ways, but you're sure good in bed."

Before his marriage Jerry had accepted, at least on the surface, his family's standards: the ideals of hard manual labor, scrupulous cleanliness and honesty, devout religious practices, and pride in being paid for hard physical work. Drunkenness was a part of virility and was proven, almost ritualistically, on weekends. His wife's family, on the other hand, tended to live by their wits and contemptuously looked down on hard manual work. They idolized cleverness, especially in making money, and their motto seemed to be, "Anything goes, as long as you don't get caught." One of the brothers had had several brushes with the law. They maintained no religious affiliation and had little interest in such activities as housekeeping.

When he married, Jerry attempted to exchange his family's standards for those of his wife's. He quit his hard furniture-moving job and looked for something easier, misrepresenting himself to get an insurance selling job and then moving into a door-to-door sales operation on the fringe of legality. Perhaps some inner turmoil was reflected in the fact that he flaunted his change in behavior in front of his brothers, trying to demonstrate his "superiority" to them. He missed no opportunity to tell them how late he slept, that he could make more money lying in bed using the telephone in one hour than they could make working hard all day. His arrogance, of course, angered his brothers, who countered with physical attack and moralistic scorn.

Although he had assumed the superficial facade of his wife's family, the change was not entirely successful. He started to feel guilty about cheating the people to whom he sold his goods. His elaborate rationalizations did not completely work. He began to worry about his two children, having thoughts that they might be injured by an irate customer. These thoughts, plus uneasy doubts about his wife's fidelity, made him feel compelled to return home frequently to check on the family. The question of birth control also became an issue. Although both he and his wife wanted no more children, the inner voice of Catholic conscience prohibited him from using contraceptives. As time passed, it became more apparent that Jerry's transformation to his wife's family's way of life was just in visible, superficial ways, and that he was in increasing conflict with the occupational, religious, and socioeconomic standards of his own family.

Jerry's new role involved another significant change. In his family, he and his brothers had been baseball players and fans. His father had been a professional player for a time and had achieved a considerable reputation as a long-ball hitter, until his drinking affected his playing. Two brothers, following in the father's footsteps, had played semiprofessional baseball. Jerry had gone through the motions of playing baseball, with a modicum of success, but the game had never meant very much to him.

When he was only thirteen, Jerry began playing golf. He caddied at municipal courses and later at a private club. He played when he could, usually a round very early or late with the other caddies. Although he played well, he was not serious. He caddied to make money and played to be sociable with the other caddies. Golf simply had not seemed an acceptable sport by his family's standards. It lacked the hard physical qualities they admired and represented the leisure classes they despised.

With his new social status he took up golf again, for it was a game that was more in keeping with his new superficial exterior. In golf he found opportunities to bet and make a fast dollar and opportunities for business contacts. But something was happening to Jerry. What was at first only a superficial attempt to find an image seemed rapidly to become a meaningful life in itself. His interest in golf was now intense, and his progress in the game was so rapid that he arranged his weekly sales schedule to include many golfing hours. The game took hold of him and proved to be an activity providing him with an outlet for aggression and opportunities for gratification hitherto unknown to him. When he was anxious or upset, a round of golf always made him feel better, and if an actual game were impossible, his fantasies of playing were almost as satisfying. As he improved, he considered becoming a professional, and his rapidly developing proficiency made this a possibility. He and his wife decided to move to California so that he could play golf the year around. He had found a personal identity in this segment of his life. Golf was not a superficial imitation or a coerced activity as most of his other undertakings had been.

The most important part of the game for Jerry seemed to be the competition and his intense desire to win. He was extraordinarily successful, although in other sports he had been a rather timorous competitor. His goal was to win the "rabbit," which was the ante each player put in for the winner's prize. The distinction between this game and the overt physical competition with which he had grown up appeared to supply him with the psychological distance necessary to allow all-out vigorous competition. This prize, the "rabbit," could be sought without fear of retaliation or abandonment.

He liked to play in foursomes and felt a special sense of satisfaction when he won in such a group. These foursomes had the same basic structure as his family competitive unit, but without the sadism and frustrations of boyhood competition with his brothers. He could now compete successfully with his chosen "brothers" and freely express rage, frustration, or contentment. He developed a good reputation at the clubs where he played and in a modest way augmented his income through his winnings. In one important way he was different from most of his companions: he had magical beliefs about his golfing abilities, feeling that he really did not need to practice outside of his fantasies. He considered himself to have an innate ability which set him apart from other players.

When playing well and when winning the "rabbit," he felt confident and worthwhile and found that his jealousy over his wife disappeared. His psychiatric disorder developed at the time of his injury, when playing golf was precluded and when golf in fantasy became blocked. This is a dramatic indication of the important role golf played in keeping him intact.

Jerry was a nice-looking, engagingly pleasant young man. He was generally cheerful and outgoing with his doctor and always eager to please. In fact, he often spent part of his treatment time attempting to entertain his therapist with the latest jokes. He perceived his doctor as being in an authoritarian position and was almost ritualistic in his compliance. His apparent gregariousness was a thinly veiled attempt to conceal the persecutory fantasies that lay just below the surface. Under stress, he had become disorganized and paranoid. His golfing, which had become a coalescing force for his personality, had now been disrupted as a result of the injury. One of the tasks of therapy was to assist him in reestablishing himself in his sport.

Before this could be accomplished, however, it was necessary for him to learn that his therapist was someone he could trust. From the first he was suspicious of his doctor's motives and continually tested the relationship to its limits. He attempted to identify his therapist with the hated police authority and kept testing to see if he would be informed upon or "turned in." When he was able to separate his therapist from the authority of his probation officer, the first stage of therapy was complete.

This accomplished, Jerry was supported and encouraged to try out his golf again. After tenuous and fearful beginnings, he discovered that he was physically able to play. In spite of the doubts, confidence gradually began to emerge again, and he was willing to risk competition. He needed considerable support during this initial period when he was shakily trying out his skills. Gradually integrity and a feeling of identity returned, and with these his jealous paranoia retreated from sight. Golf again provided him with confidence and opportunities to release the otherwise destructive aggression. As this occurred he was able to return to the approximate level of psychological adjustment he had before his accident. A relative truce prevailed at home, and he returned to work. At his insistence his wife stopped working, eliminating one source of his concern. When his doctor moved to a new facility they agreed to terminate treatment. The last information received about him was that he was getting along satisfactorily and was once again planning to take a professional job in golf. A position had been offered to him at one of the local clubs. Of course, he was in no sense cured, but he was restored to a functional level of adjustment. Beneath his adjustment there always lay a deep mistrust of himself and others, the shaky foundation on which all of his development had been based. Any slight rebuff or damage to his fragile self-esteem signaled the appearance of jealous paranoid ideas and feelings of worthlessness. They were quickly concealed, however, either through playing "his game" or through elaborate fantasies about golf. For him, golf was always there as a source of strength.

DISCUSSION

Golf has a very special public image of plush greens and tweediness. It is associated with wealth and status and the "upper crust" of society. Advertising men who wish to suggest that their products are exclusive show them with a background of a golf or country club. Golf also carries the connotation of unhurried leisure, of methodical walking in solitude over green turf, with an obedient caddy carrying clubs. Perhaps the caddy is important in the symbolism of golf: the relationship represents an island of feudalism with a master and a servant, the servant assisting his master in seeking pleasure. Although the caddy is giving way to the golf cart and the game is being played by an increasingly wide spectrum of socioeconomic groups, it has not lost its image, but remains a game of presidents and millionaires. Its greater availability, in fact, has enhanced its prestige value for the hungry status seeker.

For Jerry, golf represented an important symbol in his search for a new identity in money and leisure: a mimicry of the ideals of his wife's family and a stubborn reaction against those of his own family, who knew little of country clubs and despised elegance. It was a symbol to him of his own change in status, similar to the dream of a caddy who does not share all the same privileges as the club member but may traverse the same ground. As at the Roman feast of Saturnalia, when slave became master, on certain special occasions the caddy can assume the master's role and use the club's facilities and golf course. He may also aspire to membership if he plays well or works well. This type of status change was what appealed to our patient.

The other, more important appeal of golf was not entirely evident to Jerry. This was the driving force that made him feel, "This is my game." The sport gave him a sense of wholesomeness, confidence, and comfort he had never felt before. Golf was uniquely suited as a vehicle for the release of many of the frustrations Jerry had felt throughout his life.

In his family, fierce physical competition in fighting and baseball was fostered among the brothers. Jerry had as much aggressive competitive drive as his three older brothers, but he was bottom man in the sadistic pecking order. His aggressiveness was stimulated by provocation, but expression was blocked by the retaliative threat. In addition, he felt a primitive fear that if he were to be too aggressive and displeased his mother, she might throw him out of the house and abandom him as she had his father. He was, as a result, an erratic, fearful competitor.

In contrast to the frightening, openly physical aggressiveness with his brothers, the competition in golf was abstract. In golf there is no physical contact among players, and neither is there any opposing stance among competitors as in tennis or volleyball. The competition is parallel and is evident only by comparing the relative scores of the participants. Thus, the competition is mainly symbolic, with players close to each other only at the beginning and end of a hole. In the rest of the game on the fairway, the player can withdraw from his competitors and be aggressive and competitive through fantasy, obtaining a psychological rather than a physical release. For the individual whose aggression requires proximity to others but solitude and distance from them as well, golf has many advantages. In addition, the physical activity is not vigorous, and the club atmosphere serves to mute the possibility of violence.

These qualities of the game provided the psychological distance and safety necessary for Jerry. Distance allowed him to realize, without the fear of retaliation and abandonment, the latent aggression and competition that had been blocked. He reconstructed in his golf foursome the relationship with his three older brothers, but now the rules were different and forbade reprisals when he won.

This young man had stumbled through life in danger of falling at any moment. His identity was diffused into unintegrated fragments gathered from the attitudes of his own family and his wife's family. Was he a woman who did housework or a man who did labor? He struggled between feelings of worthlessness and delusions of power, desperately trying on the modes of life that appeared to be successful to others as if they were his own. In golf he found a personal coalition of these diffused identities; he could be genuine and totally involved. Golf became the glue that held him together and hid the underlying paranoid schizophrenia.

Because of the shaky foundation of Jerry's personality and its potential for disorganization, it is academic to discuss where things went wrong in his growth from boyhood to manhood. His development had not proceeded in an orderly manner, allowing one to distinguish the point at which it had been arrested. Perhaps one could say the flaw was at the beginning. The unstable foundation of his personality meant that subsequent development could only amount to patchwork. Golf for him was not regression into the play of childhood, retarding the assumption of adult responsibility, but rather his principal source of strength, the main unifying force of his personality.

His feminine characteristics should be seen in the same light. His fear of submission to authority was not a discrete issue as in the previous cases discussed. It was, rather, one of the many fragmented identities with which he lived. For him a unique, saving feature of golf lay in his being able to sample the pleasures of male companionship without getting too close. He could be with his competitive friends on the tees and greens, but at a safe distance most of the time while on the fairways.

As with Jolting Jack, Jerry's sports enthusiasm was related to his older brothers. Jack, however, identified solidly with the other male members of his family and had an intense desire to play football just as they did. With Jerry, the competitive struggle with his brothers, playing their game by their rules, was frustrating. Taking up golf was a spiteful reaction against them and one way of winning and breaking family ties at the same time. In contrast, Jack had always been, and wanted to remain, a member of his family. Selecting football as his sport kept him in the family group.

Jerry broke away from the family just as his parents had done when they left Ireland for America. In another era and under other social circumstances he might have become a pioneer. Breaking ties and heading for the frontier have been a time-honored way for a youth to escape family traditions. The present-day American carries many of the frontier attitudes into sports: the physical competition, the hard life, and, in some sports, the danger that characterized the westward movement. Winning or losing simulates the survival or death of the pioneers. It was fortunate for our golfer that he was able to find a sport that met his needs. Only on one other occasion, in the zealous competition for his wife, had his competitive aggression been fulfilled.

Jerry might never have become a patient had it not been for an accidental series of events. Golf had provided substance to an otherwise aimless existence. With the accident, burns, and prolonged hospitalization, his dread of being damaged and abandoned was reactivated. Further regression occurred in his delusion that his wife saw him inadequate and preferred other men. His paranoid jealousy was punctuated by two overt episodes of psychotic behavior. Had they not been blocked, the fantasies of playing golf that had carried him through other difficult situations might have sustained him during this time as well. He realized that they were only fantasies and that it was up to him to try out his golf again to determine whether he was capable of playing. Unwilling to take the risk, however, he had tried to forget the whole thing. One of the principal functions of therapy was to help him reestablish his much-needed sublimation in golf. Eventually his previous level of adjustment was regained.

10.

Membership in the Tribe: The Spectator and His City

There are men to whom it is a delight to collect the Olympic dust of the course.

—HORACE

Fan, as in *sports fan*, has a common derivation with *fanatic*: "inordinately and unreasonably enthusiastic." In a society like ours, with pluralistic institutions and values, wholehearted commitment to anything is difficult, and totally lacking in the lives of many. Thus, we can all understand when Charlie Brown, of the Peanuts comic strip, proclaims that what he wants to be when he grows up is a fanatic. As an inept athlete bewildered by a complicated world, he will likely be a sports fan when he grows up. Following is a story of a young man who, like Charlie Brown, was perplexed by his community but became a part of it through becoming a sports fan.

In a special sense, the emphasis of this chapter is a psychosocial one, drawing on both psychology and sociology. The spectator—the wild-eyed, cheering sports fan who fills the stadiums and field houses—is as significant to the psychology of sports as is the athlete on the field, but he exists in relation to a particular community. Since the community in this case, Los Angeles, is a modern American city with its own special characteristics, at once a sociologist's laboratory and nightmare, it deserves a close look before we examine its effects on one small, displaced baseball fan among its inhabitants.

Every city in the world has its own personality, and the image that Los Angeles presents to the world is especially multifaceted. To a San Franciscan, it is the hated rival, the place where the barbarians live. To the movie fan, it is the metropolis surrounding the mecca, Hollywood. To the ecologist, it is a nightmare of overpopulation and the nation's smog capital. To a majority of residents, it has simply meant sunshine, jobs, and a good place to live; and as a result, Los Angeles has been one of the fastest growing major cities in the United States, a city in which it is extremely difficult to find a native or even a long-time resident.

Los Angeles is a melting pot of Philadelphians, New Yorkers, and Chicagoans, of "Okies" and "Arkies," of Rebels and Yankees. These transplanted residents usually continue to consider themselves a part of the places from which they came, as though they were just visiting. They resemble the Greek and Italian immigrants of an earlier day who came to this country in the hope of making their fortunes and then going home, who, as exploiters rather than homeseekers, resisted assimilation and cultivated old ties and native customs. Even some who have lived in Los Angeles for a decade or more never feel at home in southern California. Thousands who neither knew nor cared about each other while they were living in their native states now anxiously await Iowa picnics or Nebraska parties, where they can feel at home. They do so, perhaps, because in Los Angeles it is not easy to feel that you belong. It is the only city in the world in which a small district, Hollywood, is better known than the city itself.

Los Angeles is like a great, sprawling amoeba which extends its pseudopodia from time to time to incorporate a new area, seemingly for no other reason than to satisfy its undisciplined appetite for growth. It has been called a group of suburbs in search of a city. A thousand people a day come to live in southern California, a majority of them in Los Angeles, and recently almost as many leave. The city is spread so widely, and in so amorphous a way, that in area it is the largest city in the world, even though it is exceeded by many others in population. Los Angeles is so diffuse that one is hard put to tell where the center of the city is or how the parts fit together. The tentacles of communication and transportation spread in every direction, but they don't seem to lead anywhere. Travel on one of the giant freeways at one edge of the city leads but to the other edge. On such a trip, one passes the endless series of look-alike houses that constitute the suburbs, clustered into a city planner's bad dream.

Cities of fifty or a hundred thousand can be distinguished from each other only by their road signs; in other respects they blend into one another without obvious differences. In these suburbs, one cannot find a center of town or a business district. Occasional shopping centers have been developed without regard to city boundaries. People do not work in relation to where they live. Many travel an hour or more on the freeway to some other part of the city to get to work, passing an equal number of others traveling in the opposite direction on the way to their jobs. Homes are no more than sleeping quarters adjacent to the freeway. Each house is designed for self-contained privacy, so the towns are analogous to bedrooms in houses that have no living rooms. City planners cry out in protest, but the city, as if with a mind of its own, relentlessly advances. It is small wonder that the citizens cling tenaciously to any identification with former cities, for those cities are at least identifiable.

It is not surprising that within this fluid, centerless mass the citizens seek, sometimes desperately, groups with which they can identify in order to bolster their feeling of belonging. Los Angeles has become the center of quackery and cultism, of evangelism and prejudice, and of political extremism, both right and left. In these spurious ways, the citizens can feel that they at least belong to something. Sports appear to have something of the same social function.

Los Angeles is described by local sportscasters and sportswriters as the sports capital of the world. Listeners to radio and television sportscasts hear this description daily. The residents of Los Angeles support their teams with a fervor probably greater than that in any other city. Los Angeles is a city of sports fans. In a single year, 1960, the city acquired a major professional football team, a major professional basketball team, professional ice hockey, and a major league baseball team. These were in addition to the already existing professional football team, major league baseball team, and a range of very popular college sports. In their first year of major league baseball in Los Angeles, the Dodgers, finishing next to last, set new attendance records. Their popularity has continued to grow, and in the 1974 season they drew over 2.7 million, the second-highest figure in Dodger history.

An explanation of this enthusiasm is that some of the citizens of Los Angeles needed the Dodgers. They needed something concrete around which to rally, something familiar yet unique, to provide identity. For many residents, the addition of a major league baseball team gave the city more substance. It helped to be able to say, "We are Dodger fans," and for those residents for whom baseball was important, the team provided a clearer picture of the place where they lived. The Angels have done the same thing for Orange County fans. Now the citizens have an opportunity to belong to a strong clan, a major league baseball team, without being branded as cultists or fanatics. As baseball fans they can, with no misgivings, be as avid as they wish, for nothing is more American and less deviant than baseball. Many who came to Los Angeles from cities that had major league teams could transfer some of those loyalties from the cities they had left to the city in which they now lived. They felt a new pride in living in Los Angeles and being Dodger fans. Separated from their families in distant cities, they found a new family. The Dodger management was quick to capitalize on this emotion. For a small price, one can buy a Dodger family portrait or a Dodger family album, or even the kind of cap worn by the members of the team.

Thus, at last, the new fans can truly belong, truly identify themselves with a family, a team, and a city. They can carry pennants which describe clearly and dramatically who they are: Los Angeles Dodgers.

In today's complex society, family ties have been attenuated and clan ties have all but disappeared. Grown children rarely continue to live in the same town as their parents; often they leave the social class in which they were born. Leaving one's roots behind makes it difficult to have a clear picture of one's place in the present and its relationship to past and future. When mobility has carried one to a city that in itself has little identity and whose citizens have all come from someplace else, the problem is even greater, for few supports remain for an already weakened identity. The greater the disruption, the greater becomes the individual's need for something with which to identify.*

The Dodgers first achieved notoriety and loyal support in Brooklyn, one of the first of the great American melting pots. Emigrants from Europe had separated themselves from their families and cultural ties by coming to America. They felt a hunger to belong to something, but it had to be something uniquely American, something rich with personal meaning. Baseball was American and easily understood; the image of the Brooklyn team—those motley, often downtrodden Bums—was ideal for the purpose. After serving Brooklyn well for many years, the Dodgers moved to Los Angeles, where they were needed even more. Although the move was made for economic reasons, the great new melting pot was hungry for them and they were embraced with loyalty and enthusiasm.

Everyone needs to feel that he has ties with others. With the dispersal of the traditional extended family, the clan, and the tribe, this need to be identified with a group of some kind has become more intense.† The sports fan has a readily available group to satisfy this need, at least in part. He has a meeting place, the stadium, where he is needed to support the team. He can gather with others, don his Dodger cap or some other identification badge, and yell at the top of his lungs for his team. He can memorize the batting averages, pitching records, life histories of the team members, and the standings of the teams, so that he gets to know the team as well as he knows his own family. By doing all this he becomes, in effect, a member of a larger, stronger family group, a collective entity comparable in some sense to the tribe or the clan.

There is a further value. Everyone needs to be able to share strong feelings

---

*After World War I, many Germans, through defeat and the Treaty of Versailles, felt a similar loss of identification. This was at least one of the forces that led to the ready acceptance of Nazism, for it did promise identity. Few will disagree that the Dodgers are a preferable identity model.

†In Japan, once a classic example of the extended family system and its attendant social stability, the mania for sports has today grown to American proportions as the traditional social forms and values have been worn away.

with others. On the other hand, the typical small American family of one or two generations promotes such intense relationships that the family members are bound in a kind of unspoken truce to restrain their feelings, and usually only impulsive moments of rage or grief break through to be expressed. In contrast, in the family with several generations under the same roof, when there were conflicts one could always find allies. Thus, if a child and a parent were locked in painful hostility, there was someone else to turn to, a grandmother or grandfather, perhaps, or an understanding uncle. In the relatively small family of today, no such neutral figure is available.

The members of the present-day family must get along with each other, or else. In a community that is new to such a family, where neighborhood ties are difficult to form, official groups—welfare agencies, churches, schools—have assumed the function of the extended family.

Official agencies often do not serve as well as those that develop spontaneously in response to a cultural need, and of the latter the athletic team, which has developed many of the characteristics of the extended family and the tribal society, is an impressive example. The fan, in relationship to his team, is like a member of a family or a tribe. He can share intense feelings in victory and defeat. He partakes of the secrets of the tribe—statistics and other team information—and he can exhibit tangible evidence of belonging. He dons his tribal headdress, his Dodger cap, and joins in the ceremonies at the stadium to support the members of the tribe as they do battle. He can complain bitterly to an understanding crowd of the fallacious decision of the chief—the manager. He can complain about the errors of some team members to other tribesmen who, like him, understand.

The fan is united with other fans in his hatred of rival teams. Where else is an American encouraged to leap to his feet, at one with a sympathetic crowd, and vehemently shout, "Kill 'em!" He knows that he does not stand alone in his intense feelings—that, in fact, such feelings are shared with a host of others. Anyone who objects must take on all of them. In victory, there is a boundless sharing of the joy which the fan experiences personally and collectively.

Keeping in mind the special function of sports in a city like Los Angeles, we turn now to a young man, twenty-five years old, whose case illustrates the psychosocial generalizations that we have been developing. We'll call him Benny.

I first met Benny when his doctor referred him to the outpatient department of a large state hospital. After four months of hospitalization, he was ready to leave, his doctor hopeful that he would make at least a marginal adjustment to life outside if he continued his treatment in the outpatient department.

That first day, although he had only two blocks to come, Benny arrived for his appointment three quarters of an hour late. He had lost his way. As he sat in his chair, almost motionless, the expression on his face was vacant and he talked in a monotone. Why had he come to the clinic? His doctor had told him to. He didn't see much point in it, himself. He didn't know just what he wanted to do. His behavior was that of automaton, but after we had talked for a time, he expressed one desire—for the only thing, apparently, that meant anything to him. Leaning forward in his chair, he said earnestly, "I want to go home. To St. Louis." He said it softly several times: "I want to go home. I want to go home."

Little by little, the story came out. I learned that Benny had been in Los Angeles for three years. He had come there with his parents from St. Louis, where he had lived all of his life. Both Benny and his father had had trouble finding jobs in the Midwest, and the promise of employment in the defense industries of southern California had drawn them there. But even though he found the work he had hoped for, things never seemed right to Benny in California. He felt alone and lost. He longed for St. Louis—for the familiar street, the familiar house, his relatives, and his friends.

It was hard for him to make friends in the suburb just off the freeway where the family now lived. He looked in vain for places where he could reestablish himself. There wasn't even a corner drugstore. To go to a movie—and in the past he had often met friends at movie houses—he had to drive for half an hour on the freeway, and even when he got there it would be a drive-in where he couldn't mix with the people.

In St. Louis, Benny had been a baseball fan who went regularly to Busch Stadium to watch the Cardinals. When he arrived in California there was only minor league baseball, and it was no fun for him to go to a small baseball park where he knew neither the teams nor the fans. It seemed to him that even the other fans weren't very interested. He tried football, the biggest spectator sport in Los Angeles at the time, but he had no interest in it. The first two times that he went to football games, he got lost trying to find the Coliseum. Somehow he never seemed to be able to get into the right lane for the parking lots. When he finally did enter the stadium, the sight, as he came out of the tunnel, of that great, gaping hole filled with 100,000 people roused him to panic, and he ran back down the tunnel and didn't even stay for the game. A thought formed in his mind: "All those people in that enormous place; I don't know any one of them and they don't know me." He was alone and lost in a sea of faceless people.

In St. Louis, when he and his father worked in the same plant, they used to ride the streetcar together back and forth to work. In Los Angeles, on the other hand, he and his father left home at about the same time, but they went in different directions and Benny never knew exactly where his father worked. At his job he tried to strike up acquaintances with the other employees, but he found that he had nothing to talk about, whereas in St. Louis there had been baseball or the movies or things that went on in the neighborhood. He was naturally shy and sensitive, and a couple of rebuffs discouraged him from further attempts at making friends.

Benny tried to explain his predicament. "I didn't know where I fit," he said. "Sometimes I felt like I must be somebody else, or maybe I wasn't anybody at all. I felt like I was beginning to come apart." He was alone in a world of strangers, his real home far away. True, he still lived with his family—mother, father, and sister—but they seemed different, too, and the house they lived in didn't seem like a house, with all that glass, that flat roof that looked like no roof at all, and every other house in the block looking just like it. Several times, coming home from work after dark, he became confused and, for a moment, didn't known which house was his.

He began writing letters to a girl he had known only slightly in St. Louis. After two or three letters, he asked her to marry him, believing that this was one way to get back to St. Louis. The girl didn't answer, but her father wrote indignantly to Benny's father, who reprimanded him for his impulsive proposal and left it at that. The next day Benny was picked up by the police, driving his car in the wrong direction on the freeway. He had been on his way to work when the feeling came over him that he was being swept along with all the other cars and had lost control over where he was going. Like a lemming, he was part of a mad, suicidal dash to the ocean. Taking the next offramp, he decided that he had to go back the way he had come. He turned back into the offramp, ignoring the Do Not Enter sign. A car that had slowed to turn off the freeway sideswiped him, forcing him into a fence, miraculously without physical injury to anyone. When the police arrived, he demanded that they let him keep driving because he had to get home. He mumbled incoherently about being controlled, and several times tried to break away to run onto the freeway in order to get home.

Just as Benny had lost his way to the hospital outpatient department, he had lost his way in life. His environment seemed unreal and unfamiliar, the people around him strangers. The others on whom he had depended for knowledge of who he was and where he was going had failed him. He had managed to survive the rigors of being in the Army where there was no dearth of people to tell him what to do, but he had lost the nameless battle in Los Angeles.

A schizophrenic reaction is an awesome thing—estrangement and loneliness, depersonalization and loss of identity; it is a profound personality disorganization with bizarre attempts to bring order from chaos. Benny's psychiatric disorder did not begin with the move from St. Louis to Los Angeles; the move, however, was the factor that precipitated it. Schizophrenia is the end product of a series of partial failures in personality development.

The failures are not easy to identify with certainty. There is evidence to indicate that schizophrenia is the final product of certain social, psychological, biological, and biochemical processes. While the proponents of each field emphasize their findings as the primary ones, the disorder is probably the result of a complex group of interrelationships among these different spheres. Benny's case history revealed the likelihood of genetic determination, psychological deprivation in his family life, and social ambiguity all of which are consistent with factors reported in the development of the schu phrenic syndrome.

There were histories of hospitalization for mental disorders in relatives on both sides of Benny's family, and, indeed, his early environment left uch to be desired. He was born to his teenage mother before marriage, and his father evidently had consented to marry under duress. To his struggling parents, their child was forever the symbol of unhappy beginnings. Although they were never overtly cruel, they tried to make believe that Benny did not exist.

The first source of identification for a growing boy is his family, but it was difficult for Benny to feel a part of a family that wished he were not there. In his earliest years, his mother performed her maternal tasks in a dutiful, if perfunctory manner, while his father, who was gregarious with others, did his best to ignore his son. When Benny's sister was born five years later, his parents had achieved a kind of equilibrium; by that time they were free to express a more normal parental affection toward their daughter. Benny no doubt suffered from this, too, but suffering that goes unrecognized eventually goes underground.

By the time Benny reached his teens, his parents had become actively concerned about the anxious, withdrawn, friendless boy in their midst, but their remedial attention was only partially effective. Moreover, there were few others with whom he could identify; his teachers were not encouraged by his withdrawal, and he failed to make friends among his peers. Identification with a religion was complicated by the mixed faiths of his parents, although periodically he became an ardent churchgoer.

The family regularly attended St. Louis Cardinal baseball games. It was here that Benny made his major social progress. In the stadium, he could join the family, especially his father, in expressions of favor and dissatisfaction. He became quite knowledgeable about the team, thereby enhancing his position in the family. Baseball thus improved Benny's tenuous relationship with the family, and he managed to find some relationships outside the home. Although still shy, withdrawn, and uncertain, he performed adequately in the Army, whose strictness was of a kind that provided direction. He had fleeting thoughts of an Army career, but he missed his home, and when his service was completed, he returned to St. Louis.

It was only a short time after Benny's return to St. Louis that his parents, lured by the warm climate and the prospect of more money, decided to move to California. Benny passively joined them.

After the first interview, Benny and I planned his return to his family and agreed to meet regularly in the outpatient department. Over the course of the next year there were a few evidences of improvement. Although at first his mother had to drive him to the hospital, he began driving himself. Occasionally now he would venture out of the house, and his medication could be cut to a lower dosage. But he was still vacant and alone. He had no interests, and the only time there appeared to be any life or enthusiasm in his sad eyes was when his psychotic thinking took over and he would say, "I want to go home to St. Louis." Even though it was also the location of his childhood deprivation, he clung to it as the best place he had known. I did not oppose his desire to return to St. Louis, but he made no effort to go, evidently realizing that there was nothing for him there. As he became more aware of his surroundings, the delusion of timeless security in St. Louis faded.

Psychotherapy was directed at supporting him and helping him to have a better picture of himself, but progress was slow. The slowness of his recovery and his inability to find meaningful relationships or activities did not make for a promising future. A year after his first acute disturbance, there seemed little hope of his being able to reach his previous level of adjustment. His parents had all but given up on him. They were willing to provide him with a home, but were unable to give him much more.

When the Dodgers moved to Los Angeles, Benny's father called me to ask if I thought it would be all right if Benny went to a game. The father was rightfully concerned about Benny's going back to the Coliseum, that gigantic football stadium which had now been transformed into a baseball park, for it was there that Benny had experienced his first panic. I suggested that he leave the matter up to Benny, who could, if he wished, talk it over with me at our next visit. Although he did not discuss it with me, Benny decided not to go.

But one day some time later, the whole family decided to go to a Dodger game. Benny, left with the unhappy choice of staying home by himself or going with his family to the game, chose to go. When he entered the stadium, he experienced none of the panic that he had felt before. The protective coat of apathy had anesthetized him. His parents noticed that he seemed to show no enthusiasm for what was going on, but they were pleased that he had come with them. Not the least of their pleasure was that no one had to stay at home with Benny and all could go to the game.

The therapeutic effect of his attending a baseball game had not impressed me except as a way of getting him out of the house to join in a family activity, and so I was not surprised by his parents' report of his apparent disinterest in the game. To me, he said not a word about the baseball game he had attended.

About a month after his first game, however, Benny arrived for his therapy hour wearing a baseball cap with "L.A." emblazoned on it. I asked him about his cap, but all he said was that he had bought it at a game. He apparently did not wish to discuss it. I viewed his wearing the cap with some concern, for such changes in dress sometimes accompany a deterioration in schizophrenic patients. In spite of this, there were no other ominous signs and, in fact, there was evidence of slow but steady progress.

It would be easy to ascribe Benny's improvement solely to the effects of psychotherapy. Indeed, a transformation had already begun with his failure to provoke in me the kind of hostility that he associated with his father. He secretly believed that I and everyone else must wish that he had never been born, and anything I could say to the contrary merely illustrated my deceit. He made every effort to prove me a liar.

Whether Benny's interest in the Dodgers started before or after he began to notice me as a person without ill will toward him, I cannot say; the two things seemed to occur at about the same time. It cannot be determined that one was cause and the other effect, for it is likely that each of us, the Dodgers and I, facilitated the other's relationship with Benny. The Dodgers symbolized a less forbidding society, while I represented the individuals in such a society who were turning out to be not so threatening after all.

Benny now wanted to tell me about his experiences. He reported that the first time he went to a game he was afraid, but he was even more afraid of staying home. He found each game he went to after that less frightening. Eventually he began to look forward to the games.

Next, he began attending games alone. He now liked being in a large crowd. He liked the idea that no one knew him, and yet that he belonged there as much as anyone else. He felt "just like everybody else."

That year Dodgers finished seventh in an eight-team league. Benny felt a kinship with the underdog team. He became interested in the players and began memorizing batting averages. One day when the crowd rose to cheer a game-winning run, Benny realized that he, too, had risen and was cheering. This was an event of great significance to him. He was at once frightened by his own public display of emotion and reassured that no one seemed surprised or concerned about it. He puzzled about this for days. At the next game he quite deliberately cheered his favorites, cursed the umpire, and shouted advice to the manager. It was his team, and he was their fan.

His next steps toward rehumanization were taken in an interesting fusion of his two new relationships, one with his team and the other with his psychiatrist. As the reader of the Introduction knows, I am confined to a wheelchair. Benny began sitting near the wheelchair section at the games. He felt more comfortable there because of his own feeling of identification with the maimed underdog—like himself, like the Dodgers, like his psychiatrist. From passively sitting near the amputees and paraplegics, he began helping them by bringing refreshments. He said that when he did, he felt that he was paying me back for helping him and that it made us "more even."

Finally, he began to talk to the other fans, hesitantly at first, but gradually with more confidence. Although he always liked to drop by the wheelchair section, he began sitting where the view was better.

Benny was beginning to find some order in Los Angeles. When he first arrived and got lost on the freeways, he could not understand their purpose. Their aimless, tortuous paths seemed to lead nowhere. When he became interested in baseball and considered the Coliseum the center of the city, he began to see a pattern and purpose in the freeways as they crisscrossed the megalopolis. He even learned alternate routes to reach the stadium. His mastery of the freeways became symbolic of the new control that he was gaining over himself.

Benny eventually was able to go back to work. At the end of the baseball season, he experienced a mild return of his symptoms—aimlessness, not knowing what to do with his time—but he managed to get through the year. The next season the Dodgers came back and won the pennant. Benny's progress, although less spectacular, paralleled the team's. His life has continued to be constricted; he does not have close friends, nor has he ever married, but he is fairly content with his life and has not had any recurrence of his illness. He works regularly, lives in his own apartment, and has many hobbies.

The Dodgers have had their ups and downs, and they have become a part of Los Angeles. So has Benny. When the Dodgers moved from the Coliseum to their own stadium in Chavez Ravine, Benny came to see me. This time he just wanted to share with me that the move had not bothered him. He even joked about it.

As Benny's need of me diminished, I saw him less frequently. He occasionally calls me, and I always receive a card from him at Christmastime. The last time I saw him, he seemed certain enough of the Dodgers (and me) that he didn't have to worry if they would be there when next season came around. He talked in an animated way about the Dodgers' pennant chances. He complained about the freeways, but it was in the same way that other Californians complain—they take too long.

The fan is an athlete once removed—an athlete in spirit, if not in fact. Through lack of capacity or desire, he is a competitor without the necessity of facing the dangers of competition. He is aggressive without threat of injury to either his body or his pride. Although his competition is vicarious, he can enjoy the pleasures of victory, the sorrow of defeat, the tension of the climactic moment. Moreover, he can, if he wishes, express his emotions verbally and even physically without fear of censure. The fan enjoys a peculiarly luxurious position between the camaraderie and the anonymity of the crowd. He can share intense feeling with strangers who understand.

There are, within the population, only a small number of persons who can become star athletes, but no matter when one ceases to participate on the field, one can continue in the stadium or by watching television. Some may never have engaged in the actual combat, while others may have been near-greats, but as fans, all may share the elemental experiences of sports.

The pleasures of the spectator are more passive than active, and they are derived mainly through the organs of sensation rather than by means of the action of the musculature. In spite of limitations in physical prowess due to age or innate lack of ability, the fan can experience the emotions of the contest. He knows what it is like on the battlefield without going into combat.

The spectator's passive sensory experiences may begin with only a single sense—auditory, for example, if he listens to the radio. Even in television viewing or listening, he is far removed from the actual scene and experiences. The newspapers or magazines provide him with only visual stimuli. Those elements of the experience that are lacking can be fabricated in the mind through fantasy, and it takes very little to set in motion a train of visual pictures or other associations that complete the experience. The spectator can be far removed from the field of action in the stadium—to the grandstand, beyond the dangers on the field, or to his own living room where even his relationship to the crowd is largely fantasy.

It is the team or the player that counts. In fantasy, the fan can take any part that suits his psychic need. He may be the haughty favorite or the downtrodden underdog, the aggressor or the defenseman. He can project onto the players the whole gamut of his emotions as they enact the competitive drama. In sports, unlike the theater, all things are possible in any role with which the spectator may identify, for there is no script. The outcome is always in doubt: as long as the game continues, it can still be won.

The team supports the player, the crowd the team. All are there for a common purpose. As in representative government, the interests of the masses are centered on the field of action, but with the distinct advantage that the crowd can see the proceedings as they occur and can make its favor or disfavor directly felt. The team influences the crowd and the crowd influences the team in symbiotic fashion. They belong to each other and rely on one another for their vitality.

The experience itself is elemental in a way that has been ascribed only to sex, crime, and sports. For modern man, social custom and the necessity of living close together preclude very much expression of primitive emotions. Regression, the return to simpler and more elemental stages of adjustment, is acceptable within the matrix of sports watching. Grown men carry banners or wear hats denoting their favorites in the same way that youngsters emulate their idols. Like alumni returning to a class reunion, they act in the stadium in ways different from the way they act in the work world, but similar to their behavior in nostalgic, bygone days. Regression, if controlled, tends to refurbish the individual for return to the monotony of his daily life.

All of these elements associated with sports watching were important in establishing and preserving the integrity of Benny's personality. They helped him to make order in himself. Baseball served as the medium of exchange in human transactions with fellow workers, spectators, and the city. Baseball had even made it possible for Benny to relate himself to the members of his own family. It is strange, indeed, that it should take a game to allow human beings to feel related to one another.

11.

The Place of Sports in Personality Development

Sports were a major force molding the personalities of each of the individuals described in the preceding chapters. Sports also played a critical part in the psychological imbalance that led each of these athletes to seek psychiatric help. The personality of any individual is the result of the cumulative interactions between that person's biological potential and the available sociocultural opportunities. The essence of a human being is the uniquely creative manner in which a personal integration is forged from these interactions. The cases described herein illustrate the important functions sports can play in these processes.

The development of a child toward the mythical goal of maturity requires the learning of certain specialized skills at the interface between the self and the sociocultural environment. Erik Erikson and others concerned with this aspect of human development have studied and described the psychosocial epigenetic tasks that must be mastered by a person as he ascends the developmental scale. The first of these is that a child, to be secure, must learn an appropriate mixture of trust and caution about self and the environment. He then faces the task of balancing his individual need for autonomy against the expectations of society and the autonomy of others. The person must also find a means for exercising initiative freely without suffering incapacitating guilt, while at the same time retaining appropriate concern for others. Then there is the matter of work and acquiring the ability to sustain industrious activities. Personal relationships require facing the complicated task of finding intimacy with another person while still leaving opportunities for individuality. Having traversed life's vicissitudes, a person must find a means of relating to succeeding generations, transmitting some of what he has learned to the young in a mutually satisfying way. Finally, near the end of life, there is the matter of acknowledging the truth of the life the person has lived and accepting death.

For centuries, those who studied children have realized that personality development is strongly influenced by the opportunities open to the individual for play. In play, an individual is able to test skills and relationships under relatively safe conditions which are less risky than those at work or in other more serious activities. The child, and later the young adult, can hone a personal integration among his physical, psychological, and social skills through trying something new and through repetition and practice. The person can also learn much about life and its depth through experiencing the varying perspectives within the game: offense, defense, winning, and losing.

Play, in America, has become increasingly institutionalized into sports with fixed rules and relatively constant roles. The result is a new, complicated amalgam of work and play. While we may mourn the loss of freedom of more elemental play, this new phenomenon offers an important functional support in a society that provides little meaningful work or responsibility to the young. As the values in our society have become more pluralistic, and as other institutions have become more open and less rigid, sports have come to play an increasingly important stabilizing role for people. They provide an orderly social framework within which an individual can grow and develop.

In our contemporary society, there are few clear social pathways for the young to follow. For many, sports have filled this void. Parents today want their children to be free, not just to follow in their own footsteps, but to be "whatever they want." The child's peer group insists upon the importance of "doing your own thing" and, reflecting the slogan of the 1960s, "Never trust anybody over thirty." Thus, the young are left without firm guidelines from adults who have traversed the same ground before them.

There is little so characteristic of our society today as the mistrust of all authority and the lack of confidence the young have in adults. Many people believe that television has played a significant role in this development. Children are very trusting of their elders initially and believe whatever they are told. The young child naively assumes that he can trust whatever he hears from adults on television, just as he believes the adults in his own environment. He literally accepts the urgings of actors in television commercials when they tell him to buy this or that candy bar or breakfast food "because it's good for you." This trust soon gives way to a crushing skepticism when he realizes that the commercial statements are really not made for his own good. This skepticism ultimately pervades all of his attitudes toward the motives of adults in general and the validity of their beliefs. The cynicism has been confirmed and increased by the revelations of the duplicities of the Viet Nam War, the criminal acts of high officials associated with the Watergate break-in, and the recent congressional investigation of unlawful acts of the CIA and FBI. Sadly for the young, they are left without authority they can trust or clear directions they can follow. They are left mainly to themselves and their peers for guidance. They have awakened from naive faith and have been left with nothing to take its place.

These developments have occurred at the very time other sources of social support have disappeared. Religious faith is declining, schools and other public services are failing, and serious doubts are being raised about the ability of our sociopolitical system to support the individual and his needs. This has placed an increasing burden on the family as the last resort to provide guidance for children. Yet, at the very moment that so much is expected of the family, it, too, is in a period of decline, with a growing frequency of one-parent families, of open marriage, and doubts about all of the traditional structures of the family.

At midcentury, Talcott Parsons identified only two functions of the family which remained out of the many functions it had served in the past. They were the *stabilization of adults* and the *socialization of children*.* Today, however, the family rarely provides either socialization or stabilization. In the face of a bewildering freedom of options, we are faced with the danger of the complete breakdown of our society. It is small wonder, then, that sports, which do provide opportunity for consistent socialization of children and stabilizing continuity for adults, have grown in importance. Sports, among the many things that can be viewed on television, remain the most credible. Perhaps it is because the actions of athletes seen on the screen are so familiar that the viewer is competent to judge the validity of what he sees. A factor unique to sportscasts on television is that the whole game is shown from start to finish, making the viewer confident that he could not have been deceived. The entire game has become so sacred to the television networks that incredible events occur, such as the delay of a telecast of a presidential address to allow completion of an NCAA basketball game. We have reached a state where a sports broadcaster such as Howard Cosell has greater credibility than major political figures. Thus, sports remain as a unique social arena in which authority is acceptable. On the playing field, the coach seems to be the last vestige of acceptable authority in our society. Athletes are much

---

*Talcott Parsons, et al. *Family, Socialization & Interaction Process* (Glencoe, Illinois: The Free Press, 1955).

more apt to follow the instructions of a coach than they are to listen to anyone else.

In a culture filled with discontinuities and change, a sports fan can return repeatedly to the relatively coherent and simple values, standards, and rules of sport. There is a place for everyone of every age, for it is an easy transition from the role of participant and player to the role of fan and team supporter. Faith in the coach becomes the belief in the wisdom of the professional supercoach. Some of the most quoted aphorisms in America today, more frequently heard than the statements of poets or philosophers, are the cryptic comments of supercoaches—as examples, the Washington Redskins' coach, George Allen's, "The future is now," or the late Vince Lombardi's "Winning isn't everything, it's the only thing."

In the case histories that have been described, we have seen how devastating it is when a person is separated from sports when he has relied so strongly on them. He is bereft without them, for they have composed the most viable support system in his life. Cal, the college basketball player, was directionless when he lost the support of the team and his fans in his senior year at college. The lives of the other athletes disintegrated when the support they received through their sports activities came to an end either through illness, graduation, coming of age, or a related developmental crisis.

As a person grows and develops, he moves through different personality stages. Each stage has a special set of opportunities, challenges, and satisfactions. To move from one stage to the next, one must be able to give up some of the old satisfactions for the promise of new ones. Difficulty arises when a stage of development has been either so frustrating that its gratifications could not be achieved and the person continues to pursue them, or so completely satisfying to the individual that he is fearful of leaving it. Thus, the child who is about to go to school for the first time must be willing to give up some of the satisfactions and securities of home and parents for the new challenges and potential satisfactions of school. Similarly, the man or woman retiring after many years of employment must be willing to give up the enjoyment and satisfactions of work for the pleasure of more leisure time. New experiences may seem empty if the person has left a part of himself behind, still holding on to past satisfactions of the earlier stage. Each stage is a little different and requires a change in the entire gestalt of the person's integration.

The growth of an individual and the changes in his capacity, skill, and social supports may proceed in orderly increments, or such changes may be more abrupt. The adolescent who grows a foot in one year experiences a precipitous change in his world; similarly, a child's life is altered greatly when he first starts to school. Sometimes accidental events may produce change without preparation, as, for example, when a loved one dies. The golfer whose burns created a personality crisis is another example of such an accidental event. It is the loss sustained, and what one is forced to relinquish, that presents problems.

Both personality transitions resulting from movement from one stage of development to another and transitions created by an accidental event may become crises. A crisis occurs when the individual becomes so disorganized or upset that he experiences temporary difficulty in functioning. He is confused and bewildered and does not know how to give up the past satisfactions for those available to him in the future. In such situations a person may need help to sort out the factors in his life, to plan for the new stage, and to be able to discharge some of his unfinished feelings.

The magnitude of a crisis is related to the magnitude of the loss sustained—that is, how important the lost experiences are to the integration of the personality. For example, the death of a distant relative usually has little impact on a person, but if an infant's mother dies, it is disastrous. Thomas Holmes, a University of Washington psychiatrist, has been able to quantify the losses people suffer. His studies have shown that when the losses are major, they are almost always followed by serious physical, psychological, or social disturbances in the individual who suffered the loss.

Sports may be an important means of support to a person as he goes through these personality transitions. They are always there to be used, and they provide special structures and special persons to guide an individual through whatever stage of development he may be in. Sports also provide an opportunity for expressing feeling, for physical activity, and for social experience. In this capacity, they often function as a consistent support. Thus, it is understandable that if something interrupts the supporting continuity of sports in the life of an individual, a major life crisis is created. In the case histories we have seen, such crises occurred in the lives of the athletes who relied on sports for much of their social support.

The case histories were of athletes or participants representing the gamut of sporting activities from the most vigorous contact sports, such as boxing and football, to the most sedentary, a spectator. The athletes described came from a range of social classes and had widely different natural athletic ability and personality makeup. The psychiatric disorders from which they suffered ranged from a mild neurotic reaction of short duration to chronic psychosis of long duration. No attempt was made to obtain a representative sample of cases, and, of necessity, those selected were chosen on the basis of their availability to me; they were persons who had come to me for treatment and whose stories I have been able to report in disguised form. The main criterion of selection was their value in illustrating the psychological aspects of sports.

Conflicts and problems as seen in the psychiatric patient are generally only exaggerations of the kinds of experiences that every person has, leading to the observation that mental disorder is a matter of magnitude and quantity rather than quality. In sports, as in any other discipline or interest, a cross section of the various degrees of mental health and disorder can be found. It might appear that athletes, actors, and showmen are more susceptible to emotional disorders than are other groups of people. It should be recognized, however, that when someone in the public eye shows signs of disturbance, his behavior receives wide publicity, thus fostering the erroneous impression that his group tends to be more disturbed than other groups. It is not my aim to uphold or dispel ideas about the amount of health or disorder among athletes or fans, but to comment on the psychosocial uses made of sports.

The cases described were athletes in basketball, football, golf, tennis, boxing, and weight lifting, and one case involved a baseball spectator. Why did each of these persons select his particular sport? In each case, the answer is not simple but probably includes a combination of factors—physical, social, and psychological.

The physical requirements of a particular sport may be highly specialized. Certainly in the case of Cal, the basketball player, his height was a determining factor. If he had been five feet seven inches instead of six feet seven inches tall, his choice of a sport would probably have been different. Similarly, one finds certain unique physical requirements in all sports. Thus, football players must be strong and rugged, with the ability to withstand hard physical contact. Linemen are generally bulky, while backfield men have to be more agile. In track, runners must be lean and shotputters strong and hefty. But within most sports, fortunately, there is a place for athletes of all sizes and nearly all physical differences. We usually take particular notice of the athlete who does not seem to fit his sport, such as a 150-pound football player, a short basketball player, or a fat tennis player. With exceptions such as these, it can be assumed that the factors which determine the selection of a particular sport are more psychosocial than physical.

Each sport also has its own special social connotation. Among the cases presented, the male tennis player and the golfer were influenced by the possibility of elevating their social positions through the sport. So, too, was the boxer, but it was the only sport available to him as a black person in the geographical area in which he lived. With the choice, he had to take on the sport's unsavory reputation. Jack, the football player, and Susan, the tennis player, also had little choice in sport selection, for this was determined by the expectations of their families. In contrast, Jerry, the golfer, did not select his sport to conform to the social standards of his family, but rather to be in opposition to them. The baseball fan was perhaps the most vulnerable of all to social influence in his selection of a sport. He was dependent upon the community in which he lived for a constant set of instructions as to how to live. His breakdown came when he became confused by the instructions. His recovery occurred when, with the aid of local baseball, he was able to find some consistency in his society. For him, baseball was the only means by which he could relate to others.

Neither social expectations nor physical characteristics alone are enough to explain all choices in sports. It was a personal decision of intrapsychic functioning that led Jack to accept the family sport and led Jerry the golfer to reject baseball and wrestling, which were associated with his family. Mike, the weight lifter and body builder, made himself look strong in order to compensate for his psychological concept of himself as small and weak. Each athlete who gains real satisfaction from his sport finds a particular constellation of maneuvers and activities that are meaningful to him. Whether the psychological meaning of the sport determines the athlete's selection of it or whether such meaning develops secondarily, after the selection, is usually not as clear as it was in the case of the weight lifter. Each sport probably provides enough latitude for an athlete to reenact his special unresolved situations.

Athletic competition often recapitulates earlier unfinished competitions. With reference to the cases discussed, it is to be noted that the first drama within the family years is often reenacted later on the athletic field. The golfer continued a psychological struggle with his brothers on the golf course; the male tennis player was, in a sense, in competition with his father and brother on the tennis court; the boxer stalked his elusive identities in the ring; Cal relived in basketball the comfort and closeness which, as a child, he had associated with his father; the weight lifter continually tried to make up for his unforgotten experiences as a weak and vulnerable child.

In the novel *Appointment in Samarra*, the principal character, on being faced with death in his own city, flees to another city which, as it turns out, is the very place toward which death is hurrying to meet him. Similarly, although one may flee from the location of an unresolved conflict, it is very likely that the same problem will arise in the new location. A familiar instance is the teenager who finds life in the family intolerable and seeks a solution in impulsive marriage, only to find similar conflicts arising there. Perhaps, in the continual testing to see if the problem still exists, it may be recreated. On the other hand, there are undoubtedly times when running away, putting potentially destructive energies into an area that is socially sanctioned, can be constructive in handling conflicts. The case of the boxer illustrates this point. His anger and frustration, which led into socially disapproved activities and might have led to much more serious ones, actually helped him become a good boxer.

Athletes have different ways of competing or inhibiting competition. There are front-runners and strong finishers, clutch players and chokers, defensive players and offensive players. Some athletes prefer team sports where their efforts are subordinate to those of the group; others enjoy the solitary competition of individual sports. All these characteristics seem to be associated with psychological events of the person's past, so much so that it would be possible to formulate the determining psychological events from how an athlete plays and what he plays. The basketball player had to subordinate his own efforts to the team, "feeding off" rather than scoring himself. Early in life he had learned that individual sports held little meaning for him. The golfer, on the other hand, needed a sport that was highly individual. His paranoid sensitivity would allow him to compete only when he was able to maintain distance from his opponents. Some athletes show reckless, aggressive abandon when they have the support of a team, while in individual sports they are self-conscious and inhibited. Others find team sports meaningless or fraught with petty intrateam competitions which preclude their effective participation.

The circumstances that led to psychiatric dysfunction in the cases discussed are worth considering. In six of the eight cases, the apparent precipitating event for the emotional breakdown was an interruption in the patient's relationship to his sport. In four, the disorder occurred almost immediately after interruption, and in the other two the effects, though delayed, were unmistakable.

It may be correctly argued that the interruption that precipitated the emotional disorders also disrupted other aspects of the athlete's life. Graduation from college, entering business, a disabling accident, moving from one city to another, marriage—all cause changes in every aspect of a person's life. In focusing attention on sports, there has been no intention of underestimating the importance of other aspects of life. It was felt, though, that in these cases sports were given overriding importance by the patient, and it appeared that the thread of continuity in the individual's life was severed when something happened to his sports participation. In every instance, maladaption replaced the previously adaptive behavior.

Through sports, the inevitable transition from boy to man or from girl to woman may be delayed or, sometimes, even reversed. The tennis player who follows the sun, playing in tournament after tournament, may achieve a temporary reprieve from entering the adult world. Old grads act like students when they return to school for the big game, while parents relive youthful experiences with their children in Little League competition. At picnics, sober adults romp in nostalgic competition with one another, only to be reminded of their age by the next day's aches and pains. The professional athlete, if he is good enough, may drink from the fountain of youth and continue to play or stay in sports almost indefinitely.

In each of the cases presented, the athlete found it more comfortable to remain a player than to turn to the seeming vicissitudes of change. Some found the transition from child to adult so fraught with unacceptable consequences that they felt anxious and empty, and they developed symptoms. Some attempted to return to earlier, happier days through their fantasies. Sports became a way of maintaining the past while living in the present, representing a place in which unfinished situations could be lived out again and again without social condemnation.

Sports provided meaning and substance to the lives of the eight athletes described. The following chapters will deal with broader observations of the millions of Americans who watch sports and participate in them, whose behavior is seen in the stadium or reported in the news.

The Psychosocial Meanings of Sports

12.

Sport as Ritual

*If Jesus were alive today, He
would be at the Super Bowl.*
—NORMAN VINCENT PEALE

In comparison with earlier times, our rituals are in a period of decline. Religious rituals especially have been affected. In this God-is-dead-or-at-least-not-very-active era there is a decreasing commitment to traditional forms of worship in America. In the past, church traditions and rites provided the principal means of celebrating and legitimizing life's transitions and developments. Various festivals and rites, such as Christmas and Easter, marked the seasons of the year; a child was baptized, confirmed, and later married and buried. Each of these events was provided with a solemn, orderly, and supportive ceremony. Today, however, some of these rituals either are not carried out at all or seem empty to many of those who still observe them.

As recently as the early part of the twentieth century, various nonreligious holidays and celebrations also offered time and provided opportunity for special expression by the people. The Fourth of July, Hallowe'en, New Year's Eve, Veterans' Day, Washington's Birthday—all were celebrated with community excitement, parades, patriotic or ritualistic plays, speeches, fireworks, and picnics. Most of these holidays seem hollow today except to the few residual romantics who try to foster the old enthusiasm. But they face impossible odds, for commercialism and cynicism have all but destroyed the last vestiges of belief in these holidays of bygone years.

Rituals are to a society as habits are to the individual life. They make life orderly and simplify routine, making it more efficient. Life would be chaotic without habit. Whether brushing one's teeth or eating dinner promptly at seven o'clock, habit affords an orderly system, freeing the person to focus his attention on other, more important matters. Similarly, society can be held together by rituals which bring the community together to reaffirm its common purposes, common origins, and common beliefs. These rituals symbolize the various historical events, religious and secular, which have sacred implications. This is true for the Christian who would celebrate Easter and the patriot who might celebrate the Fourth of July. There is a magical quality in such ritualistic worship as the gods or spirits of past glories are recalled to promote communal pride.

Yet, we live in a society that no longer believes in gods and no longer believes in religion, political leaders, or the authority of policemen, teachers, or parents. We have destroyed our heroes, and they have assisted in their own destruction, and the surviving rituals serve only to revere absent gods at deserted altars. This is a serious matter, for studies of societies that have abandoned their rituals and "left their altars untended" reveal societies in decay. They were soon gone, leaving only their artifacts by which succeeding generations might remember them. These societies abandoned their rituals for various reasons. Sometimes it was because of the migration of the people; other times the leaders were discredited or the gods failed to respond. There are important analogies to these reasons to be found in our own society, fostered by its size, complexity, level of technology, and stratification. These things have left us alienated from the sources of power, decision, and change; we feel helpless and, even worse, we seem to have no one to blame. The problem is recognized, but no one is able to do anything about it.

For a time, science seemed to promise man a way of gaining control over his environment and over life itself. It became the new and more reasonable god, replacing old, irrational ones; it offered dispassionate analysis in place of blind faith. Few old values or beliefs could hold up under its power, and few heroes or leaders could remain pure. But when science began to fail us, we were left with nothing but a powerless recognition of reality, without rituals and without goals.

In this cynical atmosphere, the rituals of sport remain among the most commonly performed and the most frequently believed in. They possess many of the characteristics of the older religious celebrations. They follow the seasons and are performed under tightly prescribed conditions with fixed roles and codified rules. Commissioners, the high priests, and coaches and officials, the lower-order priests, preside over the activities, assuring that they will be carried out in accordance with the accepted law. It has been a relatively easy transition for many Americans from the ritual of Sunday worship in church to the ritual of the Sunday game of the week on television. Sports heroes are among the most believable figures in our society and are called upon to express opinions on all manner of things: religion, politics, international affairs, and, of course, the best commercial product to buy. The credibility of sports is confirmed when the famous Protestant minister Norman Vincent Peale states dogmatically, "If Jesus were alive today, He would be at the Super Bowl." Peale's statement suggests that even the Son of God would worship in the stadium today.

Whatever the basis, the seasons today are marked as keenly by the sport that is played at a particular time of the year as by the changes in weather or foliage. The great ritual celebrations in sports serve to dignify the changing seasons—the NBA playoff games in basketball as much as the spring rites of Easter; the bowl games in football as much as Christmas.

Rites of passage marking the transitions from one stage of life to the next are also found in sport. Youngsters move from Little League to Babe Ruth baseball; the high school player graduates to college ball and, perhaps, to that ultimate Elysian field, the major leagues. Order is preserved throughout the year within the structure of sports as the weaker teams are eliminated and the stronger survive. Rankings are published daily or weekly in newspapers to clarify individual and team standings in relation to those of others. At the end of the year, the individual player can be categorized: Goof Squad, First String, Second String, Third String, All-League, All-American, etc.

This same order is also available to those who do not actually play. Americans plod dully through the week, sustained only by the anticipation of the weekend. The week begins with the "Monday blues" and ends with "Thank God, it's Friday!" But life is restored on the weekend. Each Sunday the sports fan seats himself before his electronic altar as the devout once sat in church. Like other parishioners, the sports fan sits watching while specially trained performers play out the ceremonies and the rituals. He watches with rapt appreciation, rising occasionally from his chair to cheer as churchmen once rose from their pews to recite the catechism and sing hymns. When the ritual is completed, the fan is renewed; all's right with the world, and he is ready to return once again to his mundane weekly chores.

We do not deify athletes and officials to the same extent that gods, prophets, and saints have been worshipped in the past; rather, it is that sports remain as one of the most acceptable and supportive rituals in our disenchanted society. The social value of sports and the rituals associated with them is that they hold us together. Although church pews are empty and only a quarter of the population bothers to vote, nearly our whole society eagerly follows the events of the Super Bowl and the World Series. Sports are the closest thing to traditional rituals we have to unite us.

The rituals of sport are like negative rites of worship designed to ward off evil. The evil against which we struggle is that we may fall apart collectively and our society collapse. Within the sports stadium we can see order and excitement in contrast to the often meaningless tasks of contemporary work. We sense continuity, for what we play as children, we watch as adults. There are order and cohesion, for we know the rules and what the players are to do.

We have seen in the case histories how a sport may represent a place of anachronistic refuge for an individual, a place wherein he can comfortably retain his position in the world. Sports may represent a similar anachronistic ritual for society. They maintain one of the few remaining strongholds of the archaic family structure, led by the strong, patriarchal figure of the coach. There is a community of involvement which provides a place for everyone, whatever his age or station, whether he is a fan or a player. Sport remains a locus for the expression of the competition, physical strength, and social rituals of a bygone era. This aspect of American life has remained relatively unsullied by the analysis of scientific objectivity, and we Americans continue deeply invested in our sports, whether for commercial purposes or personal satisfaction and community integrity.

If all this is true, what justification is there for examining the one remaining ritual that may hold us together? The lessons of ancient Rome should be sufficient justification for a close examination of America's athletic interest and motivation. There are many parallels between our sports and those of the declining years of the Roman Empire. A single coliseum may have served Roman spectators; today, thousands of stadiums and their satellite television sets serve almost everyone in the United States.

In the declining years of Rome, an increasing number of formerly productive rituals became focused on the sports arena. While Romans cheered their games and gladiators, their empire was crumbling. Can our national drive and our productiveness be traveling a similar path today? Perhaps if the Romans had been more willing to examine the significance of their sporting interest, they would have found viable alternatives to decadence. America's intense interest in games may signal a similar decadence, or, more hopefully, it may represent a transition from the vestiges of the constricting past to the birth of a new vitality.

13.

The Purpose of Sports

As we engage in the rituals of sport, we must wonder to what end we carry out such actions. What is it that we celebrate in the rituals of sport, and what gods do we worship by these acts? Perhaps it is inappropriate to speak of the gods we worship, for sports have much more to do with earthly concerns. More appropriately, we should consider what values we ritualize in our play of sports and in our viewing of major sporting events.

> *Winning isn't everything, it's the only thing.*
> —Vince Lombardi

The late Vince Lombardi is credited with creating the above bit of folk wisdom while he was the head football coach of the Green Bay Packers. It has since become the most frequently quoted contemporary reference to the principles embodied in American sports and has become the definitive statement of the moral and ethical values of sports. It is echoed in schools and campuses across the nation. For example, Jim Kehoe, the athletic director of the University of Maryland, recently restated the philosophy: "You do anything to win! I believe completely, totally, and absolutely in winning!" These statements leave no room for doubt about what is being taught to the young on the athletic fields throughout our nation.

To the religiously devout, God is everything; to the American athlete, it would seem, winning is everything. With no hereafter for which we must prepare by living a moral life, winning becomes a new god incarnate on earth. Since we need no longer answer to a higher power, winning is placed as an idol before us. According to this belief, each of us must get whatever we can on earth, and to the victors go the spoils. With no eternity for which we must prepare and no hell in which to suffer for evil done on earth, all rewards are here. Only those who fail to win are condemned. The strong and the ruthless shall survive—and the meek shall inherit what is left over.

Whether we view sports as a reflection of the mores of American life or as the promoter of those mores, it is a sobering analysis to consider that they may represent the end result of American pragmatism. If moral principle and high calling are embodied in winning, any manner of evil may be justified to this end. Perhaps we are, as some cynics would say, simply recognizing the essential reality of a competitive, materialistic, capitalistic society. Training the young on the athletic field to win at any cost is then ideal preparation for our world.

The implications of belief in this philosophy are profound, for it is the ultimate "ends justify the means" statement in twentieth-century America. If taken literally, it is a justification for any and all forms of action in order to reach the sacred goal of winning. (The only crime is losing; the only failure is not winning. As long as one is not caught, any form of cheating, dirty play, underhandedness or violence is acceptable.)

The belief that winning is the only thing is so pervasive that it has made a profound impact on the integrity of Americans. It would even seem to have motivated the events that surrounded the Watergate break-in, cover-up, and the ultimate resignation of President Richard Nixon, for the Committee to Re-Elect the President used as its campaign slogan the Vince Lombardi statement, "Winning isn't everything, it's the only thing." The phrase was prominently displayed at the committee's Washington headquarters for all to see. The members of this committee were all well-educated men who had at their disposal all of the great ideas from world history, politics, philosophy, and literature; yet, when it came to choosing a slogan emblematic of their beliefs, they selected one from the field of sports.

If there was ever any doubt that the leaders of the committee truly believed that winning is the only thing, that doubt was dispelled when they testified before Congress. Robert Haldeman, the President's Chief of Staff, said that he would not rule out any extreme method, including murder, to achieve his ends. John Mitchell, the Attorney General, freely declared that his justification for the illegal Watergate acts was that the other candidate might win and that such a victory by the opposing side was unthinkable. If winning is the only thing, it would then seem that the only crime these men committed was in being caught. They were losers only because they were no longer winners.

One might think that the Watergate scandals would have caused us to look more closely at the American obsession with winning. One would also think that those who insisted that we continue in Viet Nam because "America has never lost a war" would by now have seen the weaknesses in the total commitment to winning. But even Gerald Ford, whose administration followed those that were responsible for the Watergate crimes and for this country's participation in the Viet Nam War, is quoted in *Sports Illustrated* as saying: "We have been asked to swallow a lot of home-cooked psychology in recent years that winning isn't all that important any more, whether on the athletic field or in any other field. . . . I don't buy that for a minute. It is not enough to just compete. Winning is very important. Maybe more important than ever."

Bob Cousy was one of the greatest basketball players in history. In his book *Killer Instinct*, he wistfully observed that the encouragement by coaches to bend and break the rules in the pursuit of winning causes "any impressionable young person to conclude that the way to be a success is to break the rules." Reinforcement of the belief is boldly supplied to businessman in the best-selling book *Winning Through Intimidation*. Robert Ringer, author, clarifies the translation of sports to work when describing the only worthwhile goal for himself: "scoring—getting paid." He leaves no doubt about his contempt for any other values when he declares that the capacity to be a winner requires "acknowledging that honesty is a subjective, relative thing." Since we are all systematically exposed to these sports-related influences, we should not be surprised at the accelerating crime rate, whether it be violence on the street or by white-collar workers in the office.

There are good reasons to doubt that the average American fully accepts this cynical viewpoint that winning is the only thing. The indignation over the events surrounding Watergate and Viet Nam suggests that there are other values of at least equal importance to winning which remain unstated. For most people, winning is acceptable *only under certain conditions*, whether on the football field or in politics. Although Lombardi's phrase may be useful to a coach in arousing his team before a big game, to a politician seeking reelection, or to a businessman seeking sales, there are, for nearly everyone, some limits beyond which certain kinds of behavior are insufficient justification for winning. Although some values may be unarticulated, transgression of these values would be unacceptable to most people.

Lombardi's phrase about winning is interesting in itself when examined more closely. He actually adopted it from its originator, former Michigan State coach Jim Tatum. It is doubtful that either Tatum or Lombardi meant for it to be taken so literally, and they probably had clear limits in mind about what practices were acceptable toward the goal of winning. I sincerely doubt that Vince Lombardi would have condoned the murder of the opposing quarterback, even as a sure way to win a Sunday football game.

Moreover, the strength of the human relationships formed by Vince Lombardi, and the inspiration that his memory invokes in former players and fans, show that he was a man of far broader character than the simplistic statement about winning would imply. There were acts of kindness and consideration for which Lombardi is remembered which had nothing whatsoever to do with winning. A young friend of mine, when only ten years old, wrote to Coach Lombardi at a time of despair over his own athletic ineptness. The warm and supportive response expressed in a lengthy letter from the coach revealed his belief that there was much beyond simply winning football games, and that there were values beyond winning. That the busy coach, without inducement of personal reward, had taken the time to respond to the letter of a single discouraged youngster shows a man of human compassion and goodwill. *Run for Daylight*, Lombardi's personal story, reveals that there were many human qualifications which he added to the "win" philosophy and which he conveyed in many ways to his players.

A great coach insists on fighting hard, but *clean*; he promotes winning *within the rules*. He teaches that winning is not the only thing, although it is an important element. We can hardly expect a coach to provide his players with a complete statement of his beliefs each time he is encouraging them to win a game; however, we can expect that simplistic interpretations of the winning-is-everything philosophy are suspect and erroneously attributed.

The fact that the winning-is-everything philosophy is used to justify dishonesty and crime is not the only problem it creates. Perhaps even more important is its influence on the way we regard those who do not win. Bob Cousy observes that "the word 'loser' is a dirty word in our society." Just how seriously we interpret losing can be seen from what the coach of the Washington Redskins, George Allen, says about it: "Losing is a little like dying." Thus, he and others have come to regard sports, not as a game, but as a matter of life and death. A recent popular film, entitled *The Bad News Bears*, is a caricature of the way these values are taught to the young. In the film, Walter Matthau portrays a Little League manager who, in attempting to inspire his ten-year-olds prior to a championship game, says: "I'm not going to talk to you about winning, I'm going to talk to you about losing. Because if you lose, each and every one of you is going to have to live with it for the rest of your lives." We are indoctrinating the young in a philosophy wherein they are unable to distinguish between an athletic contest and the larger, more important issues in life. It is sad, indeed, for those who accept this belief that winning the game is all there is to life.

It is impossible to go through life undefeated, untied, and unscored-upon. There is only one winner in each event, and for every winner there must be many losers. If we consider only the winner to be successful, then everyone else is doomed to failure. We are all losers ultimately, for even the strongest among us eventually declines and dies. To insist that meaning in life can be found *only* through winning condemns each person to meaninglessness and emptiness. The only way to avoid being a loser is not to play or compete at all if one accepts the "winning is everything" philosophy.

Indeed, we have produced a generation in which many have elected precisely to not compete. They have dropped out, will not play the game, with a resulting loss to themselves and to the whole of our society. For others it means going through the motions of life automatically, dispirited because they are not winners. They live through days of empty work, empty marriages, and empty vacations, coming to life only when they vicariously experience a win by their favorite team. Some become like the forty-year-old who provides solace to himself with the memory of his own Little League or high school sports achievement.

The only possible reprieve from such meaningless existence is to discover that the manner in which one lives is at least as important as the outcome; that how one lives is just as important as winning.

> When the one Great Scorer comes to write
> against your name—
> He marks—not that you won or lost—
> But how you played the game.
>
> —GRANTLAND RICE
> *Alumnus Football*

This poem by Grantland Rice seems all but forgotten today, yet at midtwentieth-century, these were the words most often repeated to express the purpose of sport. The message is directly opposite that contained in the Lombardi phrase that winning is the only thing. The emphasis here is not on the final goal, winning, but on the means by which that goal is attained—how you play the game.

The generation that idealized these lofty phrases also played to win, so the words had a slightly hollow ring if taken literally. In the context of the new realism that has emerged in the last half of the twentieth century, how the game is played has been all but abandoned in favor of winning as the only thing.

Yet we have seen from the foregoing that the new realism is as hollow as the old, for the means must share importance with the ends. Both winning and how the game is played are matters of human concern shared by nearly everyone. Good sportsmanship, although somewhat neglected, is as much a purpose as is victory. In order to find greater balance between these issues, it is time to reconsider the ways in which sportsmanship is still important.

One definition of a sportsman is "a person who can take loss or defeat without complaint, or victory without boasting and gloating, and who treats his opponent with fairness, generosity, and courtesy." Embodied in this definition and in what we expect of good sportsmanship are two elements: the attitude of the player toward the game, and his attitude toward his fellow players.

To be a good sport requires strict adherence to the rules of the game and the avoidance of any unfair advantage. We see evidence of this when a tennis player turns to the umpire to report that a line call made in his favor is incorrect and that the point should go to his opponent. Such dramatic instances of sportsmanlike behavior may sometimes come at surprising times.

THE PSYCHOSOCIAL MEANINGS OF SPORTS

In the 1976 world championship tennis finals at Wimbledon, Ilie Nastase, the "bad boy" of professional tennis, made such a gesture when a linesman made an incorrect call in his favor. At his insistence, the call was reconsidered and awarded to his opponent, Bjorn Borg. This gesture of fairness had consequences which could not be anticipated and contributed to Borg's ultimate victory.

We see further evidence of sportsmanlike behavior toward one's opponent in football games, when, after a hard play, one player helps a rival to his feet. This is a show of respect and goodwill between opponents despite the desire of each to win for his side. Fairness and goodwill are shown to all people and to society in general when a player abides by the rules, for it demonstrates his respect for the rights of others even if he does not know the people personally. In treating one's opponent as oneself, as in Martin Buber's I/Thou relationship, an athlete expresses the highest ideals for relationships among people and serves equally as a model within sports and all of life.

Of course, the rules may and should be changed when they no longer serve human justice, but to disregard them solely for personal gain shows lack of regard for all those who play and live together. Respect for rules is a gesture of respect for people collectively. As religious canons have diminished in importance in our secular society, an increasing number of values have been incorporated into legal codes. Legislating the conduct of people has limitations, however, for one can conform to the letter of the law and violate its spirit at the same time. The clever competitor can always find new ways to circumvent the rules without actually breaking them, if that is his intent. Only a commitment to fair play and the attitudes of good sportsmanship will suffice.

It is remarkable that, in spite of the preoccupation of the coaches with winning and the espousal of winning as the only thing, so much good sportsmanship exists. The implication is clear that this concern for others, both individually and collectively, is an important value which is generally shared. This is true whether or not it is expressed in any particular simplistic phrase. A dramatic example occurs when two boxers battle each other mercilessly until the last round is over, and after the decision is announced, they embrace. The entire evolution of human social relationships is symbolized within this paradoxical behavior.

Primitive languages did not distinguish between the words "stranger" and "enemy"; the same word served alternately for both, since any stranger was considered to be an enemy. Perhaps the assumption that any stranger was an enemy was functional in sparsely populated forests where people lived among rival tribes, but such an assumption in contemporary urban life is fraught with serious difficulties. In large cities, people must maintain daily social relations with many different people to support them; if every stranger is an enemy, then life becomes a paranoid nightmare.

When two men met coming out of the forest in ancient times, each was concerned about the intentions of the other and a practical safeguard developed. If a man came in friendship, his open hand showed that he carried no weapon. This was confirmed when the men clasped hands so that neither could conceal a weapon from the other. The handshake thus originated both as a protective device based on suspicion and mistrust and as a gesture of friendship. The handshake represents man's hopes and fears in relation to his fellow men.

The modern handshake is a worldwide gesture of good sportsmanship used at the beginning and end of almost every sporting event, whether it be football, track, tennis, or golf. It symbolically says that even though opponents compete against each other with vigor and aggression and do anything within the rules to win, they are friends, respect each other, and feel no personal animosity.

Today, a handshake is a universal gesture of friendship. It is used when friends meet, when a business deal is completed, or when strangers meet for the first time. It is offered as symbolic of the nature of the potential relationship. Great significance is placed on the quality of the handshake: a firm handshake is believed to imply sincerity, while a limp one suggests weakness or treachery; a warm hand supposedly signifies warmth of feeling, and a cold one the opposite; a moist handshake leads to wariness.

Good sportsmanship is thus an integration of our hopes and fears in relationships. It also represents the integration of the Lombardi and Rice purposes in sport: winning as the only thing, and fairness and goodwill as an equal value. Sometimes, however, sportsmanlike behavior becomes a caricature of these hopes and fears when the sportsmanlike side is exaggerated in order to compensate for the extravagance of the victory.

Just how compelling the elements of the dilemma can be was demonstrated a number of years ago on national television. A series of weekly golf challenge matches was held in which the winner of each match would return the following week. These were important events at the time, and the prize money was great. Sam Snead, one of the senior members of the circuit, displayed his great competitive ability by winning week after week, seemingly invincible. Then, unexpectedly, he was defeated by a young, relatively unknown opponent who has since become famous.

After the match, both men appeared before the television camera to be interviewed and to receive their prize money. The defeated Snead stood with head held high, discussing the match in a matter-of-fact way. He made no excuses while congratulating his opponent, and was a classic example of a good sport.

More interesting was the behavior of the young winner. He hung his head, looked at the ground, and spoke in a low, almost inaudible voice. If there had been no sound on the television set, one would have guessed that Snead had been the winner and his opponent the loser.

The young winner was ludicrously modest. He insisted that his victory was entirely a matter of luck. When the interviewer pressed him for details on his own play, he refused responsibility for any part of it and attributed his good luck to other players, caddies, the crowd, the managers of the golf club, etc. He expressed that he was not deserving, and his demeanor seemed more one of regret than happiness, despite the large prize money he received. Most of all, he credited his opponent.

His laudatory praise of his opponent was a way of confirming that Snead had lost none of his value simply because he had lost this particular game. His modesty also displayed his regard for others as he shared credit for the victory with other tournament officials. Here was almost too much goodwill and fairness toward his opponent and toward all people.

We can interpret this good sportsmanship in relation to the dilemma between the values of winning and fairness. Having won an extravagant victory, the young golfer balanced the scales by an equally extravagant display of good sportsmanship. In his mind, the magnitude and rewards of his victory were compensated for by the great effort he took to demonstrate his goodwill, modesty, and the worthiness of his opponent. His behavior was, for him, a way of integrating a new and powerful fact into his psychological existence.

A deeper analysis of this behavior suggests a self-protective device against unconscious fears of retaliation and guilt for beating his opponent. As a young, relatively vulnerable golfer, he had beaten a powerful, almost legendary figure in the game. In a sense, he was denying the significance of his victory and thereby protecting himself against dimly felt fears that he did not deserve it and would be punished. In addition, by sharing responsibility with tournament officials, the crowd, and even the announcer, he left no base of support untended.

Whether one views sportsmanship from the standpoint of its historical significance, its social value, or its unconscious determinants, it does represent an integration of conflicting human values; it is a way of transcending the simplistic concepts of winning as the only thing, on the one hand, and fairness and goodwill, on the other. Good sportsmanship represents a level of integration beyond the slogans attributed to either Vince Lombardi or Grantland Rice.

A great coach is one who teaches sportsmanship as well as winning. John Wooden was the most successful basketball coach in college history. His seven national championship teams set him apart from his rivals and raised him to the status of supercoach. Wooden was a great competitor and a teacher of competitive skills, but he was known to be completely intolerant of any immoral or unsportsmanlike actions on the part of his players. More than once he suspended one of his stars for behavior he considered to be unsportsmanlike. In his book, *They Call Me Coach*, he enunciates his philosophy and states: "No coach should be trusted with the tremendous responsibilities of handling young men under the great mental, emotional and physical strain to which they are subjected unless he is spiritually strong."

Wooden clearly understood the limitations of the belief in winning. He put it this way: "In one way or another we are all seeking success. And success is peace of mind, a direct result of self-satisfaction in knowing that you did your best to become the best that you are capable of becoming, and not just in a physical way." He is more specific about winning: "Although I want them to work to win, I try to convince them that they have always won when they have done their best. . . . It isn't what you do, but how you do it. . . . It should be recognized that basketball is not the ultimate. It is of small importance in comparison to the total life we live." Finally, Wooden says: "We must try to prevent the pressures for winning scores from causing us to swerve from moral principles."

He explains those moral principles in which he believes in his *Pyramids of Success*. Here he makes clear the criteria that he believes show "how you play the game." In addition to such qualities as friendship and loyalty, he identifies reliability, integrity, honesty (in all ways), and sincerity. Wooden thus supports the Grantland Rice perspective that it is "not that you won or lost— but how you played the game." Coach Wooden was motivated by spiritual values, but even the most earthbound humanist may support similar values.

There is conflict between the naked desire to win and good sportsmanship. When the verbalized slogans do not include room for both, the unspoken one becomes hidden but appears in disguised form. The essential conflict in man is between selfishness and altruism, between "I" and "we." Perhaps the conflict is essentially biological, representing the conflict between the survival of the individual and the survival of the species. In our complex society, the survival of the species is contingent upon a certain degree of kindness and concern for others. Good sportsmanship is a clear expression for the altruistic side of the conflict. If we insist that winning is the only thing, this human concern for others will appear in less obvious ways; if we insist that winning doesn't matter, but only "how you play," then the "killer instinct" will emerge in some hidden form. The range of qualities that make up a human being is much greater than any simplistic slogan, and those parts of a person for which there is no meaningful social category will emerge strongly in an effort to find a place.

> The important thing is not winning, but
> taking part; the essential thing is not
> conquering, but fighting well.
> —PIERRE DE COUBERTIN

There is a historical record that the Olympic Games began in 776 B.C. and were held thereafter at four-year intervals until A.D. 394. Although winning was a great honor recorded by poets and writers of the time, participation and good sportsmanship were esteemed equally with victory. After a hiatus of over 1500 years, the Games were reconvened in 1896 through the efforts of a brilliant French educator and scholar, Baron Pierre de Coubertin. Disturbed by the horror and cruelty of the Franco-Prussian wars, he wished to establish an opportunity to bring together athletes of all countries of the world on the friendly fields of amateur sport, unmindful of national rivalries, jealousies, and differences of all kinds, and with all consideration of politics, race, religion, wealth, and social status eliminated. The Olympic definitions emphasized participation "solely for pleasure and for the physical, mental, or social benefits to be derived therefrom—without material gain, direct or indirect."

What the Baron and those who helped him found the Games wished to emphasize was "taking part" and the involvement in "friendly competition." The importance of taking part—that sense of involvement—has become an even more important issue for people in the late twentieth century. Involvement has become a *cause célèbre*, for many people today feel alienated from participation in their own lives. Our world has become so specialized that professionals are in charge of everything: politicians in charge of government, generals in charge of armies, teachers in charge of education, doctors in charge of health, lawyers in charge of justice, and even specialists in charge of our play. Seemingly everything is done for us or to us, leaving us as witnesses to the processes of our own lives without power to influence and without a sense of personal involvement in the necessities of our lives. We are left with a sense of meaninglessness.

Unfortunately, the values of participation and involvement promoted by the Baron de Coubertin in the Olympic Games have become distorted by national interests and commercialism, fostering the very things that the Games were founded to combat. Although discouraging, this makes the need to find ways of "taking part" even more relevant today. We have watched specialists take over all of the important functions of our lives, and we are relegated to watching from the sidelines. Of course, we ourselves are the specialists, each of us carrying out only a narrow segment of functions, with the remainder left to other specialists. This allows few people a sense that they are able to express their full physical, mental, and social potential during their lives.

Play and recreation are, by definition, free and without necessity or material purpose, yet that freedom has given way, in the course of specialization, to the ultimate alienation of having professional athletes who "play" for us. Experts promote and initiate that play in ever more efficient and skillful contests, relegating most people to the limited role of spectator. As spectators, we are no longer full participants even in our play.

A sense of personal participation is a vital element in life; without it, we are empty automatons carrying out programmed tasks. Indeed, many Americans complain of exactly that. There is little sense of involvement or pride in work, there is a belief that voting and political activity are purposeless, and even family life has fallen into disrepute. We are passive spectators before our television sets, watching the evening news for information about important events in our lives.

Thus, many people have given up and dropped out of conventional society. They go to the wilderness, to rural settings and communes, hoping to reestablish some sense of vitality and participation in community life. It is an unfortunate fact, however, that no matter how far one goes in an effort to escape this alienation and fragmentation, the pervasiveness of contemporary influences usually catches up.

Fortunately, an increasing number of people are choosing to stay and fight the system, to establish a revolution in which that lost sense of involvement and participation is restored. We see evidences of it everywhere in the various liberation movements: in the ethnic movements, the women's movement, the young and the old, etc. Because having others play for one strikes deeply into the heart of being human, sports, too, are experiencing their own revolution—one in which those involved demand more of a sense of participation.

One might think that the athletes themselves would be satisfied, for their rewards are enormous salaries, high status, and national adulation; yet, because of the narrowness of their participation, limited only to performance, there is growing dissension even among the players. Professional athletes have become organized into unions and present the incongruous situation of athletes paid well over $100,000 a year engaged in collective bargaining with management. One cannot comprehend what is going on solely on the basis of material benefits sought; equally important is the sense of being limited by specialization.

Curt Flood, one of the great baseball players of recent years, sacrificed his career for a principle related to this issue: he wished to be treated as a free person with full voice in all of the decisions made about him. Reggie Jackson, considered by some to be among the greatest all-around players in baseball, says of his profession that "baseball is just like any other job." This does not imply that he does not do his best; rather, that sport, as a business, has all of the arduous and even sometimes boring characteristics of work. When our play is left to a specific group of professionals, they are no longer playing; rather, they are working like the rest of us.

In high schools and colleges across the country, athletes are calling for a greater sense of participation in the decisions that are made about sports. They are attempting to recapture a sense of involvement from the officials and coaches, who, they feel, control the structure of the games.

Women, who have long been excluded from most sports activities, are now rejecting the limited roles of spectator and cheerleader which have heretofore been imposed upon them and are demanding an opportunity for full participation. Recent court decisions now require equal opportunities for women in sports at the high school and college levels. Spearheaded by the Virginia Slims Tournaments, women's tennis has become almost as popular as men's tennis, and women tennis players, once relegated to the back courts, now demand equal prize money. Participation by women in baseball, basketball, and volleyball is growing rapidly, and even that bastion of supermasculinity, professional football, has been invaded by the development of a women's league. Although with great turmoil, even Little League baseball has opened its doors to girls for the first time. The locker room is no longer the exclusive domain of males.

Some coaches, too, have revolted against the pressures and limitations of superspecialization. Ara Parseghian astonished sports followers a few years ago when he left his coaching job at Notre Dame simply because he needed time for himself, and to think. Joe Paterno, Penn State's great football coach, ignored lucrative professional offers because he preferred his involvement with his university community.

At the management level, the recent conflict between the owner of the Oakland Athletics, Charles Finley, and the commissioner of baseball, Bowie Kuhn, illustrates the new revolution. Finley sold three of his best players, Rollie Fingers, Vida Blue, and Joe Rudi, for several million dollars. His decision was overruled by the commissioner, who noted the harmful effects on players, on community relations, and on the sport in general.

Fans are perhaps the most alienated participants in sports, for they have only the role of observer and must pay even for that. Many now prefer active involvement to mere watching. In the past few years there has been a great upsurge of interest in sports that allow for individual participation. Tennis and golf have led the way. In addition, large numbers of people jog, "work out," swim, and play neighborhood games of various kinds. Today, a conversation between neighbors about sports is as likely to deal with how to improve one's backhand as it is about the number of games the Cincinnati Reds are ahead of the pack.

Television has provided sports fans with an incredible selection of events from which to choose. What one can see today in a week exceeds what was available a decade ago in an entire month. In any major city there may be as many as four or five major athletic events for the viewer to choose from in a single afternoon, each carried out by the finest athletes in that particular sport. As rich as these opportunities are, most Americans still feel deprived of something more basic—a sense of full participation. Thus, for the first time since the advent of television, there appears to be a saturation of sporting events, and the networks have noted some decline in audience interest in sports. As a result, in 1976, for the first time in many years, the National Basketball Association playoffs were not fully covered by television; only the final games were offered to the public. This decline in interest is due not only to the large numbers of events but, in addition, to the increased desire for opportunities for full participation elsewhere.

As viewers, we have come to accept the incredible excitement we can see on television almost casually. We have seen so many one-point thrillers won in the last moments of play that it is no longer novel. The players in professional sports have become truly superb, yet we have seen so much of them on television that their record-breaking performances have become routine. The only antidote to this boredom is the involvement of the individual himself in the game. We must conclude that sports are too important to be left to the professional athletes, just as we earlier realized that wars are too important to be left to the generals.

The word *amateur* is from the Latin *amator*, meaning lover, and is therefore appropriate since it is the sheer love of the game that motivates the amateur. He plays only for pleasure, without thought of material gain, and does so out of his own free choice. Many people are no longer as interested in watching the greatest athletes play as they are in having an opportunity to play themselves, no matter how clumsily. There is a limit to how much we can admire the expertise of the professional athlete and still be satisfied ourselves. The growing interest in weekend participation in sports is a move away from professionalism and toward amateurism.

"Taking part" was the value in sports that the founder of the modern Olympic Games wished to promote. It is also that same sense of participation and involvement for which Americans now cry out. To feel that one is a part of the ongoing, exciting activities in life is necessary for full satisfaction, whether as a spectator with limited participation or as an active participant. In our complicated urban environment we seize every opportunity to be involved, whether in a limited way or in a full one. One of the greatest appeals of sports is that they can provide a full sense of involvement for a person. This purpose is perhaps the most basic one for all of us, and without it all others are meaningless.

There are, of course, other purposes of sports which have become important. As a commercial venture, sports are the equal of almost any industry in America. Sports are used by some countries as an important political tool, in both national and international relations. Many other peripheral uses are made of sports as well, but they are distortions of the elemental opportunities available to people. Those elemental opportunities can be found in the slogans discussed: in Vicne Lombardi's "winning is the only thing"; in Grantland Rice's "how you play the game"; and in the Baron de Coubertin's "taking part." These, then, are the vital purposes of sport: to allow us to test our skills against others; to provide an opportunity to demonstrate our commitment to fairness and goodwill toward others; and to become involved in a full, physical, mental, and social way.

14.

The Psychology of Winning

Those who challenge the gods will be destroyed.
Those whom the gods would destroy, they first drive mad.

In the pursuit of excellence in sports, an athlete has many problems to face. These include his natural ability, the basic skills of the game, training routines, and accommodation to coaches and teammates. Finally, there is the contest itself—the pregame anxiety, pacing himself to be ready for the crucial moment, and then going all out. These problems are familiar ones to coaches and athletes, and they have devised various methods of solution. In this chapter the focus will be on an aspect of winning not quite so familiar to sportsmen, yet one that is present to some degree in all contests. It is the psychological problem of winning—the mastery of one's aggression.

The sports stadium is a nearly ideal laboratory for psychological investigation. Games are played to be observed, and the investigator has an excellent opportunity for observation just by attending an athletic event. In many experimental settings the presence of an investigator is foreign to the actual life circumstances, thus distorting the results. In most sports, however, studies can be made in the natural environment for only the price of admission. The observer is indistinguishable from other fans and has no perceptible influence on the results. The provisions for spectators, ranging from a single park bench alongside a neighborhood tennis court to hundreds of concentric rows of numbered seats in football stadiums, invite the psychologist to examine the life drama that unfolds there.

The explicit goal of all competitive sports is, of course, to win within the rules. Although the rules vary from sport to sport, this purpose remains constant. Sports like boxing and wrestling retain elements of the primitive combat from which they are derived. To win, the athlete must physically overpower his opponent. In other sports, such as golf and bowling, the competition is veiled so that there is no actual physical contact among the competitors. Football, basketball, and baseball all contain certain elements of physical contact, but the winner is determined by comparative scores. In tennis and other games played with a racket, physical contact is removed from the hand-to-hand encounter of boxing and wrestling. The opponents are separated by a net, and rather than striking one another, the players strike a ball with an instrument, the racket. Instead of hitting one's opponent in order to overpower him, as in the more elemental sports, the player hits the ball in such a way that his opponent cannot return it. In track and field events an athlete attempts to run, throw, or jump faster, farther, or higher than his opposition. Since the course is the same for each contestant, the record of each may be compared with that of all of his competitors in the event.

The capacity of the human animal to perform in any sports event is obviously limited by his physical structure. But beyond these broad limits, psychological factors play the decisive role. Nevertheless, athletes and fans usually tend to consider as physical all limitations that confront athletes in the pursuit of records or victory. There is ample evidence, however, that many of the human limitations assumed to be physical are actually psychological in origin. The skilled coach knows well the nature of these factors and intuitively works with his team to overcome them.

In track and field there have traditionally been a series of so-called physical limits. These records were believed to represent the ultimate performance within the capability of a human being. Some of the well-known physical limits of past years have been the four-minute mile, the 9.3-second 100-yard dash, the eighteen-foot pole vault, the seven-foot high jump, and the seventy-foot shot put. Performers competed, sometimes for years, at a level very near these limits, thereby confirming the theoretical assumption that the limits were inviolate.

Eventually, in each instance, someone broke through the barrier. The immediate reaction of athletes and fans to such record-breaking performances was one of disbelief. They were thought to be the result of errors in measurement or timing, of cheating or unfair tactics, such as pacers, or of secret scientific applications. An aura of magic and sorcery seemed to surround the transcendence of such records. But within a relatively short period of time other athletes equaled or bettered the unbelievable records, and surpassing the barrier soon became almost commonplace.

Thus, for example, for twenty years the four-minute mile stood as an apparently unsurpassable limit. Great runners from many countries approached but could never break through the barrier. Like many of his predecessors, Roger Bannister, then a medical student in England, trained himself for this one ultimate performance. When he finished the record-breaking race he collapsed into the arms of friends. It seemed almost as if he had extended the record beyond man's limits. Strangely, within a few months after this memorable event, several other milers throughout the world had run under four minutes—without collapsing at the finish. In 1962, when Peter Snell lowered Bannister's record by some five seconds he even continued jogging around the track. Stopping at a sportscaster's microphone to be interviewed, he hardly seemed short of breath. Today it is not at all uncommon for college athletes to break the four-minute barrier, and even high school milers are turning in sub-four-minute performances.

Of course, there have been technical advances which have facilitated the breaking of records; improved tracks, improved training regimes, and stronger and better equipment have helped greatly. But the final striking impression is that when a record is finally broken by one man, it opens the way for others to do the same. The story of the breaking of the four-minute mile is not unique in the annals of sport but is, rather, characteristic of all such barriers. Within certain broad physical limits, the obstacles are in the minds of the performers and of the fans.

Psychological obstacles are to be found not only in the assault of man against a record in time or distance. They are even more prominent in man-to-man competition. The history of sports is filled with reports of bad-luck athletes who always faltered on the threshold of victory. Lady Luck, rather than psychological disability, is magically blamed for such faulty performances. They are not limited to the untalented, either, for among those who folded in the clutch have been the most skillful and able athletes.

Just as there are those who falter at the moment of victory, so there are renowned money players or clutch players. At the moment of greatest pressure they rise to meet these circumstances and gain victory. Golfers Jack Nicklaus and, a decade before, Arnold Palmer won such reputations. Bjorn Borg can be counted on, despite his young age, to provide a pressure performance in any big tennis tournament. Parry O'Brien, the great shot-putter, could always beat opponents with superior records in face-to-face competition. Jerry West in professional basketball and Johnny Bench in baseball always seemed to be able to come through with the big performance at precisely the right moment.

Some fascinating studies have been made by Francis J. Ryan on some differences in the competitive ability of fine athletes.* Ryan was the field events coach at Yale University and a psychologist as well, and thus he had a superb

---

*Francis J. Ryan, "An Investigation of Personality Differences Associated with Competitive Ability," and "Further Observations on Competitive Ability in Athletics," *Psychosocial Problems of College Men*, ed. Bryant M. Wedge (New Haven: Yale University Press, 1958), pp. 113–139.

opportunity to make such studies. He has observed that some athletes give exceptional performances in competition, while others do poorly in spite of having at least equal potential. "To give a simple illustration of the pattern, two shot-putters may both make practice puts almost daily of 45 feet. In formal competition one may achieve 48 feet and the other 42 feet. In practice sessions their performances may again converge, only to separate once more in competition—and in the same direction as before. As another example, there are high jumpers who have frequently bettered 6 feet [in practice] and never in competition; others may have cleared 6 feet only in competition, never in practice."

Ryan sent questionnaires to track coaches throughout the country asking each to describe one of the best and one of the worst competitors he had had under him. The men described included world record holders and Olympic champions, all of whom were exceptional athletes with great natural talent in track and field events. The distinction was solely on the basis of their ability in competition. Some of the results will be summarized here.

Ryan points out that all athletes appear to compete poorly on some occasions and that there are distinguishing characteristics between the poor and the good competitors. A good competitor who has a poor performance does so because he is temporarily "overanxious." He appears to try too hard, disturbing his timing and coordination, or he expends too much effort. The poor competitor, however, who nevertheless may have much natural ability, does poorly in competition because he makes a feeble effort. Ryan observed that the prognosis for future competition in these two types is quite different. The performer who has failed because of an overanxious, violent try will eventually do well in competition. The chronically poor competitor who makes only a feeble effort has a very poor prognosis for improvement. Ryan observed that poor competitors may even negate an otherwise good performance by some unnecessary action. For example, a thrower may foul after a good effort, or a broad jumper may fall backward.

The good competitor, in the heat of battle, uses his opponent as a temporary enemy. He may even appear angry at him; some good competitors seem to require "grudge" opponents. An observation of my own of the way one of America's great tennis players reacted toward his tournament opponents gives emphasis to Ryan's statements. As a tournament would progress and he could see who his next opponent would be, he would undergo a strange personality change toward that opponent. He would avoid his potential opponent and not speak to him. If they met socially, as was inevitable, he would glare angrily and utter hostile and sarcastic remarks. In a most unrealistic fashion he accused his opponent of unfounded and petty things. Because most tournament players are of necessity close companions, it would often happen that his opponent was actually a good friend. But for several days before the match the opponent was to him a bitter enemy. His anger would disappear immediately after the match, whether he won or lost, and once again he would be affable. Although his behavior reached paranoid proportions in the accusations he made against potential opponents, after a match he would completely disregard the whole affair.

This kind of behavior is also characteristic of the attitudes of an entire campus, both team and fans, before Saturday football games. As the big event nears, the students recall or invent more and more horrendous stories of how "dirty" or "unworthy" their opponents are. By the time the team comes on the field, the event has become a grudge game.

Among poor competitors Ryan observed the opposite reaction. Rather than whipping up their anger to meet the competitive challenge, they did everything possible to maintain an atmosphere of friendliness with their opponents. In the heat of battle they would even encourage or console them, going so far as to coach their opponents, doing everything possible to avoid recognizing the contest as a competitive one. Ryan further observed that any display of anger by athletes, coaches, or spectators disturbed the poor competitors.

After a poor performance, the chronically poor competitor is in good spirits and cheerful; he accepts his defeat philosophically. A good competitor, in contrast, is morose, surly, and angry at himself or others. Precisely the reverse is true after successful performances. If the poor performer by accident has made a good mark and won, he is often upset. His next effort will almost certainly be a poor one. Ryan cites fascinating examples of the extremity of the need to lose by the poor competitors.

"A poor competitor of great natural athletic talent was entered in two field events. The first effort of his first event went extremely well. Almost before he could prevent it, he had achieved by far the best performance of his career. He appeared pained and anxious. His remaining trials were incredibly poor but, of course, the first mark stood as his performance. When the time arrived for his second event, he was not to be found. Later it was found that he had left the athletic area in a panic. He could offer no explanation for his absence."

The second example, from the pole vault, is even more dramatic. Although the heights are very low by current standards in the fiber-glass era, the events illustrate the strength of the psychological barriers to succeeding experienced by an athlete. Ryan states: "A pole vaulter routinely cleared 12'6" in competition. Just as routinely, he failed to clear the next height of 13 feet. His teammates noted that he usually had more than 6 inches of clearance at 12'6" and therefore reasoned that his inability to make 13 feet was 'only mental.' Thus they conspired to 'help him.' When his back was toward the take-off, they raised the bar from 12'6" to 13 feet. Unaware of the bar's true height, the vaulter made a successful attempt.

"Thus, as the athlete landed in the pit and the bar remained aloft, his teammates rushed toward him with cries of congratulations. When he realized his accomplishment, he was stunned; he left the area and never again vaulted."

In all cases these athletes expressed the conscious goal of winning. They directed all of their deliberate efforts to this end by preparing for competition through arduous training. But when the long-awaited opportunity was actually at hand, other forces appeared to work against victory. So strong were these forces that they overcame the expressed goal. A closer examination of the psychological forces that an athlete must master in order to win would appear to be warranted.

Competition in sports requires that aggression be focused on the goal of victory. The poor competitor has learned to fear aggression most of the time, the average competitor fears it occasionally, and the good competitor fears it only infrequently. Ryan observed that his poor competitors in field events avoided aggression in many ways both on and off the field. They spoke softly, and they avoided arguments. They tried to maintain friendly relations with their rivals under all circumstances. It is the nature of this aggression that we will now consider in trying to understand the problems faced in winning.

In the process of growing up, a child learns that under certain conditions a display of aggression has unhappy consequences. To oversimplify the situation, an aggressive attempt to take something or to destroy something is likely to be met by disfavor from parents, teachers, or other adults. Their disfavor is expressed either by retaliation in the form of corporal punishment or by the withholding of love. These consequences are very serious for the child, who is dependent on the parents or other adults for love and the material advantages that accompany it. His small size and relative weakness make him especially vulnerable to any kind of retaliation that might result from his aggression.

He soon learns to think before acting and to consider the consequences first. This represents the beginning of the development of conscience and eventually is incorporated into the child's personality as a system of conscious and unconscious "should" and "should nots." These parental admonitions to the child become translated into the rules of society as he grows older. The rules may be informal, as when he learns that he must be polite and "nice" or he will be unaccepted by others in certain situations, or formal, as in the case of laws, policemen, and religious teachings.

He also learns that "there is a time and place for everything," and especially if he is a boy, he is sometimes expected to be aggressive. In certain situations, such as sports, he is looked upon with disfavor if he is not aggressive or assertive enough. Unfortunately by the time he has sorted out when he is supposed to be aggressive and when he is not supposed to be, there has been some contamination of the sanction with the prohibition. The "should nots" have largely gone underground; they have become unconscious and generalized. In a "should-be-aggressive" situation such as, let us say, a basketball game, a player may find himself, to his consternation, reacting as though it were a "should-not-be-aggressive" situation.*

These psychological prohibitions have their effect and take their toll largely outside of conscious awareness, so that the athlete, his coach, his teammates, and the spectators are at a loss to explain some of his peculiar falterings in quest of victory. They all tend to believe that it must be that he needs to train harder, change his diet, or alter some technical aspect of his performance. Unfortunately these changes are rarely successful, except as they may alter the emotional tone of his performance.

At the deepest levels of the unconscious, aggression may be equated with violence and murder. The reader will recall the case of our tennis player, "Killer Ken," who unconsciously equated long tennis matches with killing. He could only win quickly and put his opponent "out of his misery" swiftly and mercifully, for a long match recalled too vividly his father's agonizingly slow death, an event for which he felt responsible.

Some further verifications of the murderous nature of the unconscious component of aggression in sports can be seen in the description of an effective competitor. It is said that he must have "the killer instinct." Although this is usually taken to mean that an athlete is able, relentlessly and without inner prohibition or a sense of guilt, to keep the pressure on his opponent while achieving victory, the language chosen to describe it suggests a criminal act rather than a sportsmanlike activity.

An interesting example which demonstrates the destructive nature of the fantasies associated with athletic competition appears in tennis. When two opponents enter the court for a tournament match, they enter a very restrictive setting with a myriad of inhibiting psychological factors, both conscious and uncounscious. Although the avowed purpose of each participant is to defeat his opponent, this must be done in a sportsmanlike manner. Sportsmanship dictates that outward signs of aggression toward one's opponent should be suppressed. Tennis, the gentleman's game, requires spotless white attire and polite praise for the rival's good shots; the loser is expected to congratulate the winner with a hearty handshake and a smile. Audience participation is limited by custom to applause for placements—but never for errors. This sedate atmosphere is rarely violated during a match. By contrast, in the locker room after a match where there are fewer social restrictions and the facade of politeness is removed, the intense competitive spirit of each player is clearly revealed in the language used: "It was murder." "He slaughtered him." "He killed him." One is struck by the contrast of such expressions of primitive carnage with the polite cultural setting in which the action

---

*The psychoanalytic term "superego" is technically applied to this learned guiding system. It includes the conscience, the common term for the conscious prohibitions and admonitions, as well as elements that are unconscious.

took place and to which murder, killing, and slaughter would seem to be quite foreign. Yet the selection of these terms to describe the game betrays the latent implications of the controlled aggression of the match.

Sometimes situations arise unexpectedly, and the reality of the contest coincides with the competitor's latent destructive fantasies. Under such circumstances the athletes are suddenly confronted with a demonstration of the full intensity of the violent wishes they hold, and they are appalled by what they see. Their subsequent performances bear testimony to the guilt they feel over the realization of their destructive fantasies.

A number of years ago in the finals match of the United States Tennis Championships, two splendid Australian players met to decide the championship. The same two players had met the year before for the title, and the past winner was again favored. The match was very close and the competition intense. Soon the champion of the previous year gained the upper hand and needed only a few points to complete his second consecutive championship. Then, during a particularly hard-fought point, the challenger fell, apparently having sprained his ankle. The match was delayed while the officials rushed to see how seriously the player was injured. The pained expression on the injured man's face was far surpassed by the anguish on the champion's face, who hung his head and paced nervously back and forth, the picture of dejection. As it happened, the injury was minor and the match was quickly resumed, but now the defending champion missed easy balls and was unable to regain his former standard of play. Despite his earlier commanding lead he went on to lose in a surprising upset.

Perhaps there were several determinants in the sudden change in this match, but one of them was most apparent. The turning point occurred when the challenger injured himself, but the change was not in his play but in the champion's play. The injury to his opponent produced in the champion an appearance of dejection and anguish. He hung his head, and his expression was one of guilt, as though he had committed a serious crime. It was apparent that this sense of guilt played a part in his losing the match.

An athletic injury is the calculated risk of anyone who competes. Separated by a net, as is the case in a tennis match, if one player turns his ankle, it is certainly not due to an assault by his opponent. But man's unconscious is not limited by the spatial arrangements of the game. In this case the injury was so minor that play was quickly resumed. However, the defending champion now behaved as if it had been his intent seriously to injure his opponent. His play was so disturbed that he lost the match.*

As in dreams, things that occur unconsciously are not bound by reality. For example, a dreamer may be an adult, but the dream may take place in a

---

*Arnold R. Beisser, "Psychodynamic Observations of a Sport," *Psychoanalysis and the Psychoanalytic Review*, Vol. 48 (Spring 1961), pp. 69–76.

childhood setting, and his parents who are dead may seem very much alive. In the dream he may fuse some elements of the home in which he now lives with his childhood home. Similarly, an athlete who could not actually have harmed his opponent may nevertheless unconsciously experience the opponent's injury as the result of his own deliberate act. His reactions, which may appear illogical, are not to the real situation but to its unconscious meaning for him.

An entire team may be similarly affected when an unfortunate event coincides with the team's violent wishes. The collective guilt experienced may result in a turning point in an important athletic contest. For example, a number of years ago in a playoff game in the National Basketball Association, the Syracuse Nationals and the Boston Celtics were the two rivals. The great Boston team was overwhelming its opponent by a large score when, during a wild scramble for the ball, the Syracuse star and mainstay, Dolph Schayes, was knocked down and his wrist was broken. It was indeed a terrible blow to the Syracuse team, for without their leading scorer they seemed to have little chance. They might well have expected to fold, and the Boston team to display some subdued pleasure, for the loss of Schayes presumably wrapped up the game for them. But instead, the Boston team appeared apathetic and unnerved rather than the Syracuse team. The Boston Celtics seemed to lose their will to win, throwing the ball away and missing easy shots.

In contrast, Syracuse, now in a mood of revenge, began playing better. The eventual result was an almost unbelievable finale as Syracuse beat the favored Boston team. An important factor contributing to the Boston defeat appeared to have been the guilt experienced by the players upon the realization of their violent fantasies. Afterward, in an interview with a Boston star regarding the loss, he expressed over and over again how the injury to the Syracuse star had had a detrimental effect on his own team's morale. He said he could not explain why, but that the injury had upset Boston more than it had Syracuse.

When one traces the turning point in a game, one frequently finds events of this kind.* A team, seemingly on the way to victory, loses its spark under a cloud of depression when a member of the opposing team is injured. They appear to want no more violence. This, coupled with an attitude of revenge in the opposing team, often spells the difference between defeat and victory.

Sometimes the violence which is latent most of the time erupts into deliberate attempts to kill or to do violent bodily harm to the opponent. Joe Frazier, with striking candor when talking about his fights with Mohammad Ali, said simply, "I want to kill him." In heated rivalries in football there are

---

*This occurs mainly in individual sports or small-team sports where the players are intensely involved in the whole course of the game. It is infrequent in football, with platooning and plays called from the bench.

sometimes malicious and deliberate attempts to injure an opponent. A baseball pitcher, too, may turn a brush-back into a bean ball. The fans, caught up in the excitement of the event, may yell, "Murder the bum!" or "Kill him!" Sometimes their violent wishes erupt, as was the case following a Latin American soccer event when many deaths resulted, or in the riots associated with the Stanley Cup in ice hockey several years ago. In these tragic moments, athletes or fans act as though the limited aggression allowed within the rules is license to be violently destructive. Just as in appropriate circumstances the prohibitions against aggressive displays may inhibit the aggressiveness in competition, so may the freedom to battle within the rules sometimes be confused with freedom to kill.

These examples of naked violence are the exception, however, rather than the rule, and for most athletes the destructive significance of the competition remains unconscious. Instead, it reveals itself only in the inhibitions to aggressive expression with the rules, as in inexplicable "blowing" or "choking" at the moment of potential victory.

Whenever there are seemingly mysterious forces at play, a tendency exists to attach magical significance to them. The athlete whose competitive ability is blocked by such unconscious forces looks to magic for explanation and solution. The primitive tribesman attempts to deal with the mysteries of nature, such as fertility and the weather, by magical ritual and incantation. Strangely enough, the modern athlete does the same. Unlike the primitive, however, modern athletes, in keeping with the scientific society in which they live, disclaim the importance of their rituals. Nevertheless, they continue them.

It has been said that baseball players aren't superstitious; they just don't want to take chances. They use lucky pieces, lucky clothes, lucky equipment, refuse to shave while winning, sit in special places in the dugout, and don't mention that a pitcher has a no-hitter going. Some athletes seek divine protection—a basketball player can be seen to make the sign of the cross before shooting a foul shot, or a boxer may kneel to pray in the ring before the bell. Basketball teams, before going into action, lay their hands together to symbolize their solidarity. They try to fight the unknown forces that lie within them with magical gestures.

When it comes to rituals, no one surpasses the baseball player. As he steps to the plate for his turn at bat he engages in a mixture of purposeful activity and obsessive ritual. The same ritual is compulsively repeated to its completion each time before he takes a pitch. If it is interrupted he steps out of the batter's box and starts all over again. A typical example is something like this: First, the player knocks the dirt off his spikes, then he picks up dirt for his hands, and then he hitches up his trousers. He carefully places his feet in the batter's box, he loosens his trousers around his genitals, he pulls down his cap, digs in his feet, takes back the bat—and behold, he is ready!

The order and the style of the routine may vary, but it must be repeated each time. There are many variations of the baseball ritual. For example, Dick Stuart, the former major league long-ball hitter, always bit off a piece of gum of designated size and threw it on home plate before he stepped into the batter's box. The elaborateness of the rituals in ballplayers varies considerably. The late Gil Hodges of the Dodgers and later of the Mets, in his playing days, and Roger Maris, home-run champion of the Yankees, were among the most careful in their rituals.

One of the interesting characteristics is the attention paid by hitters to making sure that their trousers are just right around the genitals. It seems doubtful that positioning the genitals should have much to do with hitting a baseball, but in the language of the unconscious the genitals are the symbols of potency and power. It appears, then, in large part to satisfy unconscious and not physical needs.*

Pitchers, too, engage in standardized routines. A pitcher leans forward in exactly the same way each time to get his signals from the catcher and goes through the same characteristic motions before throwing. Of course, some of these rituals do facilitate the actual physical action of throwing, but many primarily offer the psychological safety of routine. There are some teams where it has become a custom for the players in the dugout to switch seats constantly when the team is losing but to keep the same seats when they are winning. Maury Wills, the former Los Angeles Dodger shortstop, would wear the same trousers when he was hitting well and would not change them until his streak stopped. There were also certain subjects that he would not talk about, as a magical remedy for specific competitive problems that he encountered.

Many baseball players deliberately try to avoid thinking when they are hitting. This appears to be an attempt to dispel any disturbing fantasies that might creep into the player's mind. The "no-think" school of hitting has a large number of inherents. Yogi Berra used to say, "How can I think and hit at the same time!" If the player does not think, he cannot think anything bad that will come into conflict with his conscience. Not thinking thus serves as a protective mechanism.

I have described how guilt is one of the major difficulties an athlete faces in competing, since to win is, in the unconscious, tantamount to destroying

---

*If the person feels compelled to perform rituals of this kind and is flooded with anxiety when he does not, his behavior is classified in clinical psychiatry as an obsessive-compulsive symptom. As has been described earlier, psychological disorder is largely a matter of degree, and nearly all persons sometime in their lives perform similar rituals. For example, children commonly avoid stepping on cracks in pavement or feel compelled to touch each lath in a picket fence. Analysis of obsessive-compulsive rituals has revealed that they are performed to magically ward off certain unconscious forces that are in conflict with the superego. The preceding discussion would suggest that those rituals served to protect the athlete against the implications of his own aggression.

one's opponent. One method of avoiding the guilt is to deny that one is winning at all. Denial is a common psychological defense mechanism which is seen in many athletes in the pursuit of victory. For example, there are several world-caliber tennis players who exhibit a consistently predictable behavior when they are winning. As the match progresses, they begin to castigate themselves. They talk to themselves critically, as though to some-one else, saying out loud, "You're terrible," "You're lousy," "You can't play." This is indeed surprising to hear after a player makes a brilliant shot. It is incongruous to see a player behaving in this way on one of his best days, especially when on a bad day, in defeat, he seems to have no need to do so. This patently false denial of the true situation is a way of saying, in effect, "I'll conceal the fact that I'm winning and thereby avoid the consequences of guilt." I have asked a number of these players about their behavior, and they have told me that it is necessary for them in order to "keep the pressure on" and not to "let up." It would appear then that only by denying victory can they escape the anxiety and guilt of conscience.

One excellent tournament player, well known throughout the world, con-tinually strikes himself on the leg with his racket between points of impor-tant matches. This is traumatic enough to produce bruises which can easily be seen. Beating himself is a magical gesture by which he equalizes the situ-ation of beating his opponent. Since to beat his opponent in a tennis match has the latent connotation of physically beating him, he must satisfy his conscience by physically beating himself.

A famous Wimbledon champion regularly showed another variation of this same type of activity. Despite the fact that he was one of the best players in the world, he found it almost impossible to win an easy match. He had to struggle with each opponent and would barely win each time. His first-round matches against weak opponents were just as close as those in the finals against the best players in the world, and he appeared equally dishev-eled. Among the players it was wryly said that if his clothes weren't dirty from falling on the court and if he didn't look as if he had been beaten, he hadn't played well. There are many players in many sports who behave in a similar manner; they can only win by hairline decision, never by a wide margin. They persistently must demonstrate that there is little difference be-tween the winner and the loser. If the distinction between the players can be nullified, they are protected from the consequences of beating an opponent.

Another interesting variation of the attempt to deny the consequences of one's aggressive competition characterized a national tennis champion of some years ago. He was one of the most popular competitors among all other players, for he was always friendly with them even in the heat of battle. He would never say a harsh word about an opponent either on or off the court. In contrast, he was probably the most unpopular champion of all time with fans, for during a match he constantly berated the ball boys, linesmen, and umpires. Each of his important matches was held up by his loud and sometimes obscene criticism of them. On more than one occasion he was known to hit a ball boy with a ball or with his racket. Such unsportsmanlike behavior resulted in his being disqualified from several tournaments. He could, however, tolerate the displeasure of the fans, the tournament officials, and the ball boys, since it served a vital purpose for his personality. He accomplished a displacement of his aggression and his destructive fantasies to less threatening objects, allowing him to compete successfully against opponents. By this strange behavior he tried to demonstrate to himself that he was not engaged in combat with his opponent and that his only enemies were the ball boys and officials.

An athlete in a competitive sport must face his goal of winning. To accomplish this he must somehow master or overcome certain unconscious concomitants of winning. The aggression in the game may be tainted with implications of violence and mayhem, and the athlete has learned restrictions of conscience against such murderous thoughts. These thoughts countermand his desire to win so that he unexplainably chokes or falters in the crucial moment. Since these forces opposing victory take place outside the player's awareness, they seem magical. Even though the player logically denies the existence of magic, he finds himself bound by superstition and employing elaborate rituals to defend himself against dire consequences.

SUCCESS AND FAILURE IN SPORTS

The magic and rituals described illustrate the problems that the athlete faces in trying to win and why it is often said that a player is his own worst enemy. There are great differences in how freely athletes allow themselves to pursue victory. For some the ritual and magical gestures seem to be enough; for others no matter what kind of psychological manipulations they engage in, they still seem doomed to failure. All athletes experience difficulties sometimes, some frequently and some almost all the time. Personality is not static but dynamic, and so a poor competitor may become a good one and a good competitor may become a poor one. Other factors, such as one's coach, the crowd, or other changes in one's life circumstances, may help or hinder a player's ability to win.

Early in the athlete's career he may have more difficulty winning than he will have later, especially in important contests. Lack of experience is often one of the reasons a youthful performer falters. A player must get the feel of winning before he can be successful. If he has the physical talent and skill, there is still a psychological obstacle that must be overcome. Coaches and fans are patronizing toward youthful failures and are apt to say, "All he needs is more experience" or "What he needs is a couple of victories under his belt" or "He needs confidence." An athlete has to "think he can do it" before he can win.

The four-minute mile, the eighteen-foot pole vault, and the seventy-foot shot put are examples of how important it is for athletes to believe that it can be done. Once these records were broken it was commonplace to do so, but before that, they had seemed insurmountable barriers. The youthful performer who is uncertain whether or not he can win faces a similar problem. He must learn that it is possible and that no disastrous consequences develop when he does win. If a player finds that nothing bad comes from victory, the unconscious or only partly conscious destructive fantasies associated with winning are tempered by reality.

The history of sports is filled with stories of athletes who have not lived up to their potential. These players seem to have the talent and skill to defeat all opponents, but something always happens. For many of them a break finally comes, and once having tasted victory and found only sweetness, they continue on to be true champions. Others finally achieve that great victory, only to find themselves tortured by unexplainable forces of conscience, and they never again do well.

Sometimes fortuitous circumstances occur which seem to help a competitor over that important threshold between losing and winning, between challenger and champion. A number of years ago there was a tennis Davis Cup final between United States and Australia. Team captain Perry Jones had selected as a representative from this country a little-known Chilean player, Alex Olmedo, who was eligible only on a technicality. It was a surprising choice and one for which Jones was sharply cirticized. The player had never won a major championship, and although there was no doubt about his natural ability and talent, he could not seem to win important matches.

Sports columnists said he lacked the "killer instinct." But he astounded the tennis world by winning all of his matches, thereby also winning the Davis Cup for America. He defeated players who had always before been his masters.

The explanation he gave for his brilliant play was most revealing. He took no credit for himself, but rather attributed his victory entirely to Mr. Jones. He stated that he had played for the captain alone because the captain had done so much to forward his career. Modestly he refused the accolades for his victory, directing them all toward Jones. The confidence of the team captain had obviously been a great boost to Olmedo. He had been unable to win the big ones before, but now Jones' demonstration of faith in him made it possible for him to win.

Beyond this interpretation lies a deeper one. By attributing his victory to the team captain, Olmedo was able to transfer the responsibility for winning from himself. He was thus able to avoid the unconscious problems of conscience already discussed. These victories in the Davis Cup matches served as a turning point in Olmedo's career. In the next few tournaments he won regularly and clearly established himself as a great player. Once having crossed the barrier that separated him from victory, he had discovered that it was safe on the other side. In order to make the transition, he had needed the assistance of his intuitively wise captain, who evidently recognized his potential.

This is not a unique story, for coaches often find themselves showing faith in the ability of an athlete to overcome the personal barriers that have kept him from winning. By encouragement and by assuming the responsibility for the player's efforts, the coach is able to spur the athlete on to victory. Often this is accomplished when the coach sets a specific training or game plan for the athlete. Although the emphasis is on physical performance, the most important part of the plan is the confidence the coach conveys by saying, "If you do this, you'll win." The athlete is thus able to avoid his psychological inhibitions by "just following orders" and letting the coach handle the worries. Once the athlete has experienced victory, it is often no longer necessary for him to have such assistance.

The successful coach knows when to assume responsibility for the actions of his players and when to give them free rein. In a crucial moment, sending in the play to a football or basketball team may relieve the players of the burden of responsibility and allow them to "just play." Often, I believe, it is not that the play itself was better than one the team might have used but it provides psychological relief.

Negative effects may also result. Floyd Patterson achieved the heavyweight championship of the world under the guidance of Cus D'Amato. D'Amato expressed his boundless faith in Patterson, assuring the fighter that he was unbeatable. He encouraged Patterson to put his faith and trust in him and let him manage all the details. D'Amato accepted all responsibility for any unfortunate consequences of either winning or defeat.

Under this regime Patterson won the heavyweight championship of the world and appeared to be in for a long reign. But D'Amato became involved in a controversy with boxing officials, and Patterson's confidence in him became shaken. He began to assume responsibility for his own training and matchmaking. This was followed by a series of ignominious defeats. The former champion seemed, in these fights, especially against Sonny Liston, to lose all confidence and to be frightened of his opponents. He seemed only to be waiting for the inevitable defeat.

An athlete may work out his problems about winning outside of the athletic arena. A dramatic example is how one well-known golfer did this. Lloyd Mangrum was known as the mystery man of golf, for although he had demonstrated himself to be a brilliant performer, he had also established the reputation for blowing the big ones. His sudden failures in competition were mysterious to his fellow players and to his fans.

Mangrum was inducted into the service and was in combat in the European theater in World War II. He faced the most difficult wartime conditions over an extended period during the Battle of the Bulge but was one of the survivors of that costly encounter.

The first year, in the first major tournament after his return from combat, he played in the U.S. Open, one of golf's greatest challenges. In this tournament, in contrast to his previous strange inability to win the big ones, he displayed exceptional coolness under fire. Although the tension was great during the match, Mangrum appeared to be able to tolerate the stress without difficulty and went on to win the tournament. This great victory occurred under amazing circumstances. Mangrum had not only had a long layoff from competition in golf but also had returned after war experiences that had in other ways exhausted him. This did not inhibit his ability to win, however, but seemed to enhance it. In the war he had experienced the threat and the realities of death and destruction. The dangers he had faced as a soldier seemed to clarify his competitive activities in golf. He was now able to pursue victory on the golf course without confusing it with destructive fantasies, for he had seen the real thing. Mangrum's war experiences had brought his golf competition into a more accurate perspective and made him into a cool competitor.

Among the other forces that may play a decisive role in an athlete's ability to win is the crowd. It is well known that if the crowd is with a team or a player, there is an advantage for that team or player. So widely recognized is this fact that in making up the season's schedules in sports, careful attention is paid to giving the teams equal numbers of home games. Sports experts say that a football team playing at home has a seven-point advantage and a basketball team playing at home has a five- to ten-point advantage.

It is not encouragement and support alone that make the crowd such an important factor to the player or the team; it is the knowledge that they share with him the responsibility for his aggression. It is not just public relations or sportsmanship that stirs players to pay tribute to the fans for their part in the victory achieved by the team. The fans shout "Kill 'em!" and "Murder 'em!" thus sharing with the players the violent impulses directed against the opposition. This sharing of unacceptable aggression allows the team or players to compete fiercely. The guilt they might otherwise experience if they were alone is diluted and shared by the fans. The athlete may feel that he is only carrying out the mandate of the crowd and that any evil consequences are therefore not his responsibility. Knowing the crowd is with him is comforting and removes some of the inhibitions from his aggressive actions.

On an international scale, the tragic consequences of crowd support were seen during World War II. Nazi soldiers and their sympathizers carried out the most dreadful acts of murder and genocide against other humans. The support of the crowd gave license to many persons who probably would otherwise have retreated in horror from the ghastly crimes in which they participated. Today, without the support of the howling mob, many of these people look back in amazement at their complicity.

The player who faces a hostile crowd meets a converse situation. He may find it difficult to go all out because there are so many against him. For example, tennis fans in Italy do not generally observe the niceties expected of tennis audiences. They castigate foreign players who compete against Italians with jeers and profane comments. Many players find it so intolerable that they will not play in the famous international tournament in Rome. It is so unpopular for foreigners to win there that it is almost impossible for them to compete effectively. They find themselves losing quickly just to get off the court.

In team sports an athlete is never alone. He always has his teammates to share some of the responsibility for his aggressive action. No doubt this plays an important role in the choice an athlete makes of his sport. The reader will recall the case history of the basketball player in Chapter 3. Although he displayed amazing natural ability in individual sports, he chose not to compete in them. He needed the support of teammates to share responsibility for his aggression. The athlete in an individual sport stands alone to face whatever consequences result from his actions. Some athletes prefer this position and choose individual sports.

There are times when no amount of support or sharing of responsibility by coaches, teammates, or fans is sufficient to liberate an athlete to pursue his goal vigorously. This is not to say that athletes inhibited by conscience in their pursuit of victory do not have the same intensity of desire to win as do their freer fellow athletes. They want to win, they train to win, and they hope to win in the same way, but they are defeated by forces beyond their awareness.

Ryan describes the case of a young runner who never could reach his potential, always failing to win in important meets. In a particular event his performance meant the difference between victory and defeat for the whole team. Under great pressure the team was able to wring out a victory from him. Although successful for the team, the results were disastrous for the athlete: faced with the restrictions of his conscience, he dropped out of school.

Sometimes becoming a winner is so disastrous for an athlete that he develops a serious psychiatric disorder when success comes his way. There have been several examples of potentially great athletes who managed every time to fail at the moment of victory. A few, through either crowd support or other seemingly fortuitous circumstances, did win a great event. Following this they underwent severe personality disorganization. At the moment when a player sees victory within his grasp he may feel the most exquisite conflict.

There was once a tennis player of international reputation who consistently managed to stay just below the top. Through a peculiar series of events he found himself in the final round against a champion who was sick that day. He was within a point of victory on several occasions, and each time he would either throw away the point or make a wild attempt to put the ball away. In either case, he lost the point. Following the match, which he eventually lost, he played in only one or two more tournaments. After that he was an emotionally disturbed man and spent much of his later life in a mental hospital. He maintained the delusion that he had actually won this great championship match, but tragically it was only in his delusions of grandeur that he could allow himself to achieve the greatness that was his potential.

The reader of the sports page is aware of examples of this kind in every sport. It is the story of a promising career that fell apart at the very moment when success was at hand. Such a player is soon forgotten once he no longer competes. Athletes who fail to achieve in reality sometimes become broken men who finally rely on their fantasies for achievement. Winning is safer there. These psychodynamics of failure are not specific to athletes but can be found in other areas of life as well. It is not uncommon for the psychiatrist to meet patients in his office whose psychiatric problems are related to the athlete's problem in winning. These patients develop their psychiatric disorders at the very moment in their lives when they achieve a long-awaited and dreamed-of goal. Such psychological destruction can occur in the man whose lifelong ambition is realized—when a businessman becomes vice president of his company, or a college professor becomes chairman of his department, or a man finally has enough money to retire.

Like the athlete who becomes disturbed when he wins, such men present at first a puzzling situation. The goal, long awaited and sought, when finally achieved, creates discomfort and anxiety rather than the expected happiness. The reader may recall that in certain of the case histories this was also the case. The basketball player became disturbed in his senior year at college, the football player became depressed when his son was born and he was offered the family business, and the tennis player became anxious when he married into wealth. All these events would appear to be signals for relief, joy, and pleasure, but instead they led to tragic and disintegrating personal consequences. Although each case had its own specific and unique background which led to the predicament, there are certain general principles that may help to explain the strange phenomena.

Sigmund Freud observed early in his career that there were "those who are wrecked by success." He related such misfortunes in the adult to the unfinished business carried over from childhood, expressed contemporaneously in the joke, "I spent the happiest days of my life in the arms of another man's wife—my mother." To the adult male, certain successes are symbolic of the achievement of unconscious wishes representing the anachronistic displacement of his father and the sexual possession of his mother—the Oedipus complex. "The term, of course, has complicated matters because it compared what is to be inferred in childhood with what is to be inferred from the story of King Oedipus. The name thus establishes an analogy between two unknowns. The idea is that Oedipus, who inadvertently killed his father and married his mother, became a mythical hero, and on the stage is viewed with intense pity and terror because to possess one's mother is a universal wish, universally tabooed.'"* This statement of Erik Erikson's suggests the scientific and emotional controversy that prevails as to the use of the term. For our purposes it is sufficient to emphasize that there is almost always a rivalry between growing sons and their fathers. This rivalry is mainly on the child's part while he is too small to threaten his father physically, but as the boy emerges into adolescence, the father becomes keenly aware that he has a competitor in the home. The adolescent struggle over almost everything— money, cars, school, girls—obscures the historical roots of competition. The childhood statements of little boys who declare that they will replace their fathers and marry their mothers are patronizingly forgotten.

In the Victorian era when Freud began his work, the stereotypes of family were very different from what they are today. Although they were a composite of fact and myth, they were clearly presented: The father was the dominant member of the family. He was the provider. He was hard-working, God-fearing, and powerful.† He expected and received obedience from his wife and children. It was in this context that the Oedipus complex could be seen in full force. The tremulous weak child, looking to the power and possessions of the forbidding father, was subject to a variety of problems that are not so obvious today. Contemporary models of father-son relationships are very different.

The Victorian dictum that children should be seen and not heard has given way to what has been termed the "century of the child." Today the child occupies center stage, and his mother is the director. The boy and his father, as portrayed in fictional writing and television, are pals, and the patriarchy of earlier days has been replaced by democracy—togetherness. The father appears as a good-natured, slightly befuddled buffoon, dominated by his wife, who actually holds the family together. He is no longer sole provider, for his wife, too, may be working outside the home. The father's job is often sedentary and rather obscure. Such caricatures, although not entirely accurate, do illustrate the direction of family change since Victorian days.

Whatever the weaknesses in the Victorian family, and they were many, the roles were at least fairly clear. It was easier for boys to identify with the fathers. But today, a boy rarely relies on his father for the example of the ideal male. The image is diffused, and rather than serving as the ideal for his son, father and son together share an admiration of an ideal, frequently a baseball or football player. Erikson has described this father-son relationship in the following passage: "If a father plays baseball with his son, it is not in order to impress him with the fact that he, the father, comes closer to the

---

*Erik Erikson, *Childhood and Society* (New York: W. W. Norton & Company, 1950), pp. 82–83.

†In modern sociological terms he was an inner-directed man. See David Riesman's *The Lonely Crowd* (Garden City, N.Y.: Doubleday & Company, 1950).

perfection of a common ideal type—for he probably does not—but rather that they play together at identifying with that type, and that there is always the chance, hoped for by both, that the boy may more nearly approach the ideal than father did."*

To be a winner, a champion, an athlete achieves a position similar to that of the Victorian ideal man: strong and powerful, for otherwise he would not have won; and righteous and moral, for he is a good sport and potentially, if not in fact, a good provider. He achieves success as a man that his own father only dreamed of. He stands alone on unfamiliar ground, responsible for his aggression and its consequences.

Now this may not seem like a bad state of affairs at all. The fruits of victory include fame, admiration, and perhaps even financial success. The reader will also recall, however, that unconsciously the aggression is often tantamount to violent destruction of the opponent. So the athlete, although he basks in the glory of victory, also unconsciously stands convicted of murder.

In this unenviable position, a contemporary youth does not have the security that comes from growing up with a clearly defined masculine role— something that his Victorian counterpart did have. Although filled with problems, that Victorian role was consistent, allowing the young person to gradually identify with it. Today, the role and duties of the man are clouded by change and a disturbing relativism. No clear continuity exists for a youth to follow.

The problem faced by the champion is familiar on the contemporary scene and is fabled in the archetypal western. The cowboy who becomes known as "the fastest gun in the West" is constantly plagued by vanquished foes, relatives of his victims, "two-bit gunslingers," and "reckless kids trying to make a name for themselves." He is the winner and champion and is thus the target of attack. "Once you've reached the top there is no place to go but down." The *High Noon* story has all of the elements of the problems of a champion in sports. The marshal (the athlete) who defeated the outlaws (his opponents) reigns (is champion) in peace only temporarily. He hopes to settle down with the girl (the prize) whose love he has earned. However, his retirement cannot be accomplished, for the outlaws (his opponents) whom he sent to jail (defeated) have been freed and will come after him (challenge again) to get even. It is futile for him to run because he knows they would only track him down in order to retaliate. He turns to the townspeople (the fans) for support. After all, he did it for them while they cheered. But they are not with him; he is alone, frightened, and disappointed. He must defend the town (his championship) by himself. In the Hollywood endings, he usually kills the outlaws (wins), but he is a bitter and disappointed man.

---

*Erik Erikson, *Childhood and Society* (New York: W. W. Norton & Company, 1950), p. 273.

Of course, the young athlete meets many men—coaches and other athletes—other than his father who can serve as the image of the winner or champion. But the point is that these occur outside the home and the immediate family where he learned his first important lessons. His foundation may thus be weaker than the superstructure it is required to hold.

An "also-ran" in the game is like one of the fans, for he does not stand apart from the crowd, risking isolation from them. For him the competition may be filled with violent fantasies, but they are without the risk of becoming reality. He is like the child who may entertain the most destructive possibilities without the power and strength to carry them out. His safety comes from losing, as the child's comes from his weakness and impotence. He remains united with the others, the crowd, as the child is united with his parents, deriving his strength from their size. In his capacity for failure he receives comfort and the certainty of belonging.

It is the winner, the champion, who risks emerging from the crowd and who tangibly acts out their mutual desires. He bears responsibility for the collective aggression focused in sport. He may receive respect, awe, and deference, but great things are also expected of him and he is allowed no sign of weakness. Comfort and pity, the rewards of the child, are reserved for those he defeats. He is the man who stands alone. In America everyone cheers for and loves the underdog. When the underdog becomes champion, he loses much of his support.

If the loser is the child and winner is the man, society prepares a player for the former role better than for the latter. It is "the century of the child," and the world is organized for his benefit. His innocence and goodness are idolized by adults who hope his fate will be better than theirs. It is the paradoxes of adult life as much as the virtues of childhood that retard the maturation process. The experiences of youth are inadequate preparation for the shifting identities of adult life. Continuity from child roles to adult roles is disrupted by the possibility of social mobility and the paralyzing relativism of changing values. By comparison, the child's role seems stable and secure.

In his choice between the isolation of outstanding play and the mass solidarity and comfort of remaining mediocre, the athlete on the threshold of victory is in effect choosing between the security of childhood and the responsibilities of adulthood. The champion is the man emerging out of the crowd into uniqueness. Winning is one aspect of the enigma of maturity.

15.

The American Seasonal Masculinity Rites

Not all of the characteristics that are attributed to being male or female are, to the same degree, biologically determined. Some, considered to be basic to masculinity or femininity, are determined by the culture in which one lives rather than by obvious physical differences. In our culture, athletics are now considered the most masculine of activities. Let us turn now to a consideration of what part sexual orientation plays in the intense interest in sports in America.

Before puberty, boys can be distinguished from girls mainly on the basis of primary sexual characteristics; when puberty is reached, biological distinctions become more apparent. At that time, because of the differences in hormonal balance, the distinct secondary sexual characteristics begin to develop; boys begin to grow hair on their face, and their bodies become more muscular and angular; girls become more curvaceous and develop breasts. Primary and secondary characteristics are predictable and universal: girls' hips broaden; boys' shoulders grow wider.

Beyond these physical characteristics are others that are largely, if not exclusively, determined by the society in which one lives. These can be termed tertiary characteristics, and are transmitted from generation to generation by the examples of the men and women in the culture. To suggest, as Margaret Mead does, that the nature of maleness and femaleness, outside the physical characteristics, is culturally determined may be an extreme point of view, for differences must develop just from living in a male body which has greater physical strength, compared with living in a female body which experiences menstruation and pregnancy. Nevertheless, it is true that many of the male or female characteristics that are taken for granted in our society are determined by social custom rather than by genetics. For example, up to very recently in this country, boys wore short hair and girls wore long hair, but in other parts of the world the reverse is true.* Similarly, an American boy would hide in shame if he had to wear a skirt, whereas in Greece it is the attire worn by a particularly virile and courageous group of soldiers.

There is a story, although of doubtful validity, that nevertheless illustrates the importance of these tertiary sexual characteristics: Two children were playing outside a nudist camp. One of them discovered a hole in the wall surrounding the camp through which he could look. While he peeked through the hole, the other child excitedly inquired, "What do you see? Are they men or women?" The peeper responded in dismay, "I don't know, they don't have any clothes on!"

Tertiary sexual characteristics such as dominance, mannerisms, dress, and speech are often considered unalterable, and yet studies of different cultures reveal quite different ideas about what constitutes male and female behavior. Each culture assumes that it knows how a man or woman should act. The folklore is justified by a self-fulfilling prophecy, since parents transmit their culture's expectations to their children.

To be considered feminine in Victorian society, women had to be frail and passive, the potential victims of aggressive, lecherous males. Yet according to the stories of Greek mythology, women were as urgently sexed as men. In our own age, primitive tribes differ grossly in what most Americans consider basic masculinity and femininity. Among the Arapesh tribes of New Guinea, for example, studies in the early twentieth century found that men as well as women showed such characteristics as concern, giving, and protectiveness, which we in America associate with mothering. Their neighbors, the Mundugumor, living only a short distance away, had quite opposite attitudes; both men and women were strong, tough, and aggressive, like the idealized pioneer male in the United States.†

Another tribe in New Guinea, the Tchambuli, showed a reversal of conceptions about masculinity-femininity in another way. The male job was

---

*A remarkable change has taken place in the dress and hair styles of American teenagers and young people. Boys often wear long hair and bright, attention-getting clothing, making their dress more similar to the traditional feminine attire. Girls frequently wear trousers and male-style shirts. These changes are consistent with the reduction of differences between the sexes in our society, as discussed in previous chapters. For the purposes of this chapter, it is sufficient to note that standards of dress can change as a matter of taste, and are not inherently either male or female.

†The information in this and the following paragraphs about New Guinea is from Margaret Mead, *Sex and Temperament in Three Primitive Societies: Manus, Mundugumor, and Tchambuli* (New York: William Morrow & Co., 1939), 2, pp. 1–384, 3, pp. 164–244, 237–322, and from a lecture by the noted anthropologist Weston LaBarre.

headhunting, war preparation, and war making. To carry out their plans the men congregated daily in the "men's house." The women, on the other hand, were charged with all of the economic responsibilities in the village, such as fishing, food preparation, pottery making, and basket weaving. When the British banned headhunting and imposed a peace upon these people, the men became essentially unemployed, while the women continued their traditional activities. These women were temperamentally stable, secure, and cooperative with others, but the men, having lost their important functions, became insecure, capricious, and aesthetic. Although men could no longer make war, the preparation rituals were continued. Their interest in the cosmetic arts and in creating suitable costumes, previously an important part of war, was now used instead to make themselves sexually attractive so that they could employ charm to compete for the favors of the important sex, the women. The women were tolerant of their men, whom they viewed as gossipy, self-centered playthings.

Among the Manus, it was the father who was endowed with what in America are considered maternal characteristics. While the women were occupied with the economy and had little time for children, the father cared for and raised them. When Dr. Mead brought dolls to the children of the Manus, she found that it was the boys who eagerly played with them, while the girls were disinterested. The boys, in their play, were emulating their fathers' activities.

Largely, then, the tertiary sexual characteristics of people are socially determined and subject to considerable change from one generation to another and from one culture to another. Sometimes, however, the roles assigned to certain members of a society are intolerable, and in order for such a society to survive and maintain stability there have to be safety valves through which those who are placed in ambiguous or deprecated positions can gain some satisfaction or status.

The Iatmul were a tribe of New Guinea natives who had such a culture. The men despised women, considering them unimportant, worthless, and almost subhuman, allocating to them only the most menial and routine tasks. Men, in contrast, were considered to be the "real human beings"— strong, brave, and courageous. They, too, were headhunters. The men were expected to be proud, the women self-effacing. Everything in this culture was either all good or all bad. There were no shades of gray. To be a man was to approach perfection; women epitomized all that was to be avoided. If a man showed the slightest feminine interests or characteristics, he was considered to be sliding toward the subhuman. Such rigid standards of human behavior placed each man in constant jeopardy of losing his humanity. This dichotomy was hard on the women, but it was equally difficult for the men. Adjustment in the Iatmul society was precarious; men walked a tightrope and women were scorned.

A society like the Iatmul has doubtful durability, for the tensions and resentments engendered are at an explosive pitch. This tribe's safety valve was the ceremony of Naven,* an annual occasion in which bitterness and tensions were discharged in a convulsive reversal of the year's pressures. Naven was a ceremony of cultural transvestism during which men and women exchanged not only their clothes but also their roles. Boys who had been rigorously taught the shamefulness of femininity were now contemptuously called "wife." They were bullied in the same way that women had been bullied throughout the year. The women were given a vacation from their despised roles and identified themselves dramatically as men, wearing men's clothes and assuming their actions, strutting and swaggering. They could enter the men's house and could even beat certain designated men. They could engage in a theatrical simulation of the war games played by men. The men, who had spent the year taking elaborate ritualized precautions to avoid anything feminine, could relax during the ceremony. It was actually a great relief to assume, in deliberate fashion, the female role.

By the end of the ceremony, the tensions and resentments accumulated during the year were dissipated. The women felt better about their position in the community, and the men admired the women for having been able to assume the masculine position. For a short time the women had become human and the men could love them. Over the next year the tensions built up again, and hatred pervaded community life until the next Naven.

The Naven ceremony of the Iatmul is not unique, for other cultures have similar festivals. Rome's ancient feast of Saturnalia served a related function in discharging the year's accumulated tensions between masters and slaves. In this ceremony, slaves were waited upon by their masters and enjoyed all the privileges they were denied during the year. It is easy to understand the necessity for such rites and their vital function in preserving a culture. Beyond a certain point, tensions and resentment would destroy any community life.

The Iatmul looked forward throughout the year to their ceremony of Naven. The Romans, both slaves and masters, eagerly awaited the festival of Saturnalia. In fact, in these cultures and others with similar rites, the populace lived from festival to festival. These were the most important events in their lives. Similarly Americans, particularly many American males, mark time by their own seasonal rites: football season, basketball season, baseball season, and so on. Many men live from one sports season to the next, with sports representing the most vital part of their lives.

Iatmul men and women were in a precarious psychological balance as a result of the extreme demands that their culture placed upon them. The Naven rite offered an opportunity for the expression of strong feelings which

---

*Gregory Bateson, "The Naven Ceremony in New Guinea," *Primitive Heritage: An Anthropological Anthology*, eds. Margaret Mead and Nicolas Calas (New York: Random House, 1953), pp. 186–202.

had to be disowned throughout the year preceding the ceremony. For the women, it was denial of self-assertion and aggression; for the men, it was denial of passivity, with no opportunities for relaxation of their facade of superstrength. Naven saved the Iatmul people from the otherwise impossible demands of their culture and thereby saved the culture from extinction.

American men, as we have seen, are also on shaky cultural ground. Their position is as precarious, as a result of the contradictions in their lives. To an ever-increasing degree, American male children have close physical and emotional experiences with their fathers early in their lives. Fathers share almost equally with mothers in the maternal activities of feeding, bathing, cuddling, and comforting—activities that were once the exclusive domain of the American female. American parents are apt to take turns getting up with the baby when he cries at night. When either parent has a "night out," the other serves as babysitter. If the egalitarianism is disrupted, it is likely that bitterness will develop.

"Togetherness" has largely meant the diminution of the uniqueness of the female position as well as the male position in the family. Father is no longer the ultimate authority; he has become a "pal"; now he is not a teacher, but a co-learner. He has a voice in the collective activities of the household equal to but not greater than that of the children and his wife. The wife, who may have a job outside the home and may make as much as, or even more money than, her husband, quite naturally expects him to share the housecleaning, dishwashing, and caring for the children. The roles are diffused, and the differences between male and female, between adult and child, are diminished.

Like the Tchambuli, American men have had a change in status. The Tchambuli men lost their principal function, headhunting; American men have had to share with their wives their economic productivity as breadwinners. Tchambuli men became superfluous; the authority and uniqueness of the American man have diminished. Previously, the main way in which men were superior to women was in their physical strength. The development of modern machines has now caused male strength to become less important, almost obsolete. Machines are stronger than men, and the sexes are equally competent in running most machines. Dexterity has become more important than power, and women are at least as competent as men in this respect. As a consequence, the sex of contemporary factory and office workers is essentially insignificant.

While these changes in technology and in the family have taken place, in many ways the cultural expectations of masculinity have remained fixed as they were in pioneer days. Physical strength and agility were the qualities by which a man was measured, for then only the strong were able to survive. Obviously, such values are more appropriate to the frontier than to the office. Now, in order to fit this already obsolete image, men and boys must engage in artificial, nonproductive displays of strength.

As the real demands for what was once considered traditional male strength have decreased, the expectation of show of strength has grown. Parents have a special concern that their boys are not aggressively masculine enough. Mothers are more apt to be concerned about passive, compliant behavior in male children than about their destructiveness. They are often even relieved by, and perhaps subtly encourage, overt displays of aggression, for in that way they are reassured that their sons are not "sissies." This is quite different from the concept of several decades ago, when the good child was the quiet child.

As fathers and sons have drawn closer together, an obsessive cultural concern with homosexuality has grown. In order to avoid such taint, children are pushed earlier and earlier into heterosexual relationships. The tragedy of this parental encouragement is that it is self-defeating, since the child in latency has other business that is more important to learn than sex appeal. Premature explorations in heterosexuality often promote a sense of inadequacy within him as he recognizes his inability to perform as expected. This inadequacy, in turn, is interpreted as edging toward homosexuality, and as the parental efforts and encouragement toward aggression and heterosexuality are redoubled, the situation becomes a vicious circle.

Just as Naven helps to relieve the Iatmul tensions, American sports serve a similar function. The first man outside the home whom a boy encounters is usually a coach. In school, he meets a series of female teachers who are the purveyors of morality, knowledge, and competence. The coach is not only a man among men but, more important, a man among women teachers. Boys try to model themselves after the coach and find security in imitating him. Their roles are clearer on the baseball diamond than in the classroom, for it is on the athletic field in those seasonal masculinity rites that males become the kinds of men their grandfathers were and their mothers want them to be. Strength is king; men are separated from boys, and boys, in turn, from girls. In the best tradition of the frontier, an athlete overpowers his opponent, and the sexual roles are reestablished to conform with the traditions of the culture. Male and female are relieved of their role burdens, just as they are after the Naven ceremony. Fortunately for most people, this can be accomplished not only by participation but by observation as a spectator who identifies with the players. Men and women can both then return to the office and the home with renewed respect for the uniqueness of the sexes. Their own identities have been reestablished and remain clear until the distinction gradually diminishes and another masculinity rite is necessary.

In a subtle way, these supermasculine "frontier rites" also allow men to express among themselves the warmth and closeness that society compels them to disown. In sports, players huddle together; they caress, pat "fannies," shout affectionate phrases, and engage in activities that are scorned elsewhere but are condoned in sports. In a recent heavyweight boxing match, the victor was embraced and kissed by his manager before several thousand fans in the sports arena and perhaps several million more on television. Such behavior anywhere but in the context of sports would be highly suspect. Here, however, with full cultural approval and without detracting from the supermasculine atmosphere, men can satisfy either physically or vicariously their needs for close male companionship like that which they experienced in childhood. In this context, physical contact, either aggressive or friendly, is applauded rather than condemned. In the frenzy of American sports, males are purged of their femininity and, at the same time, provided with an outlet for close male contact.

Among the Iatmul, Naven takes place annually, and a single festival appears to take care of a year's accumulated tensions between the sexes. Fifty years ago a single sports season, namely baseball, sufficed for Americans; today, each season of the year is occupied with a different sport. Sport seasons now fuse with one another into a continuous succession of ceremonial demonstrations. The fall rite of football overlaps with the winter rite of basketball, which in turn overlaps the spring rite of baseball and track, and so on. The vacant moments are filled with transitional rites: hockey, tennis, and golf, to mention a few.

Although the potential for wild celebration is always present, the pitch of these ceremonies is somewhat lower than in the yearly Naven in New Guinea. This is consistent with the lower pitch of all activities in our sophisticated country. Very little can be termed a "special event," since we are bombarded daily with the spectacular and the overwhelming. Just as the differences between the sexes have diminished, so has the difference between holiday and weekday. Activities converge into a more integrated (for the hopeful) or amorphous (for the pessimistic) mass of ongoing activities. The Fourth of July, once fraught with danger and excitement, is now closely controlled and tame. Similarly, other holidays such as Veterans' Day and Memorial Day have lost their appeal to all but the most enthusiastic. Since the range of the pitch is lower, the exposure time must be increased. Thus, sports go on continuously from the beginning to the end of the year.

Among primitives, the transition from boyhood to manhood is accomplished in a single, brief ceremony—the puberty rite. A symbolic gesture, such as circumcision or knocking out a tooth, bears witness to the cliche, "Today I am a man." For American men the transition is quite different. Puberty, the time of traditional manhood when the secondary sexual characteristics appear, is now only the signal for the prolonged period of suspension between boyhood and manhood called adolescence. Biologically and sexually, manhood has been reached, but the technical complexity of our society requires an extension of many years of education and preparation before the productive work of life can begin. This preparation shortens the working years from one end, while mandatory early retirement advances from the other end, allowing only a relatively brief period for the adult work career.

Without clear role definitions and supports from society, young people are in moratorium, waiting for something to happen to them rather than seeking something. They become preoccupied with the here-and-now without future goals or desires. They have difficulty finding anything that sustains their interest, and they develop little sense of integrity and continuity in their lives.

Because of the nature of this moratorium, adolescence is a period of turmoil. Rebellion and confusion can be expected from the man who has not yet found a place for himself; who is suspended, seemingly for an infinite length of time, between his family of origin and his family of procreation.

But as we have seen, if a culture with contradictions and ambiguities is to survive, it must have some way of relieving and integrating its tensions. Sports form an elongated bridge across childhood, adolescence, and adulthood for American males. Although the adolescent boy may have to suspend decision and commitment on most of his affairs until many years hence, he can enter athletics with full exuberance and can play and work at sports with a dedication that satisfies his personality and his society.

Among my patients has been a successful attorney who came to treatment because his marriage was on the point of dissolution. The bone of contention between him and his wife was that he was "not man enough" in her eyes. She was bitterly disappointed that he was not handy around the house, that he did not make the family decisions, and that he was not more assertive—all qualities she had admired in her father. Her husband's competence in a learned profession seemed unimportant, while her father's physical strength, resulting from his being an unskilled laborer, was important. She feared that their son would develop into a "passive man" like her husband. The husband, too, doubted his own masculinity, shared her fears, and so sought therapy in order to try to conform to her expectations of him. The bickering that went on between them always subsided when they engaged in sports or jointly watched sports events. This seemed to adjust the perspective, and after such activity each respected the other for his or her distinctiveness.

This is not an unusual case. Wives are worried about their husbands' not being masculine enough; mothers are worried about their sons' being too passive; men fear that they will be dominated or thought to be effeminate.

In reality, men are larger and weigh more than women. They have more powerful muscles, bigger lung and heart capacities, and a sexual organ that makes them different. They are built for physical combat, for hunting, as well as for a unique sexual role. In the work and social worlds, however, this combat strength is largely obsolete. A 200-pound man can easily lose a business encounter (symbolic combat) to a 130-pound man or to a 90-pound woman. Slender feminine fingers can push the buttons on a computer as well as thick, strong, male fingers can—perhaps better. Machines are stronger than either men or women, and it makes no difference to the machine if its buttons are pushed forcefully or lightly; strength has, at least in part, lost its function and its value in society.

In sports, male and female are placed in their historical biological roles. In sports, strength and speed do count, for they determine the winner. As in premechanized combat, women are usually second place to men in sports. They can compete against one another and they can cheer their men on, but a quick review of the record books comparing achievements in sports of men and women confirms the distinctness of the sexes here.

It is small wonder that the American male has a strong affinity for sports. He has learned that this is one area in which there is no doubt about sexual differences and in which his biological strengths are not obsolete. Athletics help assure his difference from women in a world in which his functions have come to resemble theirs.

16.

The Sports Fan and Recreational Violence

A brief apocryphal review of the evolution of contemporary competitive sports will show just how far removed we are from the elemental satisfactions afforded by them, and what it is we must seek to regain. Imagine a boy who discovers a ball in a field. He is curious, and explores what he can do with the ball. He is absorbed with the potential of the object he holds in his hands; he throws it and kicks it playfully. His activity is motivated by curiosity and the pleasure of exploration, completely without compulsion. As he plays, he becomes better acquainted with the ball and learns what can be done with it; he becomes more skillful and begins to master the new experience.

Another boy comes along and joins in the play. The actions of the two become complementary, and they pass the ball back and forth. They are developing not only skill with the ball but also in the more complex relationship involving another person at the same time. They try to determine which of them can throw the ball the farthest and handle it more skillfully, and soon they begin to test their skill and strength against one another. The activity is still playful, but new purpose has intervened—the purpose of competition and winning.

The game may end when the boys tire of playing, and the experience will have been nothing more than a pleasant diversion with some sense of increased mastery in relation to another person and to a ball. One boy may also feel pride in having been the stronger, the other a sense of failure for having been less skillful. For both, there will be a sense of discovery and self-challenge.

But suppose, instead, that a small group of people are attracted by the sight of the boys playing with the ball and pause to watch. They are initially attracted by the action and energy generated, vicariously enjoying the creative part of the play. Perhaps, if they are older, they nostalgically recall similar play in the days of their own youth.

The spectators now begin to notice the competition which has been developing. They choose sides, perhaps because one boy is known to them in the neighborhood, or simply because they like the way he plays. They call out their support to him and shout with delight over each especially skillful maneuver.

The boys begin to notice the spectators and compete more aggressively, hoping to receive more approbation. Their attention has shifted so that it is no longer on the play alone, but also on how well they are performing before the audience. A critical line has been crossed which, by heightening the competition and the importance of the spectators, makes the whole process more purposeful and less free. Discovery gives way to achievement, and playfulness gives way to winning and succeeding.

Soon, one of those who paused to watch is attracted by the purposefulness of the activity and sees in it a way to gain profit for himself. He offers to bring seats so the spectators might watch more comfortably and to provide them with refreshments. He offers to arrange another game between the boys so the spectators might bring their friends, and he offers to improve the conditions of play. His services, of course, are not to be provided gratis; they require payment from the spectators.

Now he must also negotiate with the players, for up until now they have played only for themselves, when and how they wished. In order to arrange a game at a time the spectators will pay to see it, the entrepreneur now must pay the boys to perform at a given time and under specific conditions. Soon other people become involved to assure the integrity of the game; some are concerned with maintaining the rules, others with keeping score, and still others with communicating the results of the game to the people who did not attend. The whole operation becomes increasingly complex and broader in scope, each step moving the activities farther away from the original purpose of play and closer to being work for profit.

The game may continue to grow until it is duplicated in other communities, then in other states, and finally in other nations. People are employed to organize the various games and players, permanent stadiums are built, and complicated communications media are used to distribute the results of the play. The initial purpose seems all but lost; the players are no longer free, and the spectator's role is sharply demarcated and limited. Sooner or later both players and spectators will wonder where all of this is taking them, and how a simple, human activity could have become so complicated. Crucial changes began when the spectators affected the play of the game. The sports fan is born. $\sharp 1$ *fan is kids*

The sports fan is a remarkable social product of the industrial, technical society, a hybrid form which enjoys having others do his playing for him. Play, by definition, is for the pleasure of the player, yet in our highly special-ized society a special group of people have been designated to play for the rest of us. The very word "fan," as in sports fan, is indicative of just how circumscribed the role is. *Fan*, as mentioned previously, is derived from *fa-natic*, which means "inordinately and unreasonably enthusiastic; extrava-gant or intemperate zeal."

The United States has been described as a nation of sports fans. One of the reasons the role of sports fan has developed to such prominence is because of the pleasurable, perhaps even essential, opportunities it provides. Such op-portunities have become more difficult for the average person to find as our society has become larger and more complex, and the role of sports fan serves as an increasingly important diversion for those confined to boring routines within bewildering communities.

What is a fan? A fan is a spectator who enthusiastically follows a sport without actually participating in it. This strange role offers people an oppor-tunity to be involved in an activity that would be beyond their capacity oth-erwise. They are protected from the risks of actual participation and do not require the training or physical prowess necessary to actively play a game. The fan can participate vicariously through identification with the players and the action on the field while, at the same time, remaining entirely passive.

In this role, the sports fan can achieve mastery of the game and become an expert on all of its details. He can appreciate increasingly subtle aspects of the play while remaining secure in the grandstand. He can "talk" a good game without the need to prove, by action, that he can actually perform; he can even achieve a special kind of recognition from other fans as a "super-fan" because of the extent of his knowledge of the sport. He can appreciate the distinction between himself and the players, respecting his own role as well as theirs.

Despite his isolation from the field of play, the fan's role is a very impor-tant one, for it is his support of the players and of the game that allows the game to flourish. There is a mutually satisfactory relationship between those on the field and those in the grandstand, each needing and feeling supported by the other. The fan feels that he is a part of a community of involvement with the team, and he can stalwartly demonstrate his partisan loyalty. This kind of community involvement is rare in urban America and provides the fan with both enjoyment and a sense of active participation.

The fan is given an opportunity to witness, and even to experience through identification, the thrill and excitement of the contest. His enjoy-ment can come from several different kinds of thrilling experiences: there is the community excitement of having one's own team win and the sense of being involved in a part of excellence and strength; there are the excitement and sometimes awesome experience of witnessing a "great play" in which a player seems to exceed human capacity; and there is always the excitement of the unexpected, unplanned event, as, for example, when a fight breaks out or other violence erupts. These are the things that draw millions of fans to the stadium and to the television set; this is why we have become a nation of sports fans.

This very appeal of spectator sports and the popularity of the role of sports fan, however, have begun to influence sports in ways that could not have been predicted and now seriously affect the opportunities for satisfaction among the fans. As the sports establishment has grown, it has become increasingly dependent upon the fans, for it is the box office receipts that support the game. Promoters and players have become primarily interested in pleasing the fans, and various sports compete with each other for followers. The game has shifted from being player-centered to being fan-centered, and the promoters constantly try to divine what might titillate the fans the most.

Experience has shown that a winning team draws spectators, so promoters try every conceivable way to provide a winning team. Star players have box-office appeal and are an important ingredient of a winning team; thus, there is a continual competition among teams for players. They are traded from team to team and can no longer be identified with one particular community. The player is a commodity for exchange, a migrant worker who goes from city to city. While the player may be compensated by ever-larger salaries, the fan is left with increasing conflict in the matter of his loyalties; the player he identified as belonging with "his" team is suddenly playing for the opposition. The team itself may be moved from city to city if the box-office receipts are no longer profitable, leaving the fan bereft of his own team, and thereby less involved. In such circumstances the fan no longer feels that his support is vital to the team, and his involvement becomes less meaningful. Like a disappointed lover, he feels that he is loved for his money alone.

These efforts by promoters to satisfy the fans are partly self-defeating. In order to provide fans with the best performances available, players and teams may be drawn from almost anywhere in the country; thus, although the play on the field becomes more exciting, the fan's sense of distance from it increases. His diminished involvement lessens his satisfaction. The stadium grows larger and larger and the fan becomes farther and farther removed; ultimately, he sits in front of his television set watching the game alone. He has become isolated from any sense of community involvement when in the stadium, even though this was once an appealing part of his role of spectator. The fan experiences a loss of his interaction with the players and the team, and the progress of the game becomes impersonal, without human substance. A change in the standings of the team becomes no more involving than a minor change in the Dow-Jones average on the stock market.

The result of these changes is that the role of the fan has become increasingly narrow, so that now he sees more and more of less and less. He witnesses incredibly skillful performances under cliff-hanging circumstances, but with a sense of diminished participation. As his role becomes more passive, he demands more and more satisfaction for his money.

Because his money has become more important than his loyalty, and his distance from the play on the field has increased, he expects (and gets) more and more excitement. It is the sole remaining reason for his remaining a sports fan. His excitement may come in two possible forms, one legitimate and one not. A great play performed within the rules can produce a thrilling experience, and unexpected violence occurring outside the rules can be just as exciting.

The great play and the excitement of the last-minute victory have become almost commonplace. The television viewer sees only the best players and has developed a sense of having seen it all before. When the great play becomes common, it is no longer great; spectators are disappointed and feel deprived if the game is not a one-point thriller and if the players are not at record-breaking perfection.

The sports promoters have come to recognize the insatiability of the fans and employ all manner of schemes to lure them to the games. Baseball teams give away caps, bats, and T-shirts; there are fireworks displays in the stadium, door prizes, fashion shows, and ladies' nights; there are even occasions when teams offer free food and drinks to those who attend—all for the purpose of getting the fan to the stadium. But the fan is likely to become even more demanding, since it is no longer his team or his game—it is only his money.

THE RISE OF VIOLENCE IN SPORTS

Separated from the field of play, deprived of his community of involvement, and jaded about the "Great Play," unexpected violence still excites the fan. The beast in the stadium becomes the insatiable crowd.

Promoters are only too willing to provide the fan with what he wants, whether for the sake of the team or for profit alone. Sports have become more and more violent. Professional football is becoming more brutal all the time, leading one All-Pro guard to declare, "You have to play dirty" to make it. Ice hockey has enjoyed a great rise in popularity, owing largely to the violence it offers. Although fights are not officially encouraged, neither are they quickly stopped. The growing popularity of all forms of auto racing, with its potential accidents and deaths, is another example. In some cases, sports have lost fans to other sports that are based entirely upon providing demonstrations of

violence. Professional wrestling and roller derbies, for example, both caricatures of competitive sports, are deliberately organized to excite the fans with
ever more violent acts, whether spontaneous or contrived, and the demoli-
tion derby may be the most obvious of all. These sports are capturing an
increasing number of fans and providing a growing competition for the
more traditional sports.

For those who may still doubt that violence attracts crowds and that promoters seek to satisfy them with violence, the following example should suffice: European-style soccer has recently been brought to North America, and
there have been many attempts to capture fans from other sports. For many
weeks, a television commercial was shown on several channels throughout
southern California to attract fans to the game. This commercial featured
television star Jack Klugman extolling the virtues of soccer for its excitement.
The film concluded with an invitation to the viewers to come watch the
thrills of soccer and to "see the fans attack the players." On the screen
beyond Klugman, riotous fans were shown rushing onto the field to assault
the players.

Fans are actually being taught to expect violence in sports. With each effort
to satisfy their thirst for unexpected violence, their level of tolerance for it
increases; thus, they want more and more. Like someone restricted to a limited diet, the fan is never completely satisfied, no matter how violent the
contest. The crowd's growing appetite for violence is fed by the promoters'
willingness to accommodate it, and it spirals upward. This is recreational
violence, a new phenomenon which is sought for pleasure and diversion. It
is a form of entertainment for which people can be educated or which develops when other, more wholesome, forms of recreation are blocked. American sports are now being transformed to supply people with this recreational
violence.

There is little to suggest that recreational violence is an inherent human
desire, but it is one for which a population can be easily educated. Like
learning to drink beer, it is a pleasure for which one must acquire a taste,
and it appeals to an increasingly large number of people. It is a form of
recreation that is leading us into dangerous and unknown territory.

The enjoyment fans get from violence is not the only reason it pervades
sports today. Equally important are the conditions more commonly associated with the violence of revolution. Violence has been described as the last
refuge of the powerless, a tool used by one group to affect another when all
other means have failed. Whether or not such violence actually achieves the
gains sought, it does have some personal value to those who engage in it.
One feels that he is doing something purposeful; he has a sense of power
and participation and believes that he is affecting an otherwise immune system. He obtains recognition and a feeling of solidness.

The boundaries between the grandstand and the playing field have traditionally been sharply drawn to separate the spectators from the players.

There have always been moments of excitement when the spectators have affected the actions on the field of play, as, for example, by shouting support or criticism. This limited form of contact fits within the role definitions of player and spectator. There have been increasing attempts by the fans, however, to transgress these boundaries by invading the field not only by vociferous verbal comments but also by throwing beer cans, bottles, and seats. Running onto the field of play has become a common occurrence, and assaults on players and officials have become a matter of serious concern. The fan appears no longer to accept the distinction between his role and that of the players, or between his rights and the rights of the players.

It is nothing new for fans to become so excited that they fight among themselves or invade the field. In the past, however, it was in the service of partisan loyalty that a fan or group of fans became overexuberant in their support of their home team. This was understandable in the context of smaller communities where players and fans were neighbors and were likely to have other forms of contact.

Something new is happening now with regard to the violence and rowdyism. It is no longer in support of the home team alone; instead, it is directed indiscriminately at both teams. For example, on the infamous Cleveland Beer Night in 1974, hundreds of baseball fans invaded the field to assault the players. Even though the rivalry between the Texas and Cleveland teams was intense, the fans attacked the players of both teams when they rushed onto the field. The players in turn combined forces to beat them back, and were joined by the security forces of the stadium and the police. The resulting melee was like a social insurrection against the entire sports establishment. Such an event is more closely related to class warfare than it is to conflict stemming from community loyalties. This kind of violence is like a class war between the disenfranchised crowds and those figures in sports who have power and influence.

Most people spend the week laboring at unrewarding jobs, and then as fans they spend their money for the privilege of watching others play. They understandably expect to be entertained and satisfied for their money. They grow resentful when the performers seem to be disinterested in them, and are angered when a player makes such a remark as, "It's only a job." They hear of players receiving enormous salaries and they expect superior performances in return. As their distance from the players continues to grow, the situation becomes barely tolerable to them, and a disappointing performance by a team is enough to cause the smoldering resentment of the restive fans to erupt. After a bad loss suffered by the San Diego Chargers, for example, it was necessary for a squadron of police to protect the coach from a vicious drunken mob of 300 fans. Death threats to both players and officials have become almost commonplace.

The relationship between fans and players is no longer personal. Players see the fans as dangerous enemies against whom they must protect themselves, and so they have as little contact as possible with them. Fans treat players more and more as though they are less than human and have no feelings. When Bob Watson (the outfielder for the Houston Astros) was injured while chasing a fly ball, he fell to the ground, bleeding and in pain. His teammates rushed to help him, but before they could, the fans in the nearby grandstand began hurling ice cubes and beer cans at him. Further assault on an already injured player is incomprehensible unless he is regarded impersonally. The distance between the roles of player and spectator has produced just such a depersonalization of each in the eyes of the other. Without personal contact to demonstrate their essential humanness, officials and players are easily viewed as the "bad guys." And just as the crowd cheers when a movie or television villain is killed, so is it elated when some mishap befalls the actors in a sporting event.

The stadium, of course, is not divided simply into two homogeneous groups composed of players and spectators; rather, it is like a microcosm of society-at-large. Spectators are separated and located in specific areas—boxes for the wealthy and bleachers for the poor. The VIPs watch the event in the special, air-conditioned luxury of the stadium club, while other, less desirable areas are designated for the holders of lower-priced tickets. Remarkably, in the small, circumscribed area that is a stadium, the various social classes seen elsewhere are all contained, each in its place but in full view of the others. It is as though one could see and be close to all of the important social elements at the same time. Under these crowded conditions, it could be expected that we would see the enactment of the conflicts and dissatisfactions that exist in the whole of society. The same forces that seek to diminish the boundaries between groups elsewhere are also at work in the stadium.

Fans are not forced to be spectators, and there are other forms of recreation available to them. A more logical approach for dissatisfied fans would be for them to take their business elsewhere and to seek other ways of getting what they desire. Indeed, many people today are seeking to recapture the full breadth of the experience of play by becoming players themselves. A dramatic example is the growth in the number of tennis players. Over the past decade, millions of people who never before held a racket or witnessed a match have become regular players. Others have abandoned the stadium and the television set for golf, jogging, skiing, swimming, and other active sports.

Because these avenues are not open to everyone, however, many people are bound to the role of spectator. It takes courage to break away from the crowd, and the tradition of spectator sports is a strong one. It also takes money and facilities, and these are not always available to everyone. The television set and the stadium are still the most accessible opportunities for sport.

This kind of phenomenon is not new. Indeed, spectator games were the most accessible form of entertainment in Rome at the time of the decline of the empire. By contrast, in earlier times, when Rome's strength and affluence were in ascent, sports had a different meaning for the spectators and they felt privileged to support their community's representatives. In chariot races, each entrant was supported by a group of partisan followers who knew him generally and identified with him. As Rome's power grew and sport became concentrated in the Coliseum, the crowd was clearly separated from the athlete-entertainers, who, like the gladiators, formed a special group paid to perform for the crowd. The crowd demanded increasingly bloody and violent entertainment and regarded the participants on the stadium floor impersonally. The crowd would become violent when dissatisfied, and stadium riots became commonplace. As a gesture of appeasement, the spectators were offered free gifts, food, drink, money, and memorial tokens. But the crowd was still not satisfied, for it was deprived of something more fundamental—common purpose and a sense of community—so the people grew increasingly restive.

The spectator sports of Rome were also a microcosm of society-at-large as is the case today with American sports. The fragmentation and divisiveness in the stadium reflect conditions elsewhere, and if we are to learn from the Roman experience, we must find ways of restoring some of the lost satisfactions. Otherwise, the fans will continue to express their frustrations when they come to the stadium. They will in all probability continue to demand more blood and more violence, and no matter how much is done for them on the field, it will not be enough. The crowd is likely to take matters into its own hands and become increasingly rowdy and violent. Special events such as fireworks displays, free caps, and free food and drink will not satisfy that for which the crowd is hungry, and such efforts will only increase the restiveness. The outcome of one recent event reveals the mood of the crowd: When the Atlanta baseball team gave the fans free Frisbees, the toys were thrown at the players and onto the field in an attempt to disrupt the play and express dissatisfaction. More of the same kind of thing will not quiet the fans, and the attempts of the promoters and officials to appease the crowd and compensate for lost satisfactions are doomed to failure.

Hope rests on whether people's active participation or their identification with the active participants can be restored. Such a sense of involvement is necessary for people to be willing to support society's institutions by lending strength to their maintenance and revision. The stadium not only is the mirror of society but also its mentor. Attitudes learned in sports strongly affect the ways in which the young will view society, and those attitudes are continually reinforced by what adults and young people alike experience when they visit the stadium.

17.

Beyond the Game

Violence has as previously mentioned, usually been considered to be a last, desperate attempt to deal with frustrations by those who are powerless to affect change in any other way. It is a means of coping with intolerable repressive forces and is usually resorted to when all other means have failed. Today, however, we are seeing the rise of a new form of violence: recreational violence. As the term implies, this kind of behavior is a form of entertainment, one for which people must acquire a taste. This usually occurs when they are exposed to the recreational uses of violence as a readily available option rather than a last, desperate measure; it then becomes a pleasure which is actively sought out. Its use is more prevalent when other, more wholesome forms of recreation are not available or are not recognized as being alternatives. Recreational violence is a form of entertainment that is being made increasingly available in sports.

The appeal of recreational violence lies in the thrill and excitement it generates, and it is especially attractive to those whose sources of excitement are limited. Most of the uncertainties and risks in contemporary urban life have been reduced to abstractions: people worry about inflation, loss of jobs, and recessions; they worry about stretching the family budget, insurance premiums, taxes, and retirement. Today, we are apt to be protected from the intensity of experience even where real danger exists. Driving along the freeway in air-conditioned comfort, listening to soft music on the radio, one is almost completely separated from the reality of danger. The perils of cigarette smoking are known to the smoker only by hearsay when someone tells him that the habit may be dangerous to his health. These risks and uncertainties rarely produce full emotional impact; instead, they tend to be antiseptic and intellectual abstractions. People do not feel that they have encountered the vital issues and dangers in their everyday lives in a direct or meaningful way; they hunger for totally involving experiences, and they find that this desire can be partly gratified through the violence found in sports and recreation.

Perhaps the growing problem of violence in the streets is, in part, an attempt to recapture that sense of thrill associated with risk and danger. Innocent victims are assaulted, beaten, and maimed when there is no possibility of material gain; robbers shoot their victims for no reason, and gangs commit murder in senseless rites of initiation. Crimes like these lead us to conclude that they are committed solely for the sake of the experience itself, a matter of recreation through violence.

There is some evidence that the need to experience danger and excitement is a biological, deeply ingrained part of being human. Although Robert Ardrey* and Konrad Lorenz† have popularized the theory that the human being is innately violent, the evidence to support it is hardly convincing. More to the point, Sol Rosenthal, a professor of preventive medicine at the University of Illinois, has been concerned for a number of years with what he calls "risk exercise."†† He explains the need for one to encounter risky situations this way:

> Our genes are coded through evolution to receive certain stimuli (chemical or otherwise). They virtually cry out to us—Protect yourself! Live! Protect your territorial rights! Procure food! Procreate! These stimuli for self-preservation have, over the centuries, become less and less intense. . . . There built up a deficiency which "frustrates" our genes— their computers become "discombobulated"—over millions of years they have been painstakingly evolved to receive these stimuli and either they get them or else!

Rosenthal contends that sports such as skiing, surfing, hunting, mountain climbing, boating, and fencing provide this kind of total organismic challenge, and he further contends that such experiences are vital for physical health and a sense of well-being. He states that his studies have revealed that such sports produce a sense of exhilaration and relaxation which lasts for days. Rosenthal believes that in addition to the sense of well-being, the individual's body physiology and biochemistry are toned by involvement in risk exercises under well-calculated volitional circumstances. They lead to improved physical health and prevention of disease.

---

*Robert Ardrey, *African Genesis* (New York: Atheneum Publishers, 1961).

†Konrad Lorenz and Marjorie Wilson, *On Aggression* (New York: Harcourt Brace Jovanovich, Inc., 1966).

††RE (Risk Exercise): a Progress Report by Sol Roy Rosenthal, M.D., Ph.D., Medical Director of the Research Foundation (Chicago) and Professor of Preventive Medicine, the University of Illinois, 1968.

Although Rosenthal believes that readily available sports such as tennis, basketball, football, and running have somewhat less risk associated with them, these sports nevertheless possess many of the same ingredients as do risk exercises. For example, a tennis player places himself at risk and feels the excitement of the action when he rushes the net, and it is this sense of putting oneself on the line that heightens the fullness of living. Rosenthal contends that evolution has caused man's genes to come to associate risk with reward; without such risk, even reward tends to be sterile. Perhaps of more importance than whether it is of biological origin or due to psychological conditioning is the fact that such physical experiences of calculated risk do produce a sense of well-being.

If this need for risk experience does indeed exist in humans, consider the plight of the spectator, who gains his experience vicariously and not through his own actions. He tries to engage in the challenges and thrills of sport *without risk* to himself. Yet, being a sports fan who merely watches the game may constitute the most important form of recreation for many Americans who are conditioned from childhood for the role. This form of sports participation is certainly the most easily obtained. Sports fans can never achieve full satisfaction from the game if what they seek is risk and excitement of the kind that Rosenthal postulates is necessary.

We have seen how, in the past, the spectator's sense of participation was enlarged through a communal involvement and identification with his local team. This allowed him to become so engrossed in the action on the field that it was as though he were actually a part of the team and of the play. But we have also seen how these communal opportunities have been gradually and systematically taken away from him in recent years. When his favorite players are traded to other cities and other teams, as almost all professionals in sports eventually are, the fan must either experience conflicting loyalties or give up loyalty altogether. There is nothing of which he can feel a part. Now that he knows that club franchises are sold or traded away to other cities with regularity, the home team and its players have become merely another form of entertainment; all that is left for the fan to enjoy are the thrill and excitement. Without the existence of any special sense of partisan loyalty or involvement, a winning team and the skill of its players are reduced to being just that and nothing more. The spectator is distanced from the action on the field, making it little more than another of life's abstractions unless something unexpected happens to surprise and thrill him.

Even great performances become dull and routine from overexposure to them. The level of skill demanded of players and teams has risen so dramatically that a great play or a "come-from-behind" finish is a regular occurrence. Great players are selected from everywhere and trained arduously to assure superb performances on each and every occasion, and with the flip of a television dial one can see them at will. But they are distant figures, viewed with a detachment that mutes the spectator's sense of the excitement.

It takes something dramatic and unexpected to excite today's blasé sports fan; something outside the rules, such as a fight or a riot, is required to penetrate his insulation, for he feels isolated from any sense of true partnership with the team and the players. He pays to be entertained, and violence seems to be one way by which he can exact a return for his price of admission.

The sports fan has retreated narcissistically to those things that serve only himself. He sees the players as objects to be used for his personal pleasure, not people who have feelings and suffer pain as he, himself, does. An injured player is an impersonal object whose bloodshed is considered only in the light of its entertainment value.

Sports fans have always yelled "murder the bum" and "tear 'em apart" in moments of partisan loyalty, but they have rarely expected their shouts to be taken seriously. Today's fans are likely to mean it, and promoters know they not only will pay to witness violence but may even try to take part in the action. Winning alone is no longer sufficient; recreational violence seems a necessary commodity with which to both excite and appease the appetites of the fans.

We have seen how the activities in the sports stadium both reflect and influence society. The same characteristics found in sports can be found in the streets; moreover, they are a major source of the values expressed elsewhere, for sports serve both as a training ground for the young and as a way in which the values of the adult are maintained and strengthened.

There are numerous elements in contemporary society that foster the right conditions for recreational violence: the transiency and mobility of the population and changing values and roles in overcrowded, impersonal cities are some of them. Conditions such as these have taken from the individual his sense of reliance on his neighbors, and families and communities exist in name only. The *sense* of community essential for security and satisfaction has been lost, and without that sense, other people are regarded impersonally. Witness the astonishing increase in rape at the very time that sexual restrictions are loosening. The rape victim, like an injured athlete, is not looked upon as a person capable of feeling, but rather as a depersonalized object to be used solely for the gratification of a particular need. It is this very kind of detachment that provokes the incredible rise in violence and assault in our cities. Such crimes are possible only when an individual feels that he is without community support, and so the manner in which he treats other people is of no concern to him. This is the same way the sports fan now feels.

THE QUEST FOR THE BEYOND

A special kind of magic can sometimes occur in sports, and it is the possibility of experiencing such a "happening" that lures millions of people into some kind of sports involvement. This elusive magic is the element that provides athletes with the motivation to endure ruthless discipline and tedious training regimens and makes them willing to suffer physical pain and even injury. Spectators are drawn by the possibility of an experience of such intensity that enduring a hundred losing games or sitting uncomfortably for hours in a rain-soaked stadium is made worthwhile. It is what leads the fan to sacrifice time and money for the possibility of one single, glorious moment; it is even what leads athletes and fans alike to resort to acts of violence in spurious attempts to capture it. This magic is known dimly to nearly everyone drawn to sports, and those who are fortunate enough to be a part of it savor the memory for years.

These experiences are utterly and completely absorbing: the world suddenly turns bright and clear, the senses and muscles flow as one, and the person feels and functions beyond mundane limits, aware of the full potential of life in integrated vitality. Although seemingly elemental, mystical and timeless, such experiences are firmly here and now and real.

It is what John Brodie, the great quarterback, meant when he described moments when he had seemingly endless time to elude tacklers in order to throw to Gene Washington, who he *knew* would arrive at the exact spot in the end zone at the identical split second the ball did. It is what Bob Beamon experienced when he long-jumped two feet farther than anyone else had ever jumped before him. It is what the long-suffering Pittsburgh Steeler fans experienced when their team finally reached the Super Bowl and won the game.

Yet, this magic occurs not just in the great, widely publicized events, but can also emerge in a simple neighborhood ball game. It can happen at moments when an average tennis player feels his game suddenly "come together" and no longer struggles against himself or fights the ball, when a golfer concentrates perfectly, or when a ballplayer floats intuitively toward the ball. Each senses that life has been elevated to a different and more complete level of reality. It occurs when a surfer feels at one with the wave and when the skier achieves a sense of harmony with the mountain and the snow. It is what Tim Galway describes in *The Inner Game of Tennis* and what Mike Murphy illustrates in *Golf and the Kingdom*; it is what happened when the target reached out for the arrow in *Zen and the Art of Archery*.

I remember when the players on our basketball team seemed to merge together as one man, and a fast break became an elegant, aesthetic experience, the hoop forming a still-life background for effortless points. I recall tennis matches when I no longer struggled, but floated about the court with my racket, the ball, and the court all coming to life in integrated patterns. I remember being a spectator and fusing with Jim Plunkett and an underdog Stanford team in the Rose Bowl. Rising to cheer with 100,000 others was like being elevated involuntarily by a great, unseen hand. And there was the quantum acceleration of a relay team on the track that swept me and the other screaming fans along with the runners in vivid, absorbing, and magical motion, special yet ordinary as well.

These moments of awesome wonder elude the grasp, yet emerge when conditions are right and the person is open to their happening. They are experiences of transcendence into an awareness of being a part of something greater and more important, when the boundaries of the self are sharp, yet blend with all that is present, when stodgy limits are surpassed, and when the full sense of the potential in life seems within reach.

The lexicon of sport is filled with clumsy attempts to describe these phenomena with such terms as "incredible experience," "effortless play," "a perfect game." They may be hinted at when a player is called "hot" or "irresistible" or "unconscious." Indeed, "unconscious" may be close to the point, for there is an altered state of consciousness in such experiences, one in which the participant is oblivious of the irrelevant and of limiting social interpretations, yet his perception is remarkably clear and the action is all-absorbing and all-flowing.

We know such experiences under other conditions, as well, such as in moments of ecstatic sexuality and sensuality when one completely loses the self. The potential for such experiences in sexual behavior has led to a boom in the production of "how-to" sex books recommending various techniques and gadgetry. The special conditions for these elevated moments may also occur in vastly different circumstances—during a sunset in the wilderness, when a person feels at one with nature. They may also occur when one voluntarily allows himself to be swept into confluence with a crowd of others; it is what led many otherwise rational German citizens to abandon judgment and to merge with the frenzied crowd at Nazi rallies. In these ecstatic moments, dangerous social acts may occur, for there is a dissolution of valuable parts of the self, and morality is discarded for the cause of the moment. Yet these are also moments of potentially boundless goodwill when one person reaches out to another in deepest fondness. These kinds of experiences, whether benign or malignant, are known to the sports fan when his identification with the play on the field and the other fans in the stadium is complete. The sports fan who has known the wonder and awe of these moments may seek to recreate the experience when the identification with the players is no longer possible, with violence as the means, for it, too, may be so shocking as to be all-engrossing.

These experiences may be described as spiritual or religious. Indeed, throughout the history of mankind, religion has provided the conceptual framework for comprehending transcendent experiences. Phrases such as "God is one," "God is all," and "Man is in God's image" point to moments of clarity and unity when there is dissolution of social boundaries. Freud recognized such experiences, calling them "that oceanic feeling." Jung related them to collective unconscious experiences deep in human anlage which emerged in the individual, and in the more contemporary humanistic psychology, Abraham Maslow called them "peak experiences." They are also the experiences that Eastern religions call "satori."

As religious order has given way to the secular, unified concepts have given way to analytic and scientific concepts. These provide increased freedom and option, but at the expense of a framework for comprehending the special transpersonal levels of perceptions of the unity of life. In part, the ambivalent relationship of sport and religion may have its origin here, for one of the great appeals of modern competitive sports is that they may provide a focus where such unity seems possible. Player and spectator blend in common purpose with the team, with clarity of relationship between players, and with the absolute authority of the coach, like a congregation of true believers. The stadium offers a nostalgic opportunity, in a fragmented age of science and secularism, to recreate the oneness of a religious past. This clarity of good and bad, home team and rival, combined with total absorption in the play, is like restoring God to Heaven and putting all in its proper place.

We are children of our times and of our society. We have been schooled for a limited range of options to provide us with experiences of all kinds, and we are familiar with competitive sports as a source of recreation, renewal, and transcendent experiences. Sports are, moreover, the most readily available kind of recreation. But as they have become bigger, more specialized and impersonal, they have begun to collapse of their own weight. People seek more from sports than they are able to provide. High-quality play has become so routine that the fans' threshold for excitement has risen. Although Americans watch sports more, they obtain a narrower range of satisfaction and enjoy them less. They do not attain the full measure of satisfaction they once did when they were more personally identified with the players and the action, even if the level of skill was lower. The same forces at work to disintegrate society seem to be at work within sports and have diminished the opportunity for spiritual moments.

We have seen how vital these unique moments are to health and well-being. From the instant of birth, when confluence with an all-nourishing mother is cruelly interrupted, we seek to replace the loss by transcendence of the conventional boundaries that separate us from others. We seek a sense of unity and excitement in experiences that can wholly absorb us through religion, through sexuality, in nature, in crowds, in violence, and in sports. In sports, these experiences are possible when the conditions are right, and they are beyond winning, beyond the team, beyond the game, and beyond oneself.

If sports are to continue to be a vehicle for these experiences, either people will have to return to more active participation, or the great American sports spectacles are likely to become even more violent. The return to active participation is the more appealing option and, indeed, more and more people are turning to it. If the trend continues, we can also hope to see evidences of increased participation in other aspects of community life. And therein lies the hope for our society.